"*Hail to the Chiefs* is a wonderfully funny book. It reveals, among other amazing facts, that almost all our chief executives were just as weird as Richard Nixon."   —*Dave Barry*

"Along with the laughs, often encourages shrewd and touching empathy with moments of the past."   —*The Washington Post*

"[An] amusing, anecdotal volume, probing peculiarities of our presidents, past and present . . . trenchant, often wicked wit."
—*Publishers Weekly*

"Readers of any political stripe should enjoy Holland's breezy, brief, and irreverent takes on our presidents."
—*The Portsmouth (NH) Herald*

"Evokes many chuckles . . . After reading this book, you'll never again view the presidents quite the same."
—*The Oklahoman*

"Vividly gives you the flavor of each administration."
—*The Philadelphia Inquirer*

D0288337

HAIL TO THE CHIEFS

Presidential mischief, morals, & malarkey
from George W. to George W.

BARBARA HOLLAND

BERKLEY BOOKS, NEW YORK

B

A Berkley Book
Published by The Berkley Publishing Group
A division of Penguin Group (USA) Inc.
375 Hudson Street
New York, New York 10014

PRINTING HISTORY
The Permanent Press hardcover / January 2003
Berkley trade paperback edition / May 2004

Library of Congress Cataloging-in-Publication Data
Holland, Barbara.
Hail to the chiefs : presidential mischief, morals & malarkey
from George W. to George W. / Barbara Holland.— Berkley trade pbk. ed.
p. cm.
Originally published: Sag Harbor, N.Y. : Permanent Press, 2003.
ISBN 0-425-19496-5
1. Presidents—United States—Biography—Anecdotes.
2. Presidents—United States—Humor. I. Title.

E176.1.H738 2004
973'.09'9—dc22   2004045064

PRINTED IN THE UNITED STATES OF AMERICA

10   9   8   7   6   5   4   3   2   1

To my mother

THE GREATEST GLORY of our system is its dazzling variety. Like snowflakes and fingerprints, no two Presidents are exactly alike and most are totally, amazingly different. Given our national attention span, this is just as well. Every four or eight years, we get somebody new to watch.

If we voted for him, we watch to see if he's going to prove us wrong. If we voted against him, we watch to see if he's going to prove us right. We watch his goings out and his comings in, his children, his dogs, his wife. If the sun shines and the armies win, we cheer him; if the stock market hits the fan and hurricanes rage, we hiss and boo; if the times are boring, he bores us. He's our national sponge, chosen by the people to absorb the national moods and happenings. He's only a few moves away from the ancient scapegoat that soaked up our sins and troubles and then carried them away into the desert. Eight years later, at most, he disappears into the wilderness, leaving us cleansed and righteous and ready to watch the next.

Imagine having to listen to Castro's speeches for forty years. Imagine living in a monarchy. If the times are peaceful and you get yourself a young and healthy king, you could be watching the same First Family for fifty years. You would see his children born, go to school, grow up, and have children of their own, and by then you'd know more about them than your own. His majesty's portrait would be hanging on the classroom walls for generations. With luck, he'd get in scrapes occasionally, perhaps have a mistress to keep you awake for the evening news, but most modern kings lead exemplary lives.

When he finally dies, nobody gets to guess who's next; his eldest son succeeds, and you've been hearing about this prince for as long as you can remember and nothing he does will surprise you.

Americans would never stand for this. Even sixteen years of George III was too much to bear. However exciting a President may be, eight years of the same show is plenty. We are not naturally monogamous. Americans pine for fresh fields and pastures new, different clothes in the White House closets, somebody else to think about.

Sometimes the process coughs up a hairball, sometimes events overpower a perfectly decent fellow, but the system gives us chance after chance after chance, and always we keep our eye on the horizon, waiting to see who's next.

The Founding Fathers invented a glorious game.

CONTENTS

★　★　★

GEORGE WASHINGTON

★ ★ ★

1789–1797

YOU'RE WRONG ABOUT George Washington. Nathaniel Hawthorne was wrong too. He said, "He had no nakedness, but was born with clothes on, and his hair powdered, and made a stately bow on his first appearance in the world."[1] People rarely feel all warm and cozy about Washington. They look at pictures of his wife and think he must have been a stranger to the tender passion, and maybe the birds and the bees do it but George didn't.

To all this I say, then what about Sally Fairfax?

As a young country colonel, George fell in love with several pretty girls who wouldn't marry him.[2] Then he met Sally. She was said to be a bit of a flirt and had excellent family connections. However, she was married to a friend of his. In the evenings George hung around Belvoir, the Fairfax place, dancing[3] and playing cards and staring at Sally until the Fairfaxes got quite cross. Even when he was off soldiering he couldn't stop thinking about her and wrote her such unsuitable letters that her relatives felt obliged to complain. Just before he married Martha, he wrote to Sally promising lifelong devotion, and the year before he died, when she was sixty-eight, he wrote saying that nothing in his career "had been able to eradicate from my mind those happy moments, the happiest of my life, which I have enjoyed in your company."

---

[1] Hawthorne wasn't born until 1804. He was just guessing.
[2] There was talk about a Mary Phillipse, heiress to enormous tracts of land along the Hudson. George always felt enormous tracts of land gave a girl a certain something.
[3] Yes, dancing. He was younger then.

So there.

Martha was short and dumpy and had more than the usual number of chins, but she was pleasant enough. Her grandson said she had nice eyes, always the essential compliment for those with little else. By an odd coincidence, she was also the richest widow in Virginia. She liked to putter around the kitchen lifting the lids off the kettles and tasting things and helping the slaves fix George's favorite dinner—cream of peanut soup, Smithfield ham with oyster sauce, mashed sweet potatoes with coconut, string beans with mushrooms, spoonbread, and whiskey cake.

As First Lady, she gave rather stiff parties that ended sharp at nine o'clock,[4] when she blew out the candles and she and George went to bed, guests or no guests. By all reports they grew quite fond of each other. I can't imagine why they weren't blessed with issue.

In the beginning, George was born in a house with a chimney at each end, halfway between Pope's and Bridge's creeks, and he was scared of his mother. Everyone was. She was a vindictive lady with a savage temper and all her children left home just as fast as possible. She refused to go to George's inauguration and said terrible things about him every chance she got.[5]

When George was eleven his father died. I hope you've forgotten the cherry-tree story. It was invented by Parson Weems after George was safely dead and the moral—that you can commit any outrage you like as long as you confess to it afterward—has misled

---

[4] It seemed later.
[5] Once he took her to a ball in Fredericksburg, for which she wore such horrible old clothes that everyone was embarrassed. She did it on purpose.

generations of Americans.[6] Most people believed his whole book. Most people will believe anything.

We don't know any true stories about his boyhood because he didn't tell us any. He was trying to forget it. He did write a letter to Richard Henry Lee when they were both nine, thanking him for a book with pictures of elephants. He claimed he could "read 3 or 4 pages sometimes without missing a word," and added that if it didn't rain his mother might let him ride his pony, Hero, over for a visit. (I realize this isn't very exciting stuff but it's all I could find. I suppose you think you could come up with something better.)

He never went to college or learned any Latin or Greek, or got too much further than the book about elephants. In later life he had a nice library with lots of books like *Diseases of Horses, A Treatise on Peat Moss,* and *Mease on the Bite of a Mad Dog,* but basically he was more a man of action.

At fourteen he tried to run away to sea, but his mother stopped him, and when he was sixteen his half-brother got him a job surveying for the Fairfaxes, and so for several years he trudged around measuring the boondocks and rejoicing at getting away from Mother.

When he was twenty-one, Virginia was having some problems with France, and George got commissioned a lieutenant colonel in the militia. He rushed right out and attacked a French scouting party, which was silly, and accidentally started the French and Indian Wars. People forgave him, though, after Braddock's Defeat, which I don't have time to discuss right now. He was never much of a military genius, but he was brave enough and always looked

---

[6] Weems made up a lot of other pious Washingtoniana. Do you want to hear the one about God and the flower bed? Why not?

good on a horse, and that was the main thing. A strapping lad (one source calls him "a noble youth"), he was six foot three,[7] with size thirteen boots and big heavy fists with which he sometimes forgot himself and knocked unruly soldiers out cold. He'd inherited his mother's temper. From a distance he may have looked like a frozen halibut, but he spent his life grinding down his dentures and counting to ten to keep from breaking heads. When he was annoyed his language made his secretary shake in his shoes.

By age twenty-three he was a full colonel and defended the Virginia borders against the usual French and Indians.[8] When this was over he went home to take care of Mount Vernon, which he'd inherited from his half brother, and things were pretty quiet for a long time, but George didn't mind. He liked farming. First he rode around supervising his slaves for a while, and then he sat on the veranda with a tall cool one. Farming can be fun if you have the right kind of help.[9] Sometimes he sent for his hounds, Vulcan, Truelove, Ringwood, Rockwood, Sweetlips, Singer, Forester, and Music,[10] and he and his neighbors chased foxes until it was time for dinner. He always enjoyed dinner in spite of his problem.

You'll want to know about his teeth. Everyone asks. Well, before he was fifty he'd lost most of them, though he did hang on to the lower left premolar until he was sixty-five, and his dentures had a hole punched out for it to stick through. He was sentimental about it, and why not? For the rest, he tried this and that but noth-

---

[7] His bed was only six feet long. His feet stuck out.

[8] The results speak for themselves.

[9] He'd pledged never to sell a slave, so naturally he ended up with a surplus. There were over three hundred, way more than he needed, but having a lot of extras lounging around gave a nice tone to the place.

[10] If you go to Virginia today, you will find that all hounds there are still called Vulcan, Truelove, Ringwood, etc., but *they are not the same hounds.*

ing seemed to work very well. (President Harding's son wrote an article about it for the *Journal of Oral Surgery*.) One set of dentures had eight human teeth—I don't know whose—screwed in with gold rivets. One set was made with a pound of lead. The set you're thinking of, the one that makes him look so constipated in that Gilbert Stuart portrait, was carved out of hippopotamus ivory and was no good for chewing. It was just for cosmetic purposes.[11] It was held in place by a kind of spring device wedged into his jaws, but it would have fallen out if he'd smiled. It wouldn't have been proper for him to smile anyway. Eisenhower was the first military president who smiled, and that was years later.

In 1775, the First Continental Congress fingered him as commander-in-chief against the British. He hadn't been soldiering in eighteen years and was never exactly Napoleon,[12] but they wanted him because the war was being held in Massachusetts and they needed a Virginian so the South would take an interest in it.

So Washington buckled on his sword and went off to Boston to win the Revolution, with quite a lot of help from Lafayette and his old enemies, the French. He refused to accept a salary. He said he'd just send bills for his expenses instead. Everyone thought this was pretty darned noble of him, and he was so impressed himself that he kept dragging it into the conversation afterward, and even mentioned it in his will. The salary he'd turned down would have come to $48,000; the expenses he billed instead came to $447,220.[13] He did like to set an example for his starving troops, though, and drank only from a pair of very plain sterling silver goblets with

---

[11] A man who needs hippopotamus teeth for cosmetic purposes is a desperate man.
[12] Luckily the British were worse.
[13] That included a lot of Madeira wine. He was fond of Madeira, and needed to keep his strength up.

nothing engraved on them but his family crest. (His crest appears to be half a duck sitting in a crown, possibly laying an egg.)

There's a pretty story about him kneeling in prayer in the snow at Valley Forge, and you're welcome to believe it if you want, but he had a famous aversion to kneeling. When Martha dragged him to church on Sundays, he wouldn't kneel at the customary points in the service. He was a big man and this made him kind of conspicuous, but he didn't care.

After the war he went back to Mount Vernon to lead a simple life being enormously famous. He was our first celebrity and people came swarming from all over the world to make paintings and life masks of him and detailed drawings of everything he wore or ate from or sat on or wrote with during the war. They published miles of poetry calling him "the First of Heroes," "Glory's Deathless Heir," "a second Moses," and other things too embarrassing to repeat.

When he wasn't sitting for portraits, he thought about mules. Mules are the offspring of mares and jackasses, and since we didn't have any jackasses except in the colloquial sense, we couldn't have any mules. Horses are all very well, but sometimes only a mule will fill the bill. The King of Spain sent George an enormous gray jackass called Royal Gift,[14] and Gift meant well but when it came to sex he couldn't see what all the fuss was about. Then Lafayette sent him a black one named Knight of Malta with "the ferocity of a tiger" and testosterone to match, and the mule scheme was off and running.

Then in 1789 George was unanimously elected President of the United States and had to leave for New York.[15]

---

[14] Celebrities get all the best presents.
[15] Later they said New York was a sink of political vice and moved the capital to Philadelphia, but that didn't last either.

He was a good President because of being our national hero and nobody wanting to make him mad. When the Pennsylvania farmers rose up in the Whiskey Rebellion, all he had to do was *look* at them and they fell down apologizing.

He kept saying he wanted to go home to Mount Vernon, but we made him serve a second term anyway.

John Adams was his Vice President, and didn't he just hate it. He called the office "the most insignificant . . . that ever the invention of man contrived."[16]

After eight years, Hamilton and Madison wrote the famous "Washington's Farewell Address," and everyone cried. Adams delivered the reply to it and they cried harder. Some say even Adams cried. (Why do I doubt this?)

A couple of years later, George was riding around Mount Vernon thinking about mules and caught a chill, and by the next morning he had a nasty strep throat. Feeling it urgent to get bled as soon as possible, he sent for Mr. Rawlins, one of the overseers, to start the job while they waited for Dr. Craik. Martha thought maybe Rawlins shouldn't take quite so much blood, but the situation called for strong measures. Then Craik arrived and took some more, and tried to make George gargle with vinegar. By eleven he wasn't any better, so Craik bled him again, and at three Dr. Dick was called in and opened a vein the fourth time, in case there was any blood left, but even that didn't help and George was dead before midnight. (If the last word on his lips was "Sally," they wouldn't be likely to tell us.)

Your history teacher told you Washington freed his slaves in his will, but she was lying. He did free his old valet, William, who

---

[16] You either have the vice-presidential temperament or you don't.

was doubtless delighted though totally crippled by this time, but freeing slaves wasn't as simple as it looks from here. It wasn't quite like chopping the shackles off three hundred adult male stockbrokers in downtown Manhattan. We're talking about sending a colony of illiterate, semiskilled men, women, and children, with the usual percentage of them infants, elderly, or helpless, off to look for work among plantation owners as eager to hire free blacks as mine owners a hundred years later were eager to hire union organizers.

The neighbors would have broken every window in Mount Vernon.

In any case he couldn't free the slaves since so many of them were either Martha's dower slaves or related to them, and not George's to dispose of. He did say in his will that when Martha died, the slaves that had been George's when they married should be freed, or at least those still young enough to take an interest in freedom. He also left word that they should be taught to read and write, and those of suitable age be trained in carpentry or masonry or something, so as not to starve to death. He knew a lot more about the local job market than your history teacher.

It would be wrong to leave the subject of our first President without recording Washington's Joke. It seems he was sitting at dinner when the fireplace behind him got too hot, and he wanted to move away from it. Someone said merrily that a general should be able to stand fire, and Washington riposted, "But it doesn't look good when he receives it from behind."[17]

---

[17] Maybe I didn't tell it right.

JOHN ADAMS

★ ★ ★

1797–1801

IN THE BEGINNING there were Adamses all over the place, and nothing ever satisfied them. They expected a lot of themselves, and each other, and total strangers, and made life difficult for miles around.

It was never easy being an Adams, and marrying them was even worse. It was the kind of family where nobody ever said dumb things like "Hot enough for you?" or "How about those Mets?" They only talked about lofty things like political economy and astronomy and international relations. In every generation a child cracked under the strain and took to drink or suicide, and the ones who survived scarcely knew a carefree moment.

All the Adams men were very bright and had no patience with people who weren't bright enough to see things their way. They even allowed their wives to be bright, so at least one person would see things their way, but this wasn't always enough. The only wife to give full satisfaction was Abigail, and the other wives got pretty fed up with hearing about her.

Harry Truman said Abigail would have made a better president than John, but I don't know. She had a lot more charm and tact,[1] but she was a flaming radical and wanted to free the slaves, educate the children, declare war on France, and tax whiskey. She even mentioned votes for women. John said, "I cannot but laugh, you are so saucey."

---

[1] So does your average warthog.

John and Abigail met when she was a shy old maid of eighteen, and everyone says she was plain as a boot, but in her portraits she has the alert, considering look of a Jane Austen heroine and certainly didn't frighten the horses. He was no rosebud himself. He was conceited and high-minded and penniless and short and given to fits of rage and depression, but she married him anyway. Nobody else had asked her.

They were married for fifty-four years and just adored each other.[2] Their "Dearest Friend" letters make some of history's happier reading, and when she died he told his son John Quincy that without her he "could not have endured, or even survived." He wrote, "Nothing has contributed so much to support my mind as the choice blessing of a wife whose capacity enabled her to understand, and whose pure virtue obliged her to approve, the views of her husband."

If this sounds pretty pure and intellectual, it wasn't. She wrote saying the thought of him coming home made her shake all over. When she twitted him about being sixty, he wrote saying if he had her within grabbing distance he'd soon convince her he wasn't a minute past forty.

Maybe the Adamses were a nuisance to have around the house, but without them we'd be an extension of Greater Canada right this minute, and you'd be drinking milk in your tea and watching cricket matches that lasted for weeks on end.

John and Abigail and John's cousin Sam were about the only people who thought we should dump England completely. Everyone else figured we could work out something if we just sat down

---

[2] They were separated a lot and that probably helped. Spending every day with John would try the patience of a spaniel. Go ask the Continental Congress.

and talked it over like sensible adults, but the Adamses were dead set on divorce. They're the reason you think the whole Revolution happened in Boston.

John and Abigail lived in suburban Braintree[3] on a dear little farm. He chopped wood and practiced law and planted barley and talked politics. She cooked and sewed and had five children and talked politics. They were against the taxes, of course, and so are you, but you get them all muddled up. That's all right. Everyone does.

To start with, England needed some money and thought we were as good a place as any to raise it, so they sent us the Revenue, or Sugar Act, of 1764. This was a tax on foreign sugar and silk and linen and Madeira, the preferred tipple of the better sort of colonial. They followed this with the Stamp Act of 1765, which said that we had to pay anywhere from a halfpenny to twenty shillings sterling for stamps to paste on all our newspapers, broadsides, pamphlets, licenses, bills, notes and bonds, advertisements, almanacs, leases, and any other flat surface they could think of.

This was a silly nuisance and made all the more important sort of people hopping mad. John told everyone not to buy any stamps, and crowds of colonials followed the stamp officers around town calling them names, and burned them in effigy and set fire to their houses. In 1766 the English realized stamps were no way to get rich and repealed the idea, but the Revenue Act stayed, and on top of that they slapped a tax on paint, lead, paper, and tea. John said nobody should buy those things either, and people stopped painting their houses and switched from tea and Madeira to New England rum. It had a kick like an ostrich and the Sons of Liberty

---

[3] Presently it turned out to be called Quincy, after Abigail's grandfather.

joined hands and danced around and around the Liberty Tree, an elm conveniently close to Boston Common. Switching from tea to rum didn't exactly start the Revolution, but it didn't slow it down any either.

The main cause of the Revolution, aside from all those Adamses, was the quantity of feisty, short-tempered people on this side of the Atlantic at the time, and the quantity of unusually bossy, fatheaded chumps on the other side, topped by poor George III, who suffered from funny feelings in his head. After a while, though, even the English realized they were losing money because we weren't buying any of the nice things they sent us, so they repealed all the taxes except the one on tea.

They kept that just to show us who was boss.

It was only three cents on the pound, but it was the principle of the thing. They never asked us if we wanted to pay a sales tax. Now that we have our own government, they always ask us if we want to pay taxes, and we always say certainly, we'd be delighted. It makes all the difference.

The *Dartmouth,* the *Eleanor,* and the *Beaver* sailed into Boston Harbor full of tea, and the governor wouldn't let them leave again, so we threw the tea in the water and after that nobody wanted to buy it.[4]

The history books want us to think the Boston Tea Party was the social event of the season,[5] but by contemporary accounts it was pretty dull. Some sixty to a hundred and fifty persons, depending on which book you believe, dressed up as Indians and went quietly on board, and nobody tried to stop them, and they

---

[4] Boston Harbor was cleaner then, but not that clean.
[5] "Howling," "riotous," and "unruly" are the usual words.

opened the chests and deep-sixed them and went home to bed. Afterward "the stillest night succeeded, which Boston had enjoyed for several months."

Nobody ever found out who the Indians were. A lot of people claimed to know, later, but the actual participants never said a word. Probably the Adamses weren't there. At least, when John turned up the next morning, he said he'd been at Plymouth court on his circuit, and for all I know he was. Anyway, he was tickled pink.

The British were not. When it came to private property they never could take a joke, and they closed Boston Harbor and sent troops and made furious speeches. One chap in Parliament wanted every person in Boston flogged and the town "knocked down about their ears and destroyed."

Well, you all remember how the war began, with the various dustups like Lexington and Concord, where Paul Revere got his famous horse captured by the British and had to walk home. Then in 1776 somebody noticed it was the Fourth of July, so we said we were independent, but the British took no notice whatever. The *London Morning Post* gave the story six lines on an inside page.

After many exciting battles, puncutated by long lulls, we got up to 1783, and John Adams and Ben Franklin and John Jay cooked up the peace treaty in Paris. It gave us everything east of the Mississippi and in between Canada and Florida.[6] People call this the greatest diplomatic feat in the history of the United States, but all I can say is, it's a good thing Franklin was there or we'd still be sniping at redcoats. He was one smooth operator and romanced all

---

[6] Spain got Florida, but who needed it? Disney World was still crawling with rattlesnakes and you couldn't get a hotel room south of St. Augustine.

the old ladies and everyone loved him. Adams barged around being rude and impatient, and nobody liked him nearly as much, or bought him an aperitif or said *bonjour,* and his feelings were hurt. The Adamses' feelings were always hurt when people didn't like them. They could never understand it.

What with the Continental Congresses, and being envoy to France and Holland and minister to Great Britain, years and years went by when John hardly set foot on the farm. Abigail milked the cows and studied Latin so she could teach little John Quincy, and reported on the political gossip in New England. They wrote each other bales of letters full of politics and manure and cows and useful advice, like painting a strip of tar around the apple trees to keep out the tent caterpillars.[7] John wrote that all time was wasted that was "not employed in farming, innocent, healthy, gay, elegant amusement!"[8]

By 1789, things had calmed down enough for us to have a proper government, and John went off to be Vice President for eight years and President for four.

When he took office as President in 1797, he was greeted by widespread gloom. He wasn't all that popular—he'd squeaked in by three electoral votes—and everyone thought George Washington hung the moon and ought to be President forever. John moved into the presidential mansion all by himself, because Abigail was back home farming and being sick. There weren't any chairs or sheets or blankets because everything had belonged to George and Martha and they'd taken it with them. Then Rhode Island sent him

---

[7] I've tried this. It fools some of the caterpillars some of the time.
[8] Washington and Jefferson were always saying the same thing. Farming looks like more fun from a safe distance.

a cheese weighing 110 pounds and it just seemed like the last straw. Anyone would get discouraged, living in a house with a 110-pound cheese and no chairs, and besides, his teeth hurt. Abigail didn't show up to straighten things out until May, and in the meantime he just sat on the cheese and felt sorry for himself.

Thomas Jefferson was his Vice President, due to the hilarious notion of awarding this office to the first runner-up in the election.[9] Adams was a Federalist and Jefferson was a Republican, and by this time they had no use for each other. Jefferson said Adams was "distrustful, obstinate, excessively vain, and takes no counsel from anyone."[10] Jefferson, who had never met one, thought the common man had a kind of simple, natural nobility that would make the country great. Adams thought the common man was just as selfish as the rest of us and not half so well educated.

They didn't agree on anything, and neither did anyone else. Take France, for instance. By this time they'd had the French Revolution, followed by the Reign of Terror, Napoleonic Wars, and general Gallic confusion. Jefferson and half the country thought their Revolution was just as pure and high-minded as ours and we ought to rejoice in it. The Adamses and the other half complained that they'd killed off all our old buddies there and besides, it was childish to go on and *on* roasting people alive and chopping their heads off like that.[11] Some hotheads like Abigail thought we should join England in fighting France, and Washington was hauled off his veranda to be Commander-in-Chief again, just in case.

---

[9] After this misalliance they changed the rules, and now the number-two candidate gets to be Miss Congeniality instead, and weeps for joy.

[10] Especially from Jefferson.

[11] They thought a few token roastings would have been plenty. Others thought you can never have too many.

Then there were the Alien and Sedition Acts, saying that if you were a dangerous-looking enemy alien the President could send you home, and that no one should print vicious lies against the government. Jefferson said this was tyranny, and people could print all the lies they wanted, and it all just proved the individual states should run things for themselves.

It was pretty tense for a while, but then Adams arranged a sort of agreement with France and we didn't go to war after all. He said he wanted his epitaph to read "Here lies John Adams, who took upon himself the responsibility of peace with France in the year 1800." Many folks thought this was a dreadful anticlimax and went around saying that if "the old woman" had been in town, we'd be over there fighting by now, all right, all right.

Abigail spent a lot of time back home in Quincy (or Braintree) to escape from the medical attentions of Dr. Benjamin Rush. She had diabetes, and rheumatism, and chronic remitting fever, and Rush's bleedings and purges made her feel all wobbly. Dr. Rush was the most famous doctor in the country, but you couldn't convince him that people didn't contain at least twenty-five pounds of blood and ought to get rid of most of it. Actually, we've only got a bit more than twelve pounds, and he was often disappointed when his patients ran dry, but that didn't stop him for a minute.[12]

Adams stayed in Philadelphia and had awful head colds and infected teeth, scaly eruptions on his hands, and feelings of impending doom. (Washington had had smallpox, tuberculosis, pleurisy, malaria, bacillary dysentery, carbuncles, flu, typhoid, and pneumonia, though not all at once. Martha was always making everyone

---

[12] Rush made a number of important scientific advances, such as discovering that the dark color of Negro skin is actually a disease somewhat like leprosy.

take pinkroot for the ague, but pinkroot doesn't help as much as you might think. Patrick Henry felt that lots and lots of opium was the only answer, and that did help, but most people just muddled along feeling rotten.)

The newspapers were never a bit nice to poor John, and called him things like "old, querulous, blind, crippled, toothless."[13] It's true he'd lost some of his hair and his eyes bothered him, but he wasn't crippled and he certainly wasn't old, not compared to how old he got later. And they called him a spendthrift, which was silly—he had only two horses for his carriage and Washington always had six and wanted more, but does the press notice details like that?

It got worse as the next election got closer. Back then, the actual candidates didn't campaign, which would have been undignified and immodest, but their supporters made up for it in spades, broadcasting allegations of a nonpolitical nature such as we'd blush to hear today, maybe. Jefferson's backers accused Adams of listening to his wife. They called him "His Rotundity" and "a mere old woman and unfit to be President." His own side retorted that Jefferson was going to write an atheist Bible and force everyone to read it.

It took all winter to count the votes, and in the meantime the Adamses had to pack up and move to Washington, which was supposed to be finished by then but wasn't. The whole area looked like a bomb site. Cities never get finished on time.

Everyone knows Abigail hung her laundry to dry in the East Room in the White House. People go on about it as if she spent her entire life hanging laundry in the East Room, and frankly, I'm sick

---

[13] And Nixon thought they were kicking him around.

of the whole subject. Look, there was no place else to put it, not even a picket fence outside to sling the sheets over. Nothing but mud and tree stumps and construction trash. And wasn't it enough that she had to wash the stuff in the first place in water hand-hauled from half a mile away? And that the plaster was still wet and there was nobody to chop firewood and her rheumatism was killing her, and there weren't half enough candles, and no privy, and the staircase wasn't finished, and workmen underfoot the whole time? Anyone else would have let the sheets stay dirty, and I don't want to hear another word about where she strung her clothesline.

By February everyone got sick of counting votes and decided Jefferson had won. Of all the early Presidents right up to Martin Van Buren, who was an airhead, only Adams and his son J. Q. got turned down for a second term. They were completely mystified by it.

So John was finally allowed to retire with his beloved wife to his beloved farm in Braintree (or Quincy), where he lived on for years and years and years and was bored sick.

Everyone seems to think it was almost miraculously strange that Adams and Jefferson died on the same day, July 4, 1826, the fiftieth anniversary of the Declaration of Independence. I don't know why they find this so amazing. We all have to go sometime.

THOMAS JEFFERSON

★ ★ ★

1801–1809

ONLY A FEW years ago most Americans thought of Thomas Jefferson as our interesting and talented third President and author of the Declaration of Independence. Now he's just Sally Heming's boyfriend.

Hundreds, perhaps thousands, of books, articles, press releases, movies, television specials, and Web sites have spread the word. Many tell us of Sally's inmost thoughts and feelings, both bitter and tender. History books are being frantically revised. Everyone now knows that Jefferson had a thirty-five year affair with his slave—many keep referring to her as a "teenage" slave, even after all those years—and fathered her children.[1] It would be racist to doubt, but who doubts? We're strangely eager to believe, perhaps to offer up a Founding Father on the altar of white guilt, or perhaps happy to snatch off the angelic robes of our moral superior and reveal him as liar and hypocrite, if not actual rapist, and even lowlier than we are. Some want him hacked off Mount Rushmore with giant chisels.

Listen up. What the DNA tests actually did show is that Sally's youngest, Eston, born when Thomas was sixty-five, was almost certainly fathered by one of the dozen or so male descendants of Thomas's father who were on hand at the time and in and out of Monticello,[2] including a gaggle of cousins and nephews and an un-

---

[1] Sally fans feel that she was such a nice girl that all seven of her kids must have had the same father. Alas, they didn't.
[2] Virginia families still visit often and linger long.

cle, Field Jefferson, and Thomas's brother Randolph. None of these people, however, have any headline value so we never hear about them. Some say brother Randolph never stayed long enough at Monticello to do the deed,[3] others say he lived there full-time but couldn't have done it because he was retarded. Most sources don't mention him at all, and few believe Jefferson even had a brother.

On the other hand, one still-resistant historian says Randolph, twelve years younger than Thomas, was "fun-loving and carefree" and was hanging around Monticello nine months before Eston was born. A slave at the time described him as "a mighty simple man (who) used to come out among black people, play the fiddle and dance half the night." Never mind. Who can sell a movie about a slave and Jefferson's *brother*?

Here's how it started. Sally was the daughter of Mrs. Jefferson's father with one of his slaves, making her Thomas's half-sister-in-law, and he inherited her as a little girl when his father-in-law died. A slave described her later as "mighty near white . . . very handsome, long straight hair down her back." When Jefferson was minister to France he sent for his younger daughter, Polly (or Mary, or Maria), who'd been living with relatives since her mother died. He wanted her fetched by some mature and responsible lady, but instead they sent Sally. Abigail Adams met them in London and reported that she seemed unusually childish for fourteen and probably wouldn't be any use at all. Then she posted the girls on to Paris, and the first thing Jefferson did was buy both of them some new clothes.

---

[3] They don't say how long would have been long enough.

Early on, suspicious people pounced on these clothes. Why would he buy her clothes unless there was hanky-panky going on? Well, because she was a little slave girl from a farm in Virginia, and was she supposed to escort the American minister's daughter in the Champs Elysées wearing a calico apron and a hanky on her head?

Not that anyone cares, I suppose, but at the time Jefferson was madly in love with Maria Cosway.[4]

Then, several years later, when the trio came back to Virginia, Sally was pregnant. She named the baby Tom. Damning evidence. Who else can she possibly have known in France? Twelve years later, a disappointed office-seeker named Callender[5] wrote that Jefferson was having an affair with a slave—not too uncommon in that time and place. Jefferson didn't bother to answer; he said it was too silly to dignify with a denial. Nobody else paid much attention either until the recent Hemings outbreak, when Tom Jr. became exhibit A.

One thing the DNA tests did prove decisively was that the kid wasn't Jefferson's. There was Sally, alone and friendless in a bewildering land, under his wing and helpless, but apparently he was too busy thinking about Maria Cosway to take advantage of her. Maybe it didn't occur to him until later. Or maybe it never occurred to him. His teeming crowded household of family and companions never noticed anything over all those years. The man who slept in the next bedroom never heard anything but snores and no-

---

[4] She had him in such a tizzy that he was walking along beside the Seine thinking about her and jumped over a fence and fell and dislocated his wrist. It hurt for months. He was no kid.

[5] Disappointed office-seekers were an occupational hazard. Jefferson got off easy compared to poor Garfield.

body ever saw Tom hanging around Sally's bedroom. Still, we believe. It's fun to believe.

What makes it so exciting is that she was a slave, and in those days there was a sharp distinction between black slave women and free white women: the former could be beaten, raped, separated from their children, and sold by their owners, and the latter only by their male relatives, which was surely much nicer. The implication is that Sally couldn't have said no.[6] Everyone shivers with delicious horror at the thought that when Long Tom said "bedtime" she had to hop right in. Let's pull ourselves together—this is Thomas Jefferson, not Henry VIII. He had a pompous streak in him a yard wide and when it came to ethics and the moral conduct of life he thought he was the greatest thing since the star of Bethlehem. He just could never have spoken to himself again if he'd carried on like that even once, let alone for thirty-five years. And that's another thing. How many men do *you* know so stubborn they'd keep forcing the same unwilling woman into the sheets for thirty-five years?

If she could have said no, then it's none of our business, but personally I don't believe a word of it. I'm sorry, because it would be nice to think he had someone to warm up his poor bony old feet, with Martha dying so young and all, but I just can't see it. Not Tom. And I don't care if Sally had forty children, and I'm changing the subject. If you're still confused, you can go into your computer and ask for "Sally Hemings" and stagger back out weeks later twice as confused.

Jefferson's mother was a Randolph. This may not make much difference to you, but in Virginia it made a difference. Tom never

---

[6] If she'd wanted to, that is. He was a bit of a catch, if you don't mind tall, handsome, red-haired, genius Presidents who play the violin.

mentioned her in public. Probably he found her intellectually infe-
rior. She had ten children, which doesn't improve anyone's intellectual life.

As a teenager he was one of those self-righteous types, full of
maxims and resolutions about hard work, and when he fell in love
with Rebecca Burwell he worried that it might interfere with his
studies. Later he put her out of his mind and practiced law and
managed his lands and served in the Virginia House of Burgesses.

For a fellow who considered himself a simple farmer,[7] he spent
a lot of time politicking. After the Burgesses he was a delegate to
the First Continental Congress, governor of Virginia, commercial
envoy to France in charge of whale oil, salted fish, etc., and then he
succeeded Franklin as minister to France, where he tried to do
something about the Barbary pirates, but nothing can be done
about Barbary pirates. He was Washington's Secretary of State,
Adams's Vice President, and President. And whenever he got a
chance, he rushed back home to Monticello and tore it down and
started building it again differently. He spent most of his life building and unbuilding Monticello as if it was a set of Legos.[8] This was
a great nuisance to his wife, who may have died untimely from
tripping over all those stepladders and sawhorses for ten years.

He married Martha Wayles in 1772. I don't have any pictures
of her, but family tradition says she was beautiful and musically
talented.[9] He seems to have burned all their letters, so I don't have

---

[7] Or, alternatively, a simple archaeologist, architect, author, botanist, classicist, author,
ethnologist, geographer, linguist, musician, agronomist, naturalist, paleontologist,
philosopher, and surveyor.
[8] He meddled in everyone's architecture. Judging by the surviving evidence, nobody in
Virginia could even think about building a house without Jefferson barging in full of
plans.
[9] That is what families are here for.

gossip on their courtship, except that his idea of showing a girl a good time was to take his violin over to her house and play it all evening. No one will tell me whether he was any good on the thing, and few sounds are more painful than those made by a person who's only fair to middling on the violin, but anyway she married him. In the ten years before she died, she had six children. Two of them, or about par for the course, lived to grow up.

Jefferson was a father of the old school, always writing to his motherless little girls that if they expected him to like them, they'd better study harder. He wrote the younger one telling her never to go out in the sun without a bonnet "because it will make you very ugly and then we should not love you so much."[10]

His grandchildren remembered him fondly. Apparently he lightened up later.

He wrote the Declaration of Independence, or at least the first draft. Adams and Franklin made some changes, and then the congressional committee made some more. Everyone's an editor. Congress didn't get around to signing it until August, but on July 4 they'd said they liked it fine and wouldn't make any more changes, so we can go on having our Fourth of July parades on the Fourth of July.

Jefferson was a man of many interests. When he was in France and supposed to be looking after American matters there, he was often found traveling around other people's gardens and architecture and writing down what he thought of them. He wrote a large book called *Notes on the State of Virginia,* full of all sorts of things, some of them Virginian.

---

[10] The "we" was editorial, or Queen Victorian.

He liked his comforts. When he went to Philadelphia to be Secretary of State, he had to spend months rebuilding the house he was going to rent for a couple of years, so he could arrange all his things properly. He had a hundred and four crates of stuff shipped from France, including thirty-eight chairs, six stoves, a waffle iron, twenty-two bellpulls, and a hundred and forty-five rolls of wallpaper, plus mountains of books. He liked to spend his afternoons buying books.[11]

Having all that stuff to pack up again would make some people think twice about moving, but three years later he'd had enough of being Secretary of State and moved back to Monticello, where he found the fields in terrible shape. He tried all the right things, like rotating crops and planting clover to improve the soil, but nothing helped. Monticello was on top of a mountain, because Tom liked the view. There is no good soil on top of mountains. This has to do with gravity.

He planted nine hundred peach trees and opened a small nail-making shop and spent many happy hours counting and measuring nails. By 1796 he was grinding out a ton of nails a month, but nobody bought them and they kept piling up. In his spare time he pulled down some more of Monticello and added a dome and made plans to take off the roof.

But Tom was an Aries and easily bored, and pretty soon he was back in politics, and the next thing you knew he was President.[12] To show he was still just a simple farmer, he slopped around the White House in "an old brown coat, red waistcoat, old corduroy

---

[11] Adams said Jefferson was indolent, but he wasn't. He was always busy doing something or other.

[12] In his inaugural address he warned everyone against "entangling alliances" but nobody heard him. His voice was "almost femininely soft and gentle."

smallclothes, much soiled—woolen hose—and slippers without heels." Some visitors were offended, but he did change for dinner, which was nice since he went riding every afternoon and smelled of horse.

Three times a week he gave intimate little dinner parties for twelve, and everyone sat at a round table so that nobody would seem more important than anyone else. People who really were more important than anyone else were furious, and the British ambassador and his wife were so mad they moved clear to Philadelphia.[13] At dinner, topics of an enlightening nature were discussed, and Jefferson showed off scientific curiosities like his revolving shelves for sneaking food into the room, and a waterproof raincoat, and the first Baked Alaska, containing America's first ice cream.

Jefferson always wrote his own letters and speeches, so his secretary, Meriwether Lewis, didn't have anything to do but sharpen the pens and clean his fingernails with the penknife. Then Tom hit on the idea of sending him and William Clark out to walk over to the Pacific Ocean and look around. He was interested in buying a lot of real estate out there and wanted to know what he'd be getting.

When Lewis and Clark were well on their way he had Robert Livingston and James Monroe negotiate to buy the whole Louisiana Territory from Napoleon for fifteen million dollars, or three cents an acre. This was a good deal, besides settling the problem of having either France or Spain making faces at us across the Mississippi.

Lewis and Clark wrote back to say there was a whole lot of

---

[13] Once he invited his butcher to dinner. I don't know whether this was a joke or not. Probably not.

country out there, with assorted Indians in it.[14] They sent along a black-billed magpie and a prairie dog, which Jefferson forwarded to Charles Wilson Peale in Philadelphia. Jefferson didn't need a magpie, since he already had a mockingbird he'd taught to peck seed from his lips and hop up the stairs after him. (He was the first President to be followed upstairs by a mockingbird.) Lewis and Clark also sent him a quantity of large bones, some of them prehistoric and some just plain bones. Jefferson loved them all and spread them out on the floor and spent hours arranging them. Since nobody spent the summer in Washington before air-conditioning, he always went back to Monticello for a breath of air and a bit of building. When he had to return to his duties with his building lust unslaked, he revised the White House, adding two wings for stables, an ice house, and wine storage. He decided the roof leaked and replaced it, though it was practically brand-new. He put a cistern in the attic so water could trickle down through some pipes. He fixed up his clothes on a turnstile device, so his pants and jackets revolved, and built a fieldstone wall with an arch over the north entrance.

The truth was, he was getting bored again. He was a great man but he had the attention span of a gnat.

People begged him to stay on for a third term, but he said no. His excuse was that there was nothing in the Constitution to keep a President from staying forever once he'd got his hooks into the thing, and he didn't want to set a bad example.

After this, he stopped even pretending to care and started packing. He had a lot to pack, and when people came to him asking what to do about his embargo on trade with Great Britain, and

---

[14] They were still mostly friendly. They hadn't figured out what we were up to yet.

whether to leave it, or lift it, or strengthen it, or declare war, he said that was for the next man to figure out and went on packing. He said, "Never did a prisoner, released from his chains, feel such relief as I shall on shaking off the shackles of power."

When he got back to Monticello, his daughter Martha and six of her eight children moved in with him. He was so pleased at this that he built another house, Poplar Forest, ninety miles away, with no room for guests. It was all done in octagons. Even the privy was octagonal.

Then he got started on the University of Virginia, the true love of his life. It was a whole new building plan, arranged around pavilions, and he figured it would make Yale and Harvard look pretty sick.

It's not true that Jefferson introduced the tomato to the United States or publicly ate one to prove they weren't poisonous. For one thing, the tomato was native here to start with, and for another, lots of people had been eating them right along. It was just that the wrong sort of people ate them, the kind of people who probably used garlic too. They were on Jefferson's planting list, which was filled with pioneering exotica, but they were no big deal. If you care, and many hardly care at all, he did introduce brussels sprouts to the United States in 1810.

He owed everyone money. His nails weren't selling any better and his crops were full of Hessian flies, whatever they are. He invested ten thousand dollars building a commercial gristmill, but that didn't turn a profit either. He bought a spinning jenny and a loom, but it took two thousand yards a year just to make clothes for his family and slaves, and there wasn't much left to sell.

After the British burned the Library of Congress in 1814 he sold the country his books for $23,950. This left him with plenty of debts still unpaid and nothing to read. He was trying to organize a lottery to sell off Monticello when he died.

He wrote his own epitaph, which is the only way to do it if you want it done right. It says, "Here was Buried Thomas Jefferson, Author of the Declaration of Independence, of the Statute of Virginia for Religious Freedom and Father of the University of Virginia." Being President had been rather a sideline, too boring to mention.

Finicky people think that, regardless of whether he was sleeping with slaves, Jefferson was a terrible President because he believed in states' rights and a weak central government. On the other hand, he was the only President to invent the pedometer, the dumbwaiter, the lazy susan, and the swivel chair. Try to imagine America without swivel chairs.[15]

Jefferson didn't free his slaves when he died. He thought slavery was a revolting, abominable custom, and that one of these days somebody would abolish it, but in the meantime there it was and what could you do?

---

[15] Or brussels sprouts.

JAMES MADISON

★ ★ ★

1809–1817

JAMES MADISON, SOMETIMES called Little Jemmy, was not an inconsiderable person. He was a major contributing maker of these United States, an important figure at the Constitutional Convention, and sometimes referred to as the Father of the Constitution. He was the coauthor of the Federalist Papers, one of our most important shaping documents, and Jefferson's Secretary of State and personal pick for President. We ought to be more respectful of him.

Unfortunately, he looked like an inconsiderable person. He was not tall. Research shows us that in American presidential politics and the remembrances of history, barring unforeseen disasters, the tallest man always wins. For lasting admiration, or "legacy," a President should be first and foremost tall, like Washington and Jefferson and Lincoln and Roosevelt and Kennedy. Aside from Napoleon, tall means leadership. Jemmy was only five foot four and didn't weigh a hundred pounds with rocks in his hat. If it hadn't been for his splendid wife, Dolley, people would have walked straight into him in the halls and forgotten to pass the potatoes.[1]

Unlike many a President, he married the right woman.

Dolley grew up all dressed in gray in a strict Quaker family, and her father made and sold laundry starch in the front parlor. When even this modest enterprise collapsed, he locked himself in

---

[1] You yourself would have thought of him only when counting your five-thousand-dollar bills.

the bedroom for the rest of his life. He felt he was a failure.[2] So Dolley married a Mr. Todd, who died, and then Aaron Burr introduced her to Madison.

James had never thought much about women, but he was forty-three and felt it was time to get married, and he might as well marry Dolley, who was only twenty-five and had dimples. Dolley wasn't sure. It took her all summer to decide, and then when she did write to say yes it took James three days to answer her letter.

So they got married and fell in love and lived happily ever after. She called him "my darling little husband."[3] He said that whenever his official duties gave him a headache, he went and found Dolley and had a chat and felt a hundred percent better. She was that kind of girl.

Dolley didn't care a fig for politics, just for chatting and visiting and giving perfectly marvelous parties and making sure everyone was happy, but she had a knack for bringing the right people together with sometimes useful results. She'd been Jefferson's hostess when he was President, so that added up to sixteen years as queen of Washington and she loved every minute of it and it loved her. In that whole piranha tank she didn't have a single enemy except some sourpusses who hadn't been invited.[4] Even John Adams liked her.

Her portraits are disappointing—she was disappointed herself—but in person she bowled everyone over and they fought to get into

---

[2] He was.

[3] She could have broken him over her knee like a stick of kindling but she didn't want to.

[4] Plus a local preacher, who kept thundering that if she didn't quit giving parties on Sunday God was going to burn the White House down. Subsequent events much gratified him.

what Washington Irving called "the blazing splendor" of her draw-ing room. All the women wore what Dolley wore. When Dolley took snuff, everyone was charmed and took snuff too. When Dol-ley bought a pet macaw, everyone else bought a pet macaw and the jungles of South America fell silent. No murmur of scandal about her ever got murmured. She was the kindest, merriest, most gener-ous woman in town, with an endless appetite for fun, and made everyone learn to waltz.

Out in the great world, Jefferson had left us in rather a muddle with the Brits again, because he'd been busy packing. Now they wouldn't give up their habit of dragging our seamen off to work on their ships instead of ours. Some even thought they were egging the Shawnees on to do disagreeable things to our soldiers.[5] One way and another, it turned into the War of 1812, known to his enemies as Madison's War. It was a sloppy sort of war, and dragged on. Madison wanted to fortify Washington, but his Secretary of War said nonsense, the British were only after Baltimore. He didn't ex-plain what on earth they wanted with Baltimore.[6] By August of 1814 you could hear the war quite clearly from the East Room. Madison rushed presidentially off to Bladensburg to take command of an artillery battery, but when he noticed how dangerous this could be he got back in his carriage and drove away. He'd never said he was a hero.

Back home at the White House, Dolley was planning the usual dinner party, but she was having trouble rounding up guests. A Mrs. E. Jones sent regrets, explaining that her husband was busy

---

[5] The Shawnees had been pretty blistered without any outside egging.
[6] Afterwards he got fired, and replaced by James Monroe—up next.

dispatching Marines to defend the city.[7] She added, "There appears to be rather serious cause for apprehension." Dolley would have none of it.

Jemmy had left a hundred men to guard the White House but they didn't last long. The kindlier historians suggest that they all rushed off to enlist, but wherever they went, Dolley was left alone with a few servants and the steward. She postponed the party and packed up a few odds and ends—the national seal, the Declaration of Independence, the first draft of the Constitution, and a change of underwear. On second thought, she added some forks and spoons and the yellow velvet curtains, and sent her pet macaw off to enjoy diplomatic immunity at the French embassy, where it bit the hand that fed it. Then she sat down to write a letter to her sister.

The next day she was still there, hoping her dear husband would be home in time for dinner. She got herself up onto the roof to look for him, but all she could see was our gallant army running away as fast as they could. She went on with plans for the postponed dinner and finished the letter to her sister. She wrote, "Here I am, within sound of the cannon. Mr. Madison comes not . . . Two messengers, covered with dust, come bid me to fly, but here I mean to wait for him."

Finally a friend, Charles Carroll, came to drag her out bodily, but she insisted on rescuing the Stuart-Winstanley portrait of George Washington. It turned out to be screwed solidly into the wall, so she had the frame smashed, rolled up the canvas, and handed it out the door to what she described as two gentlemen from

---

[7] They didn't.

New York who were passing by.[8] Then she finished her letter: "And now, dear sister, I must leave this house, or the retreating Army will make me a prisoner by filling up the road . . . When I shall again write to you, or where I shall be tomorrow, I cannot tell!"

She seems to have had the time of her life. She never suggests for a minute that Jemmy might have stuck around to take care of the White House and other local institutions instead of making an ass of himself playing war in the suburbs. She never mentions that she was being rather stalwart to stick around holding the fort and rescuing historical items of government, not to mention the velvet curtains. She was just arranging a party, and waiting for her husband, and then she had to leave to beat the rush hour and, of course, the British, who dropped by several hours later[9] and burned down the house.[10]

They burned everything that looked official. Then it rained, and the whole city smoldered and smelled simply disgusting.

Philadelphia invited Madison to move the government back up there, and he did think about it, but Dolley was outraged. The Founding Fathers had said Washington, and Washington it was going to be.

James and Dolley moved into a nice unburned house on Lafayette Square, and Dolley gave bigger and better parties there until people complained of the suffocating crush but kept coming anyway.

Cheered and cosseted by his wife, little Jemmy lived on to be

---

[8] They did too bring it back. It isn't exactly Van Gogh's "Sunflowers" but at least we still have it, which is more than you can say for the rest of the furnishings.
[9] They found the dinner table set for forty.
[10] Moral: Don't give parties on Sunday.

eighty-five. He retired to the pretty house, Montpelier, that his grandparents had built, and nobody but Dolley could have persuaded visitors to come to dinner way down in Orange County like that, but for Dolley they'd go anywhere. She often had twenty guests just for breakfast, and on one Fourth of July she served ninety at a single long table on the lawn. A contemporary praised the Madisons' "profuse hospitality" and added that "French cooking and Madeira that he purchased in Philadelphia made a part of every day's fare." One guest said they were like "Adam and Eve in their bower."

Anxious and shy in the White House, Madison blossomed at the home he called "a squirrel's jump from heaven." He believed in parties, contour plowing, manure, and ten acres of woodland to feed every fireplace. If there was any justice, he would have gotten rich, but he just got poorer, thanks in large part to Dolley's no-good son Payne Todd, who needed great chunks of land sold off regularly to pay his gambling debts.

After he died, Dolley moved back to Washington and gave people advice about their parties. She grew to be a merry old lady, and found the perfect girl for Martin Van Buren's son to marry, and helped John Tyler figure out his social life, and played whist with John Quincy Adams, and even managed to be friends with the unfriendly Polks.

She never had been a beauty, but some people imagined she was because she made them feel so good. Even the British ambassador, meeting her for the first time, said our plump Dolley looked "every inch a queen."

Several Presidents' wives were hardly any use at all, but Jemmy did okay. If you were only five foot four, you needed a Dolley. Actually, maybe everybody needs one.

JAMES MONROE

★ ★ ★

1817–1825

AT HIS LAST New Year's reception, a Virginia lady who'd shaken hands with Monroe observed approvingly, "He is tall and well formed . . . His manner is quiet and dignified." Such a relief to have a properly tall and shapely President, after puny Madison. She added that Jefferson seemed to have been right when he said, "Monroe was so honest that if you turned his soul inside out there would not be a spot on it." This is a gratifying, though not electrifying, quality in a President.

Monroe is remembered chiefly for the Monroe Doctrine, which some consider John Quincy Adams's finest achievement. John Quincy was Secretary of State and he was sick and tired of France and Spain and England sniffing around our continent and Russians sneaking their trading posts down from Alaska as far as San Francisco.[1] His Monroe Doctrine says that since Europeans are basically different from Americans, from now on nobody but us could bully the new South American republics or set up colonies in our hemisphere or bother our neighbors, and in return we'd keep our noses out of European affairs.[2]

Nobody in Europe or South America paid the slightest attention to the Doctrine and Monroe didn't care much either. He was interested in Greece. Greece was fighting for independence from the Turks, and Monroe wanted us to go help. People got all worked up about Greece, and made their sons learn Greek in school and

---

[1] He chased them clear back up to 54-40' where they belonged.
[2] Okay, so we changed our mind about that later. It sounded good at the time.

ran around building Greek Revival courthouses and pretending they'd read Thucydides. Daniel Webster said the Greeks were a lot more fun than the "inhabitants of the Andes and the dwellers on the borders of the Vermilion Sea."[3]

John Quincy was always knocking himself out on projects that nobody else cared about.[4]

Be honest, now. Tell me three things you know about Guyana. Tell me one. Find Paraguay on the map. Find South America on a map. Well, as far as I know Monroe couldn't either. He had his own troubles, same as you and I.

James was still another Virginian, and he'd been to William and Mary College there but dropped out to go fight in the Revolution and get wounded at the Battle of Trenton. He was aide to General Stirling, a famous alcoholic, and between them they emptied many a glass. After this early training James was known as a deep, even an enthusiastic, drinker, but nobody suggested he went reeling around the White House singing improper songs. He was always a gentleman. He even looked like a gentleman, in an eighteenth-century sort of way, and kept on wearing knee breeches and buckled shoes for ages after everyone else gave theirs to the Goodwill. He had a dimple in his chin and kind blue-gray eyes and was said to resemble George Washington,[5] though I can't see it myself.

He wasn't terribly clever—John Adams called him "dull, heavy, and stupid"—but he was amiable and, as noted, honest, and people liked him.[6] He'd studied law under Jefferson, and Madison made

---

[3] There is no Vermilion Sea. Daniel Webster was a great orator, and that's the way great orators talk.
[4] He bought Florida from Spain and nobody cared about that either.
[5] This was considered a compliment.
[6] Except John Adams, but there's no pleasing an Adams.

him secretaries of State and War, simultaneously. His wife was a famous beauty and something of a mistake.

People said Elizabeth Monroe looked regal, and it's true there's a suggestion of the Tudors about her portrait, but that might be the ermine. Dolley Madison's dear friend Mrs. Seaton said Mrs. Monroe "paints very much and has, besides, an appearance of youth which would induce a stranger to suppose her age to be thirty." Actually Elizabeth's daughter Eliza would never see thirty again; nineteenth-century cosmetics can't have been as primitive as you'd think.

There was a younger daughter, Maria, born when Eliza was already seventeen, and only one child that died in between. I realize it's none of my business, but this wasn't a very generous output for a lady of the times and from what we hear of Mrs. M. she may have been a martyr to bedtime headaches. James deserved better.

Washington found her a dreadful letdown after dear Dolley. She thought the whole town was beneath her notice socially and refused to see visitors. Dolley had handed out punch and seedcake to everyone who dropped in, even if she didn't know their names, but Mrs. Monroe thought they should wait for formal invitations, and then she didn't send any. She didn't make calls, either. Eliza and her husband moved into the White House, and when somebody had to be visited, Eliza visited instead. Mrs. M. said she had a headache.

The French minister gave a grand ball to celebrate foreign troops pulling out of France, and the Monroes wouldn't go. Mrs. Monroe said Eliza might go, but only if nobody mentioned it or told the reporters. The French minister was furious.

When little Maria got married in the East Room, no one was invited. The Russian minister asked what gift he could send, and Eliza told him to forget it. The Russian minister was furious.

Everyone was furious, and kept hanging around John Quincy's office complaining so he couldn't get any work done.[7] He himself was always too busy to make calls and grumbled about "this senseless war of etiquette visiting."[8]

Pretty soon women stopped going to the White House even when they did get invited. When Mrs. Monroe gave her Tuesday-night receptions nobody showed up but her sisters, and there wasn't a sound except the teacups clinking in their saucers.

In spite of his womenfolk, everyone voted to re-elect Monroe and his administration was called the Era of Good Feeling, because there was only one political party and it was hard to scrape up much of a fight.

The main flaw was the matter of the furniture. It was kind of a furniture administration right from the start.

When Monroe was elected the first time, the White House was supposed to be all rebuilt after the British problem and ready by the following fall, but you know contractors, and even when the roof was finished there still wasn't anything to sit on. It was nice to have that George Washington portrait Dolley rescued, but you can't sit on a portrait, or at least not a portrait of George Washington. So Monroe sold the government his own furniture for $9,071.22 ½, which fixed up two bedrooms and the state dining room. It was mostly Louis Seize stuff and mighty elegant. Mrs. Monroe had expensive tastes. Then a Colonel Lane latched on to

---

[7] Surprise your friends: Monroe's Vice President was named D. D. Tompkins. He seems to have been invisible.
[8] Washington wasn't exactly Paris. If you didn't visit, you could stand around throwing sticks into the Potomac, or you could take a nap.

some money and scurried around filling in the gaps.[9] The Monroes ordered all the important pieces from France, and the French charged them prices they felt commensurate with the "President's palace."

Congress nearly choked when they saw the bills, and then, toward the end of the second term, they added them up and noticed there was twenty thousand dollars missing. Congressman Cocke asked Monroe to stop by the Hill and explain this to a committee, and Monroe sent a message back saying to "tell Cocke he was a scoundrel." Then he grandly offered to buy back his own things for the original $9,071.22 ½. This didn't quite clear the matter up and it got kind of sordid. Nobody ever did find the twenty thousand, but I'm sure Colonel Lane would have had some perfectly simple explanation if he hadn't been dead already.[10]

After they left the White House, Mrs. Monroe kept right on buying expensive decorative bric-a-brac and James got poorer and poorer until he was quite surrounded by Louis Seize candelabra and stony broke.

He died on the Fourth of July, like Adams and Jefferson, but by this time people had come to expect it.

A biographer wrote, "His virtue was not in flying high but in walking orderly, his talents were exercised not in grandeur but in mediocrity." So what's this biographer fellow done that's so special, I'd like to know?

---

[9] He had expensive tastes too. He paid $9.56 ¼ for a mustard pot, but I'm sure it was a lovely one.
[10] Nobody asked Mrs. Monroe about it. They were scared of her.

JOHN QUINCY ADAMS

★ ★ ★

1825–1829

JOHN ADAMS, BACK in the beginning of it all, had always felt that the Presidency should be, well, not exactly hereditary, which would be undemocratic, but just naturally reserved for a group of the right sort of families whose sons would be properly educated and trained up for public service, and dedicated to knowing what was best for the rest of us rabble. The idea still hangs around to this day, but at the time some people were upset when Adams' son John Quincy turned up.

John Quincy was an Adams through and through. His wife, Louisa, said sadly, "As regards women, the Adams family are one and all peculiarly harsh and severe in their characters. There seems to exist no sympathy, no tenderness for the weakness of the sex." She was a pretty girl, and a scholar, and read Greek and wrote poetry in French, and stuck it out with J. Q. for fifty years, but who was good enough for the Adamses?[1] She was said to suffer from melancholia, and no wonder. There were Adamses everywhere she turned. She saw Adamses in her sleep. Even her children were Adamses.

John and Abigail had raised John Quincy to be President and he'd worked very hard to be a credit to the family. His father was always writing him supportive advice like, "If you do not rise to the head not only of your profession but of your country, it will be owing to your own *laziness, slovenliness* and *obstinacy*." (The italics are John's.) As for his mother, his grandson Brooks says J. Q. al-

---

[1] You couldn't marry just one Adams. You had to buy the whole set.

ways loved her best of anyone in the world. I suppose he and Abigail were always going off into the kitchen for a heart-to-heart about political economy and leaving Louisa all alone muttering Greek choruses to herself.

He even looked a little like Abigail, at least for a while. In the Copley portrait he was twenty-eight and looks downright elfin, for an Adams. He looks like a poet, and in 1832 he did produce a slim volume and maybe it's not Keats but it's still the only book of poems by an American President.[2]

Later he stopped looking like his mother and lost his hair and grew a tummy and looked like his father. Later still he looked like a troll.

Way down inside he may have been a sensitive poet, but outside he was a toad, and even the nicer class of toad wouldn't have much to do with him and warned their toad children against growing up like John Quincy. He even noticed it himself. He said, "I am a man of reserved, cold, austere, and forbidding manners. My political adversaries say a gloomy misanthrope; my personal enemies, an unsocial savage."

He wore any old thing that came to hand. He wore the same hat for ten years. He got dreadful colds like his father and was always coughing and sniffling.[3] Littleton called him "doggedly and systematically repulsive. With a vinegar aspect, cotton in his leathern ears, and hatred in his heart, he sat . . . like a bulldog among spaniels."

---

[2] This may be just as well.
[3] Jefferson always soaked his feet in ice water every day to keep from catching colds, but apparently the Adamses never took this simple precaution.

Kinder folk called him "an intellectual's intellectual," meaning there were only about five people in the country who understood a word he said. He and his father and Jefferson were probably our smartest Presidents, but being smart is hardly high-priority with the electorate and if you're an Adams, it can be downright irritating. When he'd run against Monroe in 1820, most people ignored him completely.[4] When you get right down to it, he didn't even win his own election.

There were four candidates, John Quincy, Andrew Jackson, Henry Clay, who was always running for President, and a man named Crawford, and they were all Republicans.[5] Jackson got forty-three percent of the popular vote and John Quincy got thirty percent, but neither had an electoral majority, so it went to the House. The House argued the matter till February, and agreed that John Calhoun was Vice President but nobody was President. Finally Clay, who was Speaker, said Jackson wiping out twenty-five hundred Englishmen at the Battle of New Orleans in Madison's War wasn't a sufficient rèsumè, and swung the election to J. Q.

Well, the Jacksonians screamed bloody murder. They might have forgotten about it eventually, except for what Adams did next. Would you believe he made Clay Secretary of State? Naturally the whole town thought there'd been a deal, and Clay had to fight a duel about it with a hot-headed senator named Randolph, though they missed each other by a mile. The Jacksonians were beside themselves with rage and started plotting the next election right away, and vowed they'd never pass a bill John Quincy wanted, or replace the chairs and tables the Monroes took with

---

[4] The electoral count was 231 to 1.

[5] You can forget about the Federalists now, if you haven't already.

them, or say hello to him on Pennsylvania Avenue. So much for the Era of Good Feeling.[6]

It was all a misunderstanding, as Adamses are above making deals, but it made an awful mess. However, try telling an Adams he's about to barge into a giant public-relations error. Adamses are above public relations too.[7]

John Quincy felt even worse about the election than Jackson did. He thought he deserved to win it fair and square, having worked hard for the country all his life, and been minister to everywhere, and a senator, and dreamed up the Monroe Doctrine while he was Secretary of State, and his parents had always told him to be President, and now look. He thought seriously about turning it down, but not *that* seriously.

What he planned to do as President was jack up the general state of culture around here, a matter even less galvanizing than the Monroe Doctrine. He thought there should be a famous international university in Washington, with scholars and scientists clustering from all over the world like Athens or Charlemagne or something. The Jacksonians thought this was great nonsense, as they were all *non campus mentis,* or not university material. Most of all J. Q. wanted a national observatory, because there wasn't a single observatory in the whole country, and he thought if we had one in Washington we could look at the stars and that would make everything a lot nicer.[8] He called it a "lighthouse of the skies," and this struck Congress as a real thigh-slapper. People stopped each

---

[6] Washing their hands of the whole party, the Jacksonians decided to be Democrats and the two-party system was back in business.

[7] This is their main problem.

[8] Much later there was one in Cincinnati and he almost killed himself traveling out there to dedicate it, but face it, Cincinnati isn't Washington.

other in the streets and said "lighthouse of the skies," and laughed till the tears ran down their cheeks.

He also thought we should build roads and canals so people could send things from place to place and there wouldn't be any more wars.[9] Nothing came of that either. About the only legislation that squeezed through was the Tariff of Abominations, which made the Southerners mad as hornets.

Congress refused to finish building the White House or buy any furniture, but they did grade and fill the outdoors, finally, and John Quincy went out and puttered in it. He planted gardens, shrubs, orchards, exotic vegetables nobody would eat, and a whole forest of tree seedlings. It made him feel a little better. He planted white mulberries for a silkworm plantation, and Louisa sat around soaking sticky little silkworm cocoons in warm water and unwinding the threads. It gave her something to do in the evenings. J. Q. liked to read some Cicero or Milton or Plutarch and go to bed early.

He always got up before dawn and walked four or five miles and then took off his clothes and went for a swim in the Potomac.[10] One morning a lady reporter he'd been dodging saw his bald head bobbling around in the river and sat down on his clothes and refused to budge until he gave her the interview. (This story turns up so often I suppose there might be something in it, unlikely as it seems. They say her name was Anne Royall.)

If J. Q. felt bad about the election of '24, he felt a lot worse about '28. It wasn't just losing, it was Andrew Jackson. He thought Jackson was the embodiment of pure evil, and his election proved

---

[9] I forget how he'd worked that out, but it seemed to make sense at the time.
[10] This was all very healthy, but it never did a thing for his figure.

beyond question that there was no God, which meant that he, J. Q., would never go to heaven and see his mother again.

Jackson's election proved nothing of the sort, of course, and just because he couldn't spell and liked to play with guns didn't mean he was the Antichrist, but you couldn't console J. Q. He felt he was a total failure in life, because he'd always meant to "banish war and slavery from the face of the earth forever."[11] To top it off his oldest son, George Washington Adams, cracked and started seeing things that weren't there and killed himself.

John Quincy had always expected the worst, and why not?

Then, just as life seemed darkest, some kindly people came and said he could be their congressman if he wanted. The other Adamses thought it was pretty low-rent for an ex-President to go back to Washington as a humble congressman, but J. Q. said no, it was perfectly respectable, and back he went. He spent the next seventeen years there, still trying to wipe out the world's two oldest institutions with his bare hands and pretending not to mind what Jackson had done to his gardens. Sometimes he even thought he'd get invited to be President again. He never could understand why he was so unpopular, or what that had to do with the Presidency anyway.

He even died in Congress, an Adams to the end. (See POLK.)

There were still plenty of Adamses, though. His son Charles Francis had a shot at being Vice President in 1848, but his ticket lost to Taylor, who was a war hero. Adamses are never war heroes. Except for that first one, Adamses *hate* wars. After that the family tended to lurk on the sidelines complaining about the low quality

---

[11] Did I mention that Adamses expect a lot of themselves?

of Presidents nowadays and writing books with depressing titles like *The Degradation of the Democratic Dogma,* which made surprisingly little impression on the electorate.

Many Americans rarely think about the Adamses, sometimes ignoring them for weeks on end. We seem to feel it wasn't quite necessary to have two short, bald, portly, intellectual Presidents with bad manners named John Adams.

Count your blessings. If it weren't for the American public, we could have had six or seven.

ANDREW JACKSON

★ ★ ★

1829–1837

MANY OF THE wisest men in the country considered Jackson to be some kind of nut,[1] but they didn't understand. It helps to think of him as the first really *American* President, the previous samples being of recognizably English types.

Jackson was easily excited, and at six-foot-one he weighed only a hundred and forty pounds, and his gray hair looked like an eagle's nest and his blue eyes had a rather unsettling glitter. He was Scots-Irish and never stopped to count to ten, and whenever the occasion arose—and it often arose—he challenged somebody to a duel. Some say he fought in over a hundred duels, mostly about his wife.[2]

There was nothing wrong with his wife. Her name was Rachel, and it's true she smoked a pipe but that wasn't peculiar where Jackson came from. Way back in 1790, Jackson was boarding in the same house with her and her husband, one Captain Lewis Robards, and Robards started complaining in the local pubs that he thought Rachel and Jackson were holding hands behind his back. When Jackson got wind of this, he told Robards that if he ever said it again, "he would cut the ears out of his head, and that he was tempted to do it anyhow." Jackson was a man of his word in such matters, and he took to fingering a butcher's knife whenever Ro-

---

[1] "Ignorant, passionate and imbecile" and "fierce ungovernable temper" were some of the kinder descriptions. Jefferson said he couldn't possibly think of anyone worse to be President.

[2] He was so full of bullets he rattled like a bag of marbles.

bards came into the room. Pretty soon Robards left town, glancing anxiously over his shoulder.

Jackson and Rachel found they had a lot in common, and after they heard it on the grapevine that Robards had gotten a divorce in Virginia, they got married.[3]

Two years later it turned out that Robards hadn't quite gotten this divorce after all, and so when it finally came through they had to go get married all over again. It was embarrassing, but it could happen to anyone.

Jackson was touchy about this lapse, and when a man named Dickinson made some catty remark he challenged him to a duel, though Dickinson could drill a dime at fifty yards and Jackson had terrible eyes on him and could hardly *see* a dime. He let Dickinson shoot first and the bullet broke one of Jackson's ribs, and then he took extra-careful aim and shot Dickinson stone dead. He said, "I intended to kill him. I would have stood up long enough to kill him if he had put a bullet in my brain."

In 1828, when he was running for President against John Quincy, the whole Rachel story was nearly forty years old, but don't you know people went and dug it up? The *Cincinnati Gazette* rolled its eyes and said, "Ought a convicted adulteress and her paramour be placed in the highest office of this free and Christian land?" People raged on and on about it, and when they got tired of abusing Rachel they said Jackson's *mother* was "a common prostitute brought to this country by British soldiers."[4] It's a wonder anyone bothered, since a child could have seen that Jackson

---

[3] At least they said they did, and I believe it, even if nobody ever did find the records.
[4] It's a crying shame the way our modern campaigns have grown so nasty and personal, compared to the genteel olden days.

was going to wipe up the floor with J. Q. and his lighthouse of the skies. But Rachel was sick as mud about it all, and it made her so nervous and depressed that shortly before he took office, she died.

Naturally Jackson blamed John Quincy, but it wasn't Adams who started the talk, any more than it was Jackson who said Adams lurked around Catholic churches talking Latin with priests and nuns. In those primitive days, the candidates didn't have to tell horrible lies about each other in person. Their fans and favorite newspapers did it for them, and they really put their backs into it.

The inauguration was the party of the year. Jackson was Old Hickory, hero of the Battle of New Orleans, the only happy part of the War of 1812. He stood for all the manly American virtues like cockfighting, horse racing, drinking, gambling, and shooting at people. He was the candidate of just plain folks, and they'd all[5] voted for him and they all came to town to see him sworn in. The men had hickory-wood stirrups and their wives wore strings of hickory nuts around their necks. They camped out all over the town and threw chicken bones around and galloped up and down firing guns. Some fastidious observers said it put them in mind of the barbarian hordes at the gates of Rome, while others thought it was more like the French Revolution, with the peasantry howling for blue blood.

After the ceremony, everyone followed Jackson home and crashed the White House party. They nearly killed him fighting to shake hands, and they squeezed in through the windows and climbed on the chairs with their boots on, and women fainted and got trampled, and thousands of dollars worth of china and glass got smashed, and various accessories got swiped for souvenirs, and

---

[5] All except non-folks like women, blacks, and Indians.

the carpets and upholstery got all squishy with mud and tobacco juice.[6] Finally enough of them were lured outside with washtubs full of punch so that Jackson could escape to a hotel.

He couldn't complain, of course, because he'd always said he was crazy about the common man. He didn't mean they had to stay common, though. He only meant that they, like Jackson, could be born in a log cabin out in howling nowhere between the Carolinas and still grow up to be a lawyer and judge and famous general and senator and own miles of land in Tennessee and armies of slaves and stables full of fancy horses. And not need any sissy universities to do it, either. He thought people should have a chance to grab up all the public lands dirt cheap and be a success like him.

This was the birth of the American dream, and one in the eye for the Adamses.

Jackson believed in the Constitution, states' rights, no taxes, paying off the national debt, preserving the Union, and enjoying his personal comforts. Congress said he could have all the money he wanted, so he fixed up the White House in the grandest style you ever saw. He spent ten thousand dollars in the East Room alone, with some extremely splendid chandeliers, blue satin upholstery, and gilded tables. His enemies said it looked like a palace and called him "King Jackson," but his friends liked it. They spoke sneeringly of poor J. Q.'s decor, full of "cobwebs, a few old chairs, lumbering benches and broken glass."[7]

Sometimes Jackson had a thousand people drop by for drinks. Suppers were served on silver-plated dishes, with turkeys and fish

---

[6] Historians refer to this as "Jacksonian Democracy."
[7] They figured John Quincy had it done up like that on purpose, so the common man couldn't come in and get comfortable.

and canvasback ducks, partridges, cold chicken "interlaid with slices of tongue and garnished with salled," "a monster salmon in waves of meat jelly," and more than enough wine and brandy.

He threw out everything that reminded him of John Quincy and built a stable for his favorite racehorses, Emily, Bolivia, and Lady Nashville, on top of John Quincy's garden. He fired everyone who'd voted for John Quincy and gave their jobs to people who'd voted for him.

The second thing he did was send the whole town into fits with the Peggy O'Neal business.

"Pretty Peggy O'Neale" was a blue-eyed brunette who made the most of her figure. She was the daughter of a tavern-keeper who ran a popular watering-hole and she met a lot of interesting people that way.[8] She met John Eaton, and married him, and then Jackson made him Secretary of War. This caused a social problem, as who wanted to invite a tavern-keeper's daughter to dinner, and besides, there was some question about her chastity, always one of our most pressing national issues. Peggy had been married to a naval purser named Timberlake who was away at sea a lot, and a girl does get lonely. Apparently she'd already been friends with Eaton before Timberlake had the grace to die, but nobody could prove anything and Jackson didn't believe it for a minute. It reminded him of the fuss over poor Rachel. He said Peggy was "the smartest little woman in America" and invited the Eatons to dinner all the time. Nobody else did, though. Mrs. Calhoun, the Vice President's wife, stayed home in South Carolina rather than risk run-

---

[8] Jackson had stayed there himself, and spoken highly of her singing and piano-playing. He didn't know much about music but he knew what he liked.

ning into Peggy in Washington.[9] The only person besides Jackson who was nice to Peggy was little Martin Van Buren, Secretary of State. He had his reasons. He used to go out riding with the President every day and tell him the whole thing was Calhoun's fault.[10]

It was all very absorbing and nobody got any work done for ages. It was known as "Eaton malaria." All they did on the Hill was stand around talking about Peggy. Jackson called a special Cabinet meeting about her, and said she was "chaste as a virgin" and read testimonials about her character, but nobody was impressed.

Finally things got so bad that Van Buren persuaded the whole Cabinet, including himself and Eaton, to resign. Jackson sent Eaton off, Peggy in tow, to be governor of Florida, and then all the way to the legation in Spain.[11] This simplified matters.

Van Buren went to be minister to England for a while, and then imagine his surprise when he found himself the new Vice President, with Calhoun and Floride nowhere in sight.

Henry Clay ran against Jackson in 1832, saying he should never have dissolved the Bank of the United States as unconstitutional, since nobody knew what to do without it. Most of the voters kept their money in the sugar bowl anyway and didn't care. Jackson stayed in the White House.

He felt that the eastern Indian tribes took up too much room and should stop hanging around underfoot and seek their fortunes out West. He told the Creeks and the Cherokees that all the land

---

[9] Her name was Floride.

[10] Jackson was an honest, simple fellow and he always listened to Van Buren because he thought Van Buren was clever. He was plenty clever.

[11] Peggy had a marvelous time there too. She was a grand girl and did funny imitations of famous people.

west of the Mississippi belonged to him personally,[12] and he'd let them have it if they'd go there, but if they didn't,[13] he couldn't be responsible for what happened. A lot did happen, as the white settlers were naturally irritated by Indians taking up space they needed in order to get as rich and successful as Jackson. So finally the Cherokees, who were serious homebodies and hated traveling, had to be rooted out with bayonets and set out on the interstate Trail of Tears, which was full of potholes and rivers without bridges. Some[14] died on the way of cholera and cold, or just plain unhappiness, because they were only Indians and didn't understand that it was all for the good of the country.

The Florida Seminoles, on the other hand, dug in and put up a nasty fight, taking unfair advantage by hiding out in the swamps where we couldn't find them. We only managed to capture their chief, Osceola, by pretending that the flag of peace he was waving was probably an undershirt hanging out to dry. In the end we gave up on the Seminoles. The place was all swampy anyway, and who knew how the real estate prices would go up later?

With Jackson around, there was never a dull moment. There was the Alamo, for instance, where a hundred and eighty-eight gallant Texans, including the famous slave-smuggler Colonel James Bowie and the famous professional backwoodsman and publicity hog Davey Crockett, held off Santa Anna and three thousand Mexicans before the famous wipe-out. Then in Part Two, Sam Houston ambushed Santa Anna at the San Jacinto River and captured him, and said Texas was an independent country[15] and he was its Presi-

---

[12] It didn't.
[13] They didn't.
[14] Well, quite a lot, actually.
[15] Most Texans still believe this.

dent. This was fine with Jackson. It was the kind of entrepreneur-
ial spirit he liked to see.

Jackson was the first President to decide that a President can
veto a perfectly constitutional bill just because he doesn't like it,
and he was like a kid with a new toy. He vetoed more bills than all
the previous Presidents put together and left a fine, fierce legacy for
the future.

When he left office, Philip Hone, a contemporary busybody,
called his administration "the most disastrous in the annals of the
country." That's *his* opinion. One of the problems Jackson left behind was that after paying off the national debt, we still had thirty
million dollars from the public land sales hanging around in the
treasury. People were afraid this would be a temptation to the un-
scrupulous, just piling up in there. It was a lot of money back then.

One of Jackson's early biographers called him "A democratic
aristocrat. An urbane savage. A ferocious saint." In short, he was
baffled.

On the way out Jackson said, "I have only two regrets: that I
have not shot Henry Clay or hanged John C. Calhoun."

They don't make them like that any more.

MARTIN VAN BUREN

★ ★ ★

1837–1841

WHEN YOUR CHILDREN ask you where Van Burens come from, don't blush and stammer and hush them up with some fairy tale. Just tell them straight out that Van Burens are not a sickness but a perfectly normal, natural part of growing up and being a democracy.

Little Matty was, frankly, a politician. After all those farmer-statesmen and farmer-soldiers, he was our first politician President. He'd had a sort of law practice once, but basically with Matty it was politics for breakfast, lunch, and dinner. In New York he'd invented the political machine, called the Albany Regency, and made himself senator and governor and anything else he could lay his hands on, and then he swam into the public view just behind Jackson's right ear like a pilot fish.

Jackson was a simple frontiersman and didn't know what to do about problems he couldn't shoot. It's counterproductive to shoot voters, since they can't vote dead except in Boston and Philadelphia, so Matty took over for him and invented modern politics. He invented speeches, rallies, barbecues, smoke-filled rooms, ward heelers, sing-alongs, fund-raisers, leaflets, posters, billboards, buttons, bumper stickers, and other basic tools of government as we know it today. He was called "The Little Magician" because everything he touched turned to gold, or votes, which are much the same thing.

Jackson gets credit for inventing the spoils system, under which people who helped you get elected find all sorts of nice surprises under their pillows, like jobs that can make them very rich. Well, maybe it was Jackson, but it sounds like Matty to me.

It's hard to see how even the magician could convince voters he was a simple Jacksonian Democrat from the outback when he was really a Republican from New York who knew a thing or two about French wines and which sauces go on what, but that's politics for you. He didn't exactly slouch around in homemade coonskins, either. Somebody described him in "an elegant snuff-colored broadcloth coat with a velvet collar; his cravat was orange with modest lace tips; his trousers were white duck, his shoes were morocco; his neat-fitting gloves were yellow kid; his long-furred beaver with a broad brim was of a Quaker color."[1]

The ticket was balanced by his Vice President, Richard Johnson, who told everyone he'd killed the great Shawnee chief Tecumseh, and maybe he did. (Somebody did.) As a sign of statesmanship, killing Indians was just as good as being born in log cabins, and Matty needed him because he himself was born in an ordinary house and he'd been too busy politicking to kill much of anyone.[2] His supporters advertised the future Vice President by singing "Rumpsey-dumpsey, rumpsey-dumpsey, General Johnson killed Tecumseh!"

You may still not believe that anyone could possibly vote for a man in yellow gloves and a lace-trimmed orange necktie, but you're forgetting Jackson. Jackson was still very much the flavor of the month with most folks, and when he said, "Vote for my little Matty," they set down their jugs and laced up their boots and did so.

---

[1] His enemies accused him of wearing corsets too. They didn't say how they knew.
[2] When he was running the Senate during Jackson's second term, he always wore a brace of pistols because of the slavery discussions, but the record shows he shot few, if any, senators.

Being nice to Peggy Eaton had been a good idea. Van Buren was full of good ideas. Oh, some people sneered—Calhoun said, "He is not of the race of the lion or the tiger; he belongs to the lower order, the fox"—but you'll notice Calhoun wasn't President and Van Buren was.

When Matty walked into the White House he stepped smack into the Panic of '37, caused by various factors too financial to discuss. Banks and businesses closed down and people lost all their money and rioted for bread in the streets until even Van Buren had to take notice, though it was rather sordid and not his thing at all. He called a special session of Congress, and it authorized an issue of temporary treasury notes, and presto, there we were in debt again. From what people tell me, I understand we still are.

On account of the depression, Matty lay low and canceled the larger White House parties and kept the curtains drawn while he changed a thing or two in the decor. Privately he'd always thought Jackson's taste a bit garish, and also eight years of hosting the common man had been hard on the furniture.[3] He auctioned off some old tables and things and got another twenty thousand from Congress for new rugs and a thorough housecleaning. When he invited the public in to see, they were disappointed. They'd liked Jackson's furniture better and besides, there was nothing to eat. Van Buren didn't want to encourage riffraff hanging around,[4] but his private parties were something else again. He had a perfectly wizard chef, and even Calhoun couldn't resist a dinner invitation. Van Buren himself got quite tubby.

---

[3] They never wiped their feet and they spat on the carpets a lot. They thought cuspidors were sissy.

[4] Congressmen were allowed in only twice a year.

He had four sons, Abraham, John, Martin Jr., and Smith. They came to live with him, and Dolley Madison was incensed at the thought of five bachelors in the White House with no proper hostess.[5] She sent at once for a pretty niece named Angelica and bundled her straight over. Angelica decided Matty was too old for her so she married Abraham, and everyone agreed she made a charming hostess but still there were no slam-bang public parties as in the good old days.

People started murmuring disconsolately. Maybe after all Van Buren wasn't such a good old straight-shooting Jacksonian. Maybe he was a snob. Maybe he was a sissy.[6] They started calling him "Petticoat Pet." Maybe the depression had all been his fault. The Whigs, who were new on the scene and made up of assorted anti-Jacksonians, called him "Martin Van Ruin."

He didn't appear to take much notice. He was peculiarly apathetic about actually *being* President, and never vetoed a single bill or offered any opinions except Jackson's. He may have felt that getting there was more than half the fun. I mean, people climb up Mount Everest, but there's nothing much to do when you get there except leave a message in a bottle and start back down. He said himself, later, "As to the Presidency, the two happiest days of my life were those of my entrance upon the office and my surrender of it." Nobody expects you to settle down and *live* on Everest.

In the spring of 1840 Mr. Ogle, congressman from Pennsylvania, made a speech that lasted three days and really cut loose on how Matty Van's lifestyle was putting us in the poorhouse and dis-

---

[5] Some historians insist that Van Buren had had a wife for twelve years, but he wrote a painfully detailed autobiography and never once mentioned any wife, and surely he ought to know best.

[6] Maybe they'd just noticed that necktie.

gustingly decadent besides. He said the White House "glitters with all imaginable luxuries and gaudy ornaments . . . a palace as splendid as that of the Caesars and as richly adorned as the proudest Asiatic mansion." He'd heard that Matty had had a reservoir put in the basement with a pump to pull water upstairs for washing dishes and bathing, and he was revolted. He shuddered at the Greek and/or Roman luxury of the President lolling about in his "tepid bath" and spraying his bushy sideburns with a French cologne called *"Triple Distille Savon Daveline Mons Sens."*[7]

He saved his best shots for Matty's dining habits, bragging that he, Ogle, liked nothing fancier than "fried meat and gravy, or hog and hominy," and he wouldn't touch the Frenchy vittles served on Pennsylvania Avenue.[8] He said there were "knives, forks and spoons of gold, that he might dine in the style of the monarchs of Europe," and "green finger cups, in which to wash his pretty, tapering, soft, white lily fingers."[9]

Van Buren's people said he'd actually cost the government less than any other President, and I seem to remember those spoons from Mrs. Monroe's reign, but no matter. It was a real zinger of a speech.

Matty had beaten Harrison in '36 and in '40 Harrison beat him. That's politics for you. Matty got along famously with the new man. A good politician gets along famously with everyone.

In '48 he ran for President again on the Free-Soil ticket, just to keep his hand in, and didn't carry a state.

Van Buren did leave us a lasting legacy. His home was in Kinder-

---

[7] I don't know how he'd know, and I can't *imagine* how he pronounced it.
[8] Who'd asked him to?
[9] It seems clear Ogle had a mole in the kitchen, and possibly another in the bathroom.

hook, New York, and his good friends had always called him "Old Kinderhook." So back when Jackson was still top dog and Matty was looking after him, the initials "O.K." started turning up here and there. They stood for Old Kinderhook, and got to be kind of an inside joke among the Jacksonians. The Whigs couldn't figure it out, so they said, sneering, that they probably stood for the way Jackson would spell "all correct," and then this got to be an inside joke among the Whigs. For some reason a lot of people believed this pleasantry, including people who write dictionaries and ought to know better.[10]

---

[10] It's true Jackson couldn't spell for shucks, but *nobody* has ever spelled "all correct" as "oll korrect."

WILLIAM HENRY HARRISON

★ ★ ★

1841–1841

THE ELECTION OF 1840 was marvelous fun. Nobody had any sort of platform or mentioned any issues,[1] they just partied and sang.

Harrison the Whig had been the hero of the Battle of Tippecanoe, where he killed numerous Indians. He'd also liberated a lot of land from Indians who probably wouldn't have known what to do with it anyway, so he was a strong candidate right from the start.[2] He ran with a Virginia pol named John Tyler, and the Whigs went around chanting "Tippecanoe and Tyler too" and calling Van Buren a pantywaist.

An opposition newspaper made the mistake of saying that all Harrison wanted in life was a two-thousand-dollar pension, plenty of hard cider, and a log cabin. The Whigs gleefully seized the idea and set about selling Harrison as yet another barefoot boy from the backwoods. They claimed that he'd been *born* in a log cabin, which doubled his qualifications and made him the man to beat.

Luckily most voters had never visited Harrison's birthplace. It's a serene and stately brick mansion, far grander than the White House, build by his distinguished grandfather on thousands of fer-

---

[1] There was only one issue at the time, but it wasn't a good idea to mention it.

[2] He hadn't done much lately, except lose to Van Buren. He said himself, "I am the clerk of the Court of Common Pleas of Hamilton County at your service. . . . Some folks are silly enough to have formed a plan to make a President of the United States out of this Clerk and Clod Hopper."

tile acres along the James River, with two equally noble entrances, one up through the terraced formal gardens for those who came by boat and one along a tree-lined drive for those in carriages. All of our first ten Presidents were entertained lavishly there. I suppose there might once have been a log cabin among its various out-buildings. If so, I assume it contained the usual rubbish—broken lawn mowers, empty paint cans, wasp nests, mason jars with spiders in them, rusty hedge clippers, mice—and was no place to go to be born. Harrison himself didn't actually say he was born in it, but he didn't say he wasn't either. He just smiled.

His supporters got up parades with floats carrying log cabins and barrels of hard cider, and wore log-cabin badges and sang log-cabin songs and poured rivers of hard cider down the throats of prospective voters. They sang,

> *"Let Van from his coolers of silver drink wine*
> *And lounge on his cushioned settee.*
> *Our man on his buckeye bench can recline;*
> *Content with hard cider is he."*

Harrison thought hard cider was nasty, and his running mate, Tyler too, had an extremely sound wine cellar and read poetry and played the violin, but nobody noticed. The best the Democrats could think of in answer was to send Vice President Johnson out to run around in a red shirt he said he'd ripped from Tecumseh's body after he killed him. It was good but not good enough.

At his inauguration Harrison stood out there in one of those freezing northeasterly March winds with lashings of rain and spoke for two solid hours. Naturally he caught a dreadful cold, just as his mother would have warned him, and so did everyone else who had to hang around till he finished.[3]

There's a charming tale that while he was in the White House he did the family shopping and carried the groceries home in a basket. Maybe he said he was going to, but he can't have done it often. His cold had gone into his chest.[4] Besides, the job-hunters were driving him crazy morning, noon, and night. Job-hunters were a major headache for early Presidents, and lurked on the stairways and hid in the linen closets and sprang out brandishing their résumés. They were everywhere and there was no dodging them.

By the end of March he'd developed pneumonia and on April fourth he died, muttering and flailing away at imaginary job-hunters.

In his portrait he has the anxious, strangled look of a man trying to swallow a sizable goldfish, but he might have made a fine President anyway. Thirty-one days isn't much to go on, not when a person has a rotten cold the whole time.

There is one worrying sidelight on his character, though. Way back when he was a general in the War of 1812, he went to Washington to ask Madison something or other, and then Madison sent him on back to his troops. Later Dolley mentioned that he would be at her party that night, and Jemmy said, "But he should be thirty or forty miles on his way west by now." She said, "I laid my command on him, and he is too gallant a man to disobey me."[5]

---

[3] His wife had stayed home. She thought he was an old fool to want to be President anyway.

[4] He was sixty-eight years old and I hope he had sense enough to take two aspirin and go to bed.

[5] Isn't it amazing how these intimate dialogues get all over town?

"We shall soon see whose orders he obeys," said Jemmy, and they soon saw.

Harrison danced the night away and had a lovely time, but I ask you, what kind of future President would rather dance than fight?[6]

---

[6] Assuming we believe the story to begin with. There are days when I hardly believe anything anymore.

JOHN TYLER

★ ★ ★

1841–1845

ACCORDING TO SOME gossip that's making the rounds, when people went down to tidewater Virginia, to tell John Tyler he was President, they found him on his knees playing marbles. They felt this was frivolous and inappropriate to the occasion, though a Vice President's duties are not onerous and you have to fill in the days doing *something*.

Tyler had eight children at that point, and if he was playing marbles with the younger ones, definitely not a paternal custom in 1841, then he was a pioneer in the quality-time fatherhood concept and way ahead of his day. On the other hand, if he was playing marbles all by himself because he couldn't think of anything more statesmanlike to do, it was worrying.[1] The gossip doesn't specify.

He doesn't look like a marble-player. He was a fifty-one-year-old tobacco planter, formerly governor of Virginia like his daddy before him, also congressman and senator. His eyes are set a bit too high in his long bony face, putting you in mind of a sheep's skull left out bleaching in the sands, but he was a record-breaking sire so you shouldn't jump to conclusions. He must have had his lighter moments.

The general public thought it had voted for a cider-drinking, tobacco-spitting backwoodsman and found itself instead with not one but *two* tidewater aristocrats from fine old Virginia families. It was a shock.

---

[1] You never caught the Adamses playing marbles, did you?

Tyler lived right down the road from the Harrison mansion. His place was originally called "Walnut Grove," but he changed it to "Sherwood Forest" when his fellow Whigs started calling him a political outlaw, and at three-hundred-and-one feet long it's the longest frame house in the country. Virginians are house-proud and Virginia voters felt it was an important statement of solidity to have a fine big venerable family residence surrounded by boxwood bushes. Boxwood grows slowly, and many hedges of mature specimens mean that your family's been around for a while and you plan to stay put. The tomcat smell of boxwood is the true scent of a Virginia statesman.

He had some trouble taking over from Harrison. It had never happened before, and nobody was quite sure whether the Vice President turned into a real President or stayed strictly ornamental.[2] Tyler insisted he was real and tried to prove it by vetoing bills left and right, especially anything to do with federal improvements like harbors and canals and such, being a states'-rightser, and anything at all to do with banks. He didn't even want to *think* about banks.

A lot of people thought he went too far. He was supposed to be a Whig, but even the Whigs thought he went too far. Congress said it was "executive usurpation"[3] and wanted to impeach him. They even made him pay the White House utility bills himself. The only reason he was there at all was that "Tyler too" sounded good with "Tippecanoe," but that wasn't enough to veto bills with.

The very sight of Tyler made John Quincy Adams feel sick all over. He wrote, "Tyler is a political sectarian of the slave-driving,

---

[2] They called him "His Accidency."
[3] They'd said that about Jackson too, but Jackson just laughed.

Virginian, Jeffersonian school, principled against all improvement, and with all the interests and passions and vices of slavery rooted in his political and moral constitution."

He'd had a nice Whig cabinet to begin with—Clay and Daniel Webster had picked it out for Harrison, with Webster as Secretary of State—but they started quitting on him. They hoped he'd follow their example and quit too, but it never occurred to him. He just replaced them with Democrats.[4]

Pretty soon he could hardly find anyone to eat lunch with. His wife, Letitia, stayed in her room. Some first ladies stayed in their room from pure cussedness, but Letitia had had a stroke and was partly paralyzed and couldn't help it. Presently she died.

Then one fine day Tyler and a whole gang of Cabinet members, senators, diplomats and fair ladies were cruising down the Potomac on the brand-new frigate *Princeton* when one of its twelve-inch guns exploded. A couple of Cabinet members and a former state senator bit the dust, and the state senator's daughter, Julia Gardiner, was flung into Tyler's arms with a force that would have flattened a lesser man.[5] So Tyler replaced the Cabinet members with some more Democrats and married Julia.

She was five years younger than his oldest daughter and very pretty, with an hourglass figure that was much admired before she had seven more little Tylers, for a grand Tyler total of fifteen. In the White House she queened it up considerably, with a dozen maids of honor and much courtly folderol, and had Tyler dancing waltzes

---

[4] He thought maybe the Democrats would nominate him for a term of his own. Fat chance.

[5] Some insist that she was standing somewhere else and they only got cozy later while he was hanging around consoling her on her father's death, but that version lacks dramatic clout.

and polkas till the small hours.[6] It was Julia's idea to have the band play "Hail to the Chief" whenever he poked his sheep's face into the room. It gave the band something to do besides sample the punch, and it still does.

John Quincy said Tyler and his child bride were the laughing-stock of the whole town, and Tyler's original eight children went home to Virginia and had no comment for the press, but Dolley Madison, who was seventy-five and fit as a fiddle, thought it was just like the good old days.

Tyler has been called obstinate, commonplace, and narrow-minded by those who remember to mention him at all, but he wasn't all bad. Charles Dickens stopped by to visit him and said he was "unaffected, gentlemanly and agreeable." And after all, who established the United States Weather Bureau, so we could start having weather like other countries? Who stamped out Dorr's Rebellion in Rhode Island so hard Dorr was sorry he even thought of it? And don't forget it was Tyler who first noticed that Hawaii is actually in our hemisphere, like Mexico and Guatemala and so on, and therefore covered by the Monroe Doctrine and nobody's business but ours. He even straightened out the fuss over where Canada stopped and Maine started, a problem long obscured by thick woods, irascible lumberjacks, and horrible little stinging blackflies. And just before he left office, he signed the bill annexing Texas so it wouldn't keep floating around loose.

After he finished out ninety percent of Harrison's term, nobody wanted to see him again, ever, so he went home to Virginia to have some more children, and eventually seceded and got elected to the Confederate Congress.

---

[6] He felt like a kid again.

No, he didn't free *his* slaves in his will, either, and I wish you'd quit asking. Who do you think was going to pick up after those fifteen children, for heaven's sake? I'll tell you who freed his slaves. Robert E. Lee did, that's who, and he didn't wait till he was dead to do it, either, and now I don't want to hear another *word*.

JAMES POLK

★ ★ ★

1845–1849

JAMES POLK WAS not much fun and neither was his wife. They had no sense of humor. They were pious and didn't drink, or dance, or play cards, or have children. They never went out and never entertained if they could possibly help it. Sarah's receptions were so genteel that she not only didn't serve punch, she didn't serve anything to eat either. There was nothing to do but stand around, or slip across the park to Dolley Madison's instead.

At the inaugural ball, when the Polks walked in the dancing and music stopped, and for two solid hours you could hear a pin drop. Then they went away and the party resumed.

They worked hard. They put in twelve- or fourteen-hour days for four whole years, locked up together in the office, scribble, scribble, scribble. Polk said, "I prefer to supervise the whole operations of the Government myself rather than entrust the public business to subordinates, and this makes my duties very great." He was disgusted with his Cabinet, who frivoled away untold hours eating, sleeping, etc., so he and Sarah did all their work and everyone else's too.[1] No one knows why. Plenty of Presidents don't seem to do any work at all. Coolidge made it a firm rule never to work more than four hours a day, and I could name others who scarcely set foot in the office and things seemed to go along just as well or maybe better.

---

[1] Their Vice President was George M. Dallas. They didn't let him do *anything*.

James and Sarah took it seriously. They did everything but wash the dishes.[2]

Polk always needed a haircut badly and looked a bit weedy— he thought he'd seem bigger if he bought his suits a size too large[3]—but he was considered attractive enough, at least when he took office.[4] Sarah was said to be a raven-haired knockout with creamy skin, but the hairstyle of the day didn't do a thing for her, or for anyone else either; you parted it in the middle and slicked it down to the ears and then let it collapse in a drizzle of ringlets. Her clothes were called "rich but chaste."

No one was quite sure how Polk got to be President, except that it had a lot to do with Andrew Jackson,[5] and also with Sarah, whose idea it seems to have been. He was nominated on the ninth ballot and people went around saying "Who?" They'd never heard of Polk and wondered whatever happened to people they *had* heard of, like Buchanan, Van Buren, Johnson, Cass, and Calhoun.

Actually Polk had been right there in Congress for fourteen years, and Speaker from '35 to '39, but he was busy working and nobody noticed him.

He'd always been serious-minded. He was born in a dismal-looking shed near Pineville, North Carolina, and it warped his personality. Later he majored in math, back when nobody fun majored in math, and graduated at the head of his class. His classmates didn't cheer because they'd never heard of him either.

---

[2] Sarah was a dreadful housewife. Sometimes when people came to dinner there were no napkins on the table. She never noticed.

[3] It didn't work. Someone called him "the merest tangible fraction of a President." People think Presidents should be, at the very least, big.

[4] Four years later he looked just *awful*.

[5] He was still Old Hickory. He tried to get people to call Polk "Young Hickory" but it didn't stick.

He beat Clay, but that doesn't signify. So did everyone else in town.

Right from the start, he was a real-estate President. He said Oregon was really ours, because Lewis and Clark had spent the whole winter of 1805–06 there. Besides, in 1834 a couple of bird-watchers had gone out with an expedition and come home to write about how nice the birds were there. England said it was hers, because her Hudson's Bay Company had been cheating the Indians there for simply ages. We won. Many people didn't care much one way or the other. It was rainy and infested with Nez Percés, but the salmon fishing was first-rate.

Then Polk said Texas belonged to us too, and maybe California and New Mexico and some other places he'd think of in a minute.

The idea of all this suburban sprawl had everyone cranky and irritable, and there were fistfights and occasional gunfire in Congress. People worried about whether the new places would be slave and vote with the South, or not and not. Besides, getting Texas looked like war with Mexico, who thought it was theirs.

Polk didn't really want to fight Mexico because he was trying to cut a deal with them on California, but it wasn't easy. They kept having juntas and military takeovers and nobody knew who was in charge from one day to the next and Sarah didn't know where to send the letters. So in the meantime, James sent Zachary Taylor and some of the boys down to the Tex/Mex border, just to keep an eye on it and make sure it stayed put, and shoot beer cans and hang out. Naturally there was some scuffling back and forth[6] and some

---

[6] Boys will be boys.

people got hurt. Polk said that "the cup of forbearance has been exhausted," and there we were at war.

The Mexican generals were very stuck on themselves and went around saying *they* were noblemen in fancy uniforms and *we* were just a bunch of farmers in dirty overalls. For farmers, our boys did okay, thanks to the old American custom of playing around with guns; when they shot you, you stayed shot. It served some people right.

For a long time Polk kept telling himself we were only fighting to defend American soil, but we weren't. Any fool could see we had both feet in Mexico,[7] and virtuous killjoys started calling it aggression. Abraham Lincoln was in Congress and said this wasn't a nice way to act, and John Quincy Adams was in Congress too and jumped up to complain and keeled over and died.[8] Thoreau refused to pay taxes for the war, though actually he hadn't paid taxes for years *before* the war either, and went to jail for it. The next morning his aunt came down and paid his taxes for him and he went right home and wrote *Civil Disobedience*.

Meanwhile, back in Mexico, our stout senior generals were Winfield ("Old Fuss and Feathers") Scott and Zachary ("Old Rough and Ready") Taylor. They'd brought along a star-studded cast of extras—Robert E. Lee, George McClellan, Ulysses S. Grant, Matthew Perry, and much, much more.

Taylor scored a rousing victory at Buena Vista, emerging a shoo-in for the next President. Then Scott whipped Santa Anna[9] at Veracruz and struck off cross-country for Mexico City. Like many

---

[7] You could tell by the dysentery.
[8] Well, he was eighty, and there were plenty of Adamses left.
[9] Remember the Alamo? He was back. Don't ask.

subsequent tourists, a lot of his men didn't feel very well[10] but Scott pressed on and knocked off the capital and it was all over.

A fellow named Trist negotiated the treaty. The Mexicans got to keep their serapes and a couple of cacti. We got Texas. And New Mexico. And upper California, later subdivided into California, Arizona, Nevada, Utah, and most of Colorado and Wyoming. We paid fifteen million for the package.[11] Polk was cross and fired Trist—he'd wanted northern Mexico too—but people were bored with it all and made him sign the treaty as is.

Polk was a wreck. Wars are hard work. People tried to talk him into taking a few days off and going down to the Chesapeake to "eat soft crabs and oysters," but he just waved them away and went on working.

Historian Page Smith calls him "a petty, conniving, irascible, small-spirited man." Historian Bernard DeVoto says, "Polk's mind was rigid, narrow, obstinate, far from first-rate."

Maybe so, but imagine how flat life would be without Texas and California. Imagine Jesse James in Delaware. Imagine Lyndon Johnson in Maryland or Hollywood in New Jersey. Now, I ask you.

Polk tottered out of the White House and was dead in three months. Sarah was made of sterner stuff. She was last heard from at eighty-eight, and she's probably still around somewhere, working like a dog all day and banging on the neighbors' doors all night to make them stop dancing in there.

---

[10] All told, we lost 1,721 in battle and 11,155 from diarrhea.

[11] Nowadays you could hardly get even *Nevada* for fifteen million. It's criminal what's happened to real-estate prices.

ZACHARY TAYLOR

★ ★ ★

1849–1850

VIRGINIANS CLAIM TAYLOR as one of their impressive hatch of Presidents, but that's cheating; he paused there only just long enough to get born, and then continued on to Kentucky with his family. Later he had a plantation in Mississippi, but being regular Army he didn't exactly have a home in the Virginian sense of the word.

He didn't exactly have any politics either. He'd never voted for anything or anyone and thought politicians were pond scum. When they came to ask him, he said, "The idea that I should become President seems to me too visionary to require a serious answer. It has never entered my head, nor is it likely to enter the head of any sane person."

Another problem was that he wouldn't pay postage due on his mail. The Whigs were determined to run him whether he wanted to run or not, and sent him a letter to that effect, but it came with ten cents due so he sent it back unopened. Some sources say it was July before he found out, and by then it was too late to say no.

A third problem was that as a candidate he refused to answer any questions whatsoever or offer any opinions on matters of state.[1] You'd think this would discourage voters, but no. They thought he had hidden depths.

The Whigs had decided on him rather than Webster or Clay, who were only statesmen and not war heroes. The Democrats picked Lewis Cass, who wore a red wig that didn't fit. The Free-

---

[1] He may not have had any. He'd been in the Army for forty years.

Soilers[2] went for a rerun of Van Buren, co-starring John Quincy Adams' son Charles Francis. They sang,

> *"He who'd vote for Zacky Taylor*
> *Needs a keeper or a jailer.*
> *And he who for Cass can be*
> *Is a Cass without the C."*

It didn't work.

Taylor was plump and bow-legged, with curly sideburns and a battered straw hat he must have found in the trash. Some say he looked like a muskrat. Besides, he was wall-eyed, so that he seemed to be gazing off in two directions at once. This can be disconcerting. He tried to hide it by half closing the wandering eye when he was talking to you up close.[3] He'd never gone to college, but then, neither did Washington, Jackson, Van Buren, Fillmore, Lincoln, Cleveland, or Truman. Andrew Johnson never even got to kindergarten; his wife taught him to read and write. It makes you wonder.

As President, Old Rough and Ready couldn't seem to find any clean shirts and he chewed tobacco pretty much all the time, but neatly. A visitor observed that he "never missed the cuspidor once, or put my person in any jeopardy." Out on the lawn his war-horse, Old Whitey, ambled around eating grass and looking a little like his owner; he needed a good brushing. Tourists pulled hairs from his tail for souvenirs but he didn't mind.

On the whole, Taylor was pretty sensible, for a general. In his first address to Congress he said that the African slave trade should

---

[2] Formerly the Barn-Burners. Are you following this?
[3] That can be disconcerting too.

be abolished,[4] and somebody ought to build a railroad across the country, and there should be a Department of Agriculture. He closed by urging Congress not to talk about slavery—"abstain from the introduction of those exciting topics of a sectional character," he said, deftly avoiding the S word.[5]

Just then a lot of people were on their way to California. They didn't want to break into movies, they wanted gold, and lived in places with picturesque names like Grub Gulch and Red Dog and spent the day sloshing the creek bottom back and forth in a wash-basin. Other people followed, to sell them goods and services at the end of a hard day's sloshing, and soon there were so many of them they decided to be a state. Taylor agreed. They drew up a constitution saying there wouldn't be any slavery allowed, which made the South mad, especially South Carolina, which was always flying off the handle about something or other and stamping out of the room in a snit.

Some people think Taylor was wishy-washy on the North/South thing, but he did say he would personally lead the Army against any state that tried to secede and instantly hang any rebels he could get his hands on. This is a fairly clear policy statement.

Yes, there was a Mrs. Taylor, but she didn't contribute much to the merriment. She refused to meet anyone or even leave her room, and sat in there huddled over the fire shivering and muttering that the whole presidency business was "a plot to deprive me of his society and shorten his life by unnecessary care and responsibility."[6]

---

[4] He didn't say *slaves* should be abolished. He had over a hundred of them down on his cotton plantation.
[5] Naturally nobody abstained. It was *the* hot topic and senators went right on punching each other on the Senate floor and brandishing revolvers.
[6] She'd been an Army wife for a long time. It takes its toll.

As it turned out, care and responsibility didn't get a chance.

When Taylor had been President for less than a year and a half, he went to a Fourth of July bash on the Monument Grounds. Well, you know Washington in July, and there's no shade out there, and the speakers droned on and on and Taylor was mopping the old brow. When he got home he called for a lot of ice-cold milk and cherries and, some say, pickled cucumbers, and he really lit into them. One account says his doctor begged him to stop, but I can't see why the doctor would have dropped by just to watch him eat. Probably it was an afterthought, the doctor being anxious to cover his tail. Anyway, Taylor put away a great quantity of the stuff and died on the ninth.[7]

Kindly authorities call it, variously, gastroenteritis, typhus, and even cholera. Others say the doctors did it, stuffing him with ipecac, calomel, opium, and the most amazing doses of quinine while they were draining out his blood, but remember, the doctors wouldn't have had a chance at him if he hadn't made a pig of himself.

Still others, muttering discontentedly far into the future, thought it was poison. They thought his Vice President did him in, and indeed it's a wonder more Vice Presidents don't try this. Just a few years ago they finally insisted on digging up his mortal remains and testing them. Unable to take a urine sample, they tested his hair, and found only the amount of arsenic usual at the time, considering all the arsenic floating around. Then they put him back.

Some were disappointed. Imagining plump and placid Millard Fillmore as a closet Lucrezia Borgia had been fun, and a good dollop of arsenic would have put the poor fellow on the map.

---

[7] Ever since, a popular superstition holds that consuming milk and pickles at the same meal will kill anyone. It won't. Only a select few.

MILLARD FILLMORE

★ ★ ★

1850–1853

MANY PEOPLE ARE almost indifferent to the subject of Millard Fillmore. It's his name. They think if they'd known a kid in school named Millard, he wouldn't have been a barrel of laughs, but they're just guessing. Millard was his mother's maiden name, though I admit that's a pretty thin excuse.[1]

He wasn't a bad man—in fact, he was quite nice. He was just wrong a good deal of the time. He couldn't help it.

The only right thing he did was get born in a log cabin.[2] His family was very poor and indentured him to a wool-carder and cloth-dresser, and being indentured wasn't at all the same as being apprenticed. It was much nastier. By the time he finally bought his freedom and got to school, he was a big boy nineteen years old and fell in love with the teacher. They waited for each other for seven years while he clerked in a law office and then set up his own practice. (It wasn't what you'd call a classical education, but don't forget he could card wool and dress cloth too.)

He wasn't interested in politics until the Anti-Masonic party came along. At the time, everyone got very excited about the Masons and the Anti-Masons, because a bricklayer named Morgan had disappeared and some hysterical types said the Masons had done him in. In the nineteenth century, whenever *anything* happened the bystanders got together and formed a political party

---

[1] He named his own son Millard. I can't think of *any* excuse for that.
[2] See also Jackson, Taylor, Buchanan, Lincoln, and Garfield. Cynics believe they were all born in the same log cabin, rented out for the occasion to ambitious mothers by a real-estate entrepreneur. This is probably not true.

about it. For alternate entertainment, they could read the Bible or rub goose-grease into their boots.

Millard went to the New York State Assembly as an Anti-Mason.[3] Presently he found himself in Congress, and one day in 1848 the Whigs were looking around for a vice-presidential type to run with Taylor and their eye lit on Millard. They thought he'd help them carry New York. Besides, he had nice blue eyes and a deep voice and was modest and handsome and a Capricorn, and what more do you want in a Vice President? He may look a bit jowly to you, and it's true that if his waistcoat were larger it wouldn't strain at the buttons like that, but in 1850 nobody cried shame to a middle-aged man who put on a few pounds, or told him to count his cholesterol. They thought it looked much more dignified[4] than poor little Polk floating around loose in his oversize suits.

Anyway, he was a perfectly acceptable choice. Who could know Taylor was going to overdose on cold milk?

In July of 1850 Millard found himself President and hit his stride at being wrong. For starters, he gave the wrong answer to the Slavery Question.[5] He thought it was a terrible idea, personally—he'd been indentured and that was no picnic either—but he said the states were old enough to decide for themselves. He was a peaceable fellow and hoped he could stop the Civil War from happening.[6] It was also a mistake to try to enforce the Fugitive Slave Act, under which runaway slaves were returned to their owners like a

---

[3] It was the wrong thing to be, naturally.
[4] "Stout but not corpulent," they said approvingly.
[5] By this time there was no right answer.
[6] Five hundred thousand Americans died in it, compared to a mere four hundred thousand in World War II, and it cost around twenty billion. *Just* the kind of thing he hated.

lost earring or the Steinway grand caught hightailing it up the road. This was not only wrong, it was impossible.

Another idea he had was opening up world trade. He sent Commodore Perry to Japan to suggest, by means of the heavily armed frigates *Mississippi* and *Susquehanna,* that they buy things from us. The Japanese hadn't spoken to anyone at all for hundreds of years and they liked it that way. They were perfectly happy alone on their island eating sushi and kicking each other in the ear and having tea ceremonies. Sometimes, for excitement, his loved ones would try to poison the emperor, but mostly life just jogged along. Millard's idea was that, with a little arm-twisting, they'd eventually wind up with an island-full of Pontiacs and RCA stereos and we'd wind up with a vault-full of yen. His whole career was like that.[7]

His other international triumph was about Peruvian guano. Guano is a substance deposited by seabirds on rocks and offshore islands and park benches, and people used it for fertilizer. Millard intervened between the Peruvians and some squabbling American businessmen and negotiated a treaty so we could import more guano. Then everyone started using Miracle-Gro instead.

Mrs. Fillmore wasn't feeling well, but she did notice that there wasn't anything in the house to read, not even a dictionary. She'd been a schoolteacher, so she sent word to Congress that there ought to be some books around the place, and got an appropriation for sets of Dickens and Thackeray. She still felt lousy but at least she had something to read.[8]

---

[7] When the Japanese finally said yes, we gave them a barrel of whiskey and a copy of Audubon's *Birds of America.* I expect they were terribly pleased.

[8] I've been told she also installed the first White House bathtub, but if so, then what was Van Buren lolling around in, a soup kettle? You can't believe everything you hear.

Millard had his domestic side. He called the White House his "temple of inconveniences" and ordered a fancy great patented cookstove with all the modern improvements and valves and flues and drafts and a clever place to keep the ashes. Even that was wrong. The cook ignored it completely and went right on using the open fireplace and getting ashes in the soup.

In 1852 the Whigs decided Millard was the wrong President and flatly refused to nominate him. His feelings were so hurt that he joined the Know-Nothing Party, a group that claimed to know nothing about what it was doing and believed that only people who were born here, and Protestants, should be allowed to vote or get elected or hold any nice jobs or have any fun at all. He ran for President on the Know-Nothing ticket in '56 and carried Maryland.

He still thought there shouldn't be any Civil War, so he wouldn't support Lincoln, so his remaining friends stopped speaking to him.

After that he moved to Buffalo, New York, and as far as anyone knows he was happy as a clam there and nobody noticed that he was wrong. When his wife died he married a rich widow and got elected the very first President of the Buffalo Historical Society. *They* thought he made a perfectly swell President.

FRANKLIN PIERCE

★ ★ ★

1853–1857

SUDDENLY JOHN CALHOUN, Henry Clay, John Quincy Adams, Andrew Jackson, and Daniel Webster were all dead, creating one of those flat spots when the conversation lags and people look around and say, "Hey, where is everybody?"

The Whigs hauled out Old Fuss and Feathers Scott, the last available war hero. He'd been a real rouser of a general, but personally he was a frightful bore and politically he was simply absurd.

Still, he was a candidate, and the Democrats had trouble finding *anybody.* The convention went into terminal gridlock and the delegates got more and more frazzled. New Hampshire had thrown in Pierce's name as one of those favorite-son, token-of-respect gestures people sometimes regret, and after forty-eight ballots when everyone was dead for sleep, somebody said, "All right, so what about this fellow Pierce or Price or whatever?" and that was that.

Franklin Pierce wasn't really nobody. He'd been in the state legislature at twenty-five, and gone on to Congress, and by thirty-three he was the youngest senator on the Hill. He had this wife problem, though.[1] Jane Pierce was a thoroughly dismal lady. She was a religious fanatic who complained constantly about her nerves. She hated politics[2] and she hated Washington, and when Franklin was in the Senate she stayed home in New Hampshire and he had to live in a boardinghouse and eat meat loaf every night.

---

[1] He was called "Handsome Frank" and looked like a poet, but that cut no ice with her.
[2] We can't all be Abigail Adams.

They'd had two children who died in infancy, so when son Benjamin was born in 1841, Frank had to resign his Senate seat and go home to help Jane change diapers and keep tiptoeing into the kid's room to see if it was still breathing. Polk offered him a Cabinet post but he said no, he couldn't leave Jane.[3]

In 1852 when he found himself nominated for President he had some fast talking to do. He told Jane he was just as surprised as she was. He said he hadn't known a thing about it. Then he mentioned that it might be fun for little Benjamin to grow up in the White House. She just sighed and pressed her lips together.

During the campaign the Whigs made a great to-do about heroic old Fuss and Feathers, and called Pierce "the hero of many a well-fought bottle."[4] They said he'd run away from his only engagement in the Mexican War. This was a barefaced lie. What happened was, his horse shied and threw him forward so the pommel of the saddle punched him in the groin. Naturally, he fainted from the pain, and then the horse fell down and broke its leg, and Pierce hurt his knee. That's all.[5]

He won the election, because it's the thing about elections that *somebody* has to win. Then Jane found out that he really had asked for the nomination and stopped speaking to him. Then in January Benjamin, their eye-apple, got killed in a train accident and she went completely round the bend. She said God had done it on pur-

---

[3] She wasn't about to go live in Washington just because Frank was Secretary of something.

[4] So he had a little drinking problem. Suppose *you* were married to Jane Appleton Pierce?

[5] It could have happened to anyone. Alexander the Great, Genghis Khan, anyone.

pose, so the kid wouldn't distract Frank from his presidential duties.

She wouldn't come to town for the inauguration. After the reception was over the White House servants all went away, and there were dirty dishes everywhere and canapes trod into the rugs, and Pierce had to grope his way upstairs with a candle to find his bedroom all by himself.

When Jane did move into the White House, she went straight up to her room and stayed there, all dressed in black, and spent her time writing letters to Benjamin and mailing them up the chimney. It got on everyone's nerves, and mostly people went over to Jefferson Davis's house instead. He was Secretary of War and his wife knew a thing or two about Southern hospitality, which was a good thing, since Dolley Madison had gone off to teach the angels how to polka in 1849 and there had to be *somewhere* to go for a laugh.

Frank Pierce was the first President to have a Christmas tree in the White House. He was trying to cheer Jane up. It didn't work. He even had central heating installed, but still she wouldn't speak to him. There may have been days when he thought longingly of the boardinghouse and its meat loaf. There may even have been days when he ducked into the pantry for a nip of brandy. He was arrested for running over an old woman with his horse—the policeman let him go when he saw who it was he'd collared—and I'm not suggesting Frank wasn't perfectly sober at the time, but just the same it's funny no other Presidents rode down old ladies. On the other hand, he does seem to have been the world's worst rider, drunk or sober.

Jane wasn't his only problem. There was Kansas, for instance.

Under the Kansas-Nebraska Act it was supposed to vote for itself whether it wanted to be slave or non-slave.[6] So of course the pros and antis all swarmed in to vote for their respective sides, and a lot of people who didn't even live there made long journeys just to vote. At one point in the confusion there were two official state governments, both of them illegal. Some folks lost their tempers, and everyone behaved in an ungentlemanly manner and killed each other with giddy abandon.[7] This gave rise to the phrase "Bleeding Kansas." It also gave rise to John Brown, whose body later got so famous,[8] and Abe Lincoln came back out of Illinois, where he'd been brooding ever since he said the wrong thing about the Mexican War.

Harriet Beecher Stowe had published *Uncle Tom's Cabin* and it was still on every coffee table in the North. People who previously hadn't even asked themselves the Slavery Question read it and cried for hours and hours.

The Civil War had pretty much already started and was oozing east from Kansas like The Blob. Maybe nobody could have stopped it by this time. Certainly Pierce couldn't. He couldn't even get his wife to come out of her room.[9]

Later on she died and he drank himself to death, some say from grief but I wouldn't bet the farm on it. He may have been celebrating.

---

[6] Nobody asked the Wichitas and Pawnees, who used to call it home.

[7] We were taught to think of Abolitionists as kindly, reasonable, Quakerly types, but apparently some of them were quite human.

[8] He was a man of strong convictions and hacked four people into tiny pieces at the Pottawatomie Massacre.

[9] Taylor had had the same problem, but he didn't have Kansas.

JAMES BUCHANAN

★ ★ ★

1857–1861

BUCHANAN WAS A bachelor. This condition has led millions of people to conclude that he was homosexual. They take it as a given, like Jefferson and Sally. I can't imagine how they know, since it's only recently that people have found their personal sex lives an interesting topic for memoirs, confessional talk shows, special prosecutors, and conversations with total strangers. In those primitive days, it was bad manners to tell people these things.

However, Buchanan had more enemies than a dog has fleas and they called him all sorts of opprobrious names, and if his sex life was non-standard, I'm sure they would have brought it up at the time. They didn't.

Back in 1819, he was engaged to a girl named Anne Caroline Coleman, but they had a spat about something or other and she gave him back his ring and went home and committed suicide. Many men would shrug such an incident off lightly, but perhaps Buchanan took it to heart and let it color his future relationships. His enemies said he'd been so upset he tried to hang himself, damaging his neck so he carried his head funny. He didn't. He carried his head funny because he had one eye set higher in the socket than the other, and a weak eye muscle, and besides, he was nearsighted in one eye and farsighted in the other and when he didn't carry his head funny he felt dizzy.

Bachelorhood quite aside, many people consider James Buchanan the very worst President ever. I suppose they think *they* would have done better. I suppose *they* wouldn't have let Dred Scott happen, or

John Brown, or secession, and there wouldn't have been any Civil War and everyone would have lived happily ever after. Too many Monday-morning quarterbacks, that's what we've got.

The difference between a good President and a bad one has very little to do with character, leadership, or experience. It's almost entirely timing and luck.

In a thunderstorm, you wouldn't want to stand next to Buchanan.

He'd been ambassador to Russia and to Britain, and Secretary of State, and he'd tried for the Democratic nomination three times before and finally made it because perseverance pays off, just as your parents told you. The new-born Republican party nominated John Fremont, as in "Free Speech, Free Soil, and Fremont."[1] Buchanan won, and Fremont went off to become one of the worst generals in the Civil or any other War.

Many people felt the best thing about Buchanan was the niece, Harriet Lane, that he brought along to be his hostess.[2] She was young and charming and had violet eyes and she was *perfectly healthy*. The whole country marveled at her health. She never had nerves or migraines or locked herself in her room talking to people who weren't there, and she gave such swell parties that even the Prince of Wales came to visit. She liked flowers, and had a nice greenhouse built that would be there to this day if we hadn't set the West Wing down on top of it. She grew camellias and orange trees and pitcher plants, and made tasteful arrangements all over the house. People were entranced. To judge from her pictures, she was

---

[1] *His* claim to fame was that he'd once taken a long walk in California, and when he got back he had his wife write him a book about it that sold like hotcakes.

[2] She'd been his ward since she was nine, and they were very close and had long private conversations, though due to some journalistic oversight this never caused a scandal.

only average-looking, but she was such a relief after certain first ladies who shall remain nameless that she knocked them dead. Numerous popular entertainments and songs like "Listen to the Mockingbird" were dedicated to her, and a flower, a racehorse, a warship, and whole regiments of babies were named after her. Sometimes people thought so much about Harriet they forgot to think about Buchanan at all, which was just as well.

He was a Pennsylvanian, but he thought it was okay to be a Southerner and have slaves if that's the way you wanted it. He even thought it was okay to have them in Kansas, which was still bleeding pretty briskly. (He tried to help matters by sending them assorted governors and Congressional committees, but the results were about what you'd expect.)[3]

Presidentially speaking, he should have stayed in bed. There was Dred Scott, for instance. Dred Scott was all about a slave named Dred Scott who thought he was free because he'd been traveling around free territories like Wisconsin with the boss. The Supreme Court had a southern majority at the time and ruled it was unconstitutional to say you couldn't have slaves in the territories, or the new states, or anywhere else you felt like having some slaves. This was one-up for the South and made the Abolitionists wild with rage.

Then there was the depression of '57. I'm not sure what this had to do with Buchanan, but it can't have lightened the mood much.

Then John Brown came East, immediately behind the most menacing set of whiskers you ever saw. He looked like those chaps

---

[3] Congressional committees never stop anything from bleeding. Try one yourself and see.

who reel down the sidewalk shouting strange words to themselves and waving their arms, and you remember an errand on the other side of the street.[4] Not content with adding to the blood supply in Kansas, he showed up in Harpers Ferry to start a slave rebellion by bumping off the mayor and holing up in the arsenal with some odds and ends of people. No slaves offered to join the rebellion, but he brought a couple of sons.[5] The following shootout would make a television crew dance for joy, with Robert E. Lee galloping around on the outside and Brown's men getting butchered inside, and fine dramatic rivers and mountains for scenery.

Brown survived, and got tried and sentenced to hang. It was a perfectly fair trial and he had excellent lawyers, but just the same it was probably a mistake to hang him. Ralph Waldo Emerson said it would "make the gallows more glorious than the cross," and he had a point there.

Buchanan wanted to distract people's attention by buying Cuba, but his bad luck held and Congress wouldn't let him. They thought it might have something to do with the slave trade. They may have been right. Still, buying the place might have prevented a problem or two in the future.

Otherwise he tried to do as little as possible about anything so as not to rock the boat. He thought if he just sat still and kept his mouth shut, things wouldn't fall apart before he could hand them over to the next man and run like hell. He almost made it.

---

[4] The smart money crossed the street when they saw Brown coming too. He said he was an instrument in the hand of God and could kill anyone he wanted to kill.

[5] He had lots. His mother, his grandmother, an aunt, and three of his uncles were all raging certified lunatics, and this might make some people stop and think before having nineteen children, but not John Brown.

Unfortunately, the South didn't much like the election of 1860. An Atlanta newspaper put it in a nutshell: "Let the consequences be what they may—whether the Potomac is crimsoned in human gore, and Pennsylvania Avenue is paved ten fathoms deep with mangled human bodies, or whether the last vestige of liberty is swept from the face of the American continent, the South will never submit to such humiliation and degradation as the inauguration of Abraham Lincoln."[6]

Then in December South Carolina passed an "ordinance of disunion" and marched off waving torches and singing songs of an inflammatory nature. In January, Mississippi, Florida, and Alabama left too, and then Georgia, Louisiana, and Texas seceded, and there was poor Buchanan still nominally President, with great globs of the country we'd given him leaking out through his fingers like a fistful of custard.

Senator Jeff Davis said goodbye to his dear friends in Washington and went home to be President of the new country.

Some of us have a dim, confused feeling that when states secede they go away somewhere, out to sea probably, floating majestically off like a fleet of giant icebergs while the sundered friends and family on either shore stand waving and hallooing sadly across the widening waters, but it wasn't like that. The southern states stayed right where they'd always been. Anyone could see this was going to cause a problem.

Buchanan kept doing less and less and trying to make himself invisible. He was almost seventy and may have felt it had all been

---

[6] Somehow history manages to blame Buchanan for this too.

a mistake. Nobody except Harriet liked him any more, and folks said, "Buchanan has a winning way of making himself hateful."[7]

In his last speech to Congress he said, "I at least meant well for my country." Nobody thought this was half good enough.

At his final White House reception he made a valiant last-ditch effort to prevent the Civil War by having the Marine Band play both "Yankee Doodle" and "Dixie." It didn't work.

When the next man moved in, Buchanan said, "If you are as happy, Mr. Lincoln, on entering this house as I am in leaving it and returning home, you are the happiest man in this country."

If Lincoln had had a lick of sense he'd have turned right around and left with him.

---

[7] He didn't mean to be hateful. His nerves were shot. Yours would be too.

ABRAHAM LINCOLN

★ ★ ★

1861–1865

BELIEVE IT OR not, there really was an Abraham Lincoln. Many of us get muddled and think he was just one of those nice ideas, like Santa Claus and King Arthur and the Tooth Fairy,[1] but Lincoln was real, and a good thing too, because otherwise we'd have to invent him or, worse, one of us would have to volunteer to be him.

Lincoln is our national hero and everyone loves him, now that he's dead. We never even wake up on a rainy morning and wonder, "Why Lincoln? Why not Rutherford B. Hayes?"

The answer is, because Lincoln is just like us. He's Mr. Us. As *Harper's Weekly* mused at the time, he "illustrated the character of American civilization." We look in the mirror and there he is, strong and tall, honest, independent, uneducated, ambitious but modest, rough-edged but kindly, careless of appearances and indifferent to ceremony, natural story-teller and cool-headed leader in time of danger. It's uncanny—he's us to the very life. National-image-wise, Lincoln hits the spot.

We even like his looks. Us good old Americans are no dandified European pretty-boys. Face on him like a chunk of firewood. Loaded with character, just like us.

Mind you, we've grown accustomed to his face. No living American can remember seeing a picture of Lincoln for the first time, but back when people were first seeing him in the flesh he was

---

[1] No, there isn't any Tooth Fairy. What would a fairy want with all those teeth? Fairies don't even chew.

kind of a shock. "Grotesque" was a word that sprang to people's lips.[2] When he went around speechifying, a lot of folks turned out just to see if he really looked like that, and he did.

He was six feet four inches tall and carried a floppy black umbrella that wouldn't stay closed and an old gray shawl in case the weather turned chilly. His ears stuck out and his pants were always too short, which made his feet look even bigger. Shortly before his election a little girl wrote to him saying he'd look better with whiskers, so he grew some and it did help, but not much.

Most of us know a lot about Lincoln, some of it true. Yes, he was born in a log cabin, and later he did try to shoot Indians in Black Hawk's War but he couldn't find any. We all remember his school days, and how he walked forty miles each way, and scratched his math problems in the soot on a shovel, and the snow blew in through the chinks in the walls and spoiled his homework, but since he said himself that all his school days together didn't add up to a full year, we've simply got to stop worrying about it. Think of what *we* went through.

He had a gray-and-white cat named Bob. He grew up in blue jeans doing all those old-time country things voters love: killing hogs, milking cows, cradling wheat, pitching hay, clearing land, riverboating, rail-splitting, mud-wrestling, and throwing a crowbar.[3] Later he tried running a store, but he always had his nose in a law book and wouldn't wait on customers. Then he tried running a still but he kept letting the whiskey boil over. Finally he got ap-

---

[2] "Gorilla" was another.
[3] He was very good at throwing a crowbar. Why does nobody throw crowbars any more? That's probably what's wrong with the country, kids don't throw crowbars the way they used to.

pointed postmaster, which gave him a chance to read all the newspapers before he passed them out. The mail was always late.

Some said Ann Rutledge was the great love of his life and died of malaria before he could marry her. Others, including his wife, said "nonsense." Certainly he was upset when she died, and Herndon, his law partner and later biographer, said it made him think twice about the existence of God.

At twenty-five he was elected to the Illinois General Assembly, and then he passed the bar and set up practice with Herndon in an office over a belting-and-cutlery shop.[4] For sixteen years he drove his partner up the wall with his messiness and infuriating habit of reading the newspapers aloud for hours. He kept all his really important papers in his hat, and after he had kids he brought them to the office on Sunday and let them tear the place apart. Sometimes he got so depressed he was afraid to carry a pocketknife. Herndon said his black moods were probably due to heredity, environment, slow blood circulation, constipation, thwarted love, or all of the above. He wrote, "The whole man, body and soul, worked slowly as if it needed oiling."

Yes, yes, you're saying, but why don't we know more about his sex life? The recent commercial success of Jefferson's sex life has left us quite frantic for details of Lincoln's. Well, we don't know more because, odd as it seems, certain people didn't tell us.

While he was working on Lincoln's biography, Herndon kept two sets of notes. The second set, in two little memorandum books

---

[4] You will have noticed that in the olden days you could be a lawyer without going to law school, or even college, or even school at all. This greatly leveled the playing field and gave us many Presidents and other celebrities who nowadays would face a career flipping burgers.

that he called "secret and sacredly private," has disappeared, at least for now. He did let a couple of friends look at them, though, and one, a Lincoln fan named Caroline Dall who was going to make a speech about him, was so shocked by the "debauchery" that she canceled the speech.

A lot of the notes were rumors and dark allegations that Herndon kept trying to track down. Our hero may have contracted syphilis from a premarital prostitute. He may have been illegitimate. His *mother* may have been illegitimate. He had a "terrible passion" for women and may have been unfaithful to Mary Todd, and she to him.

Hardly worth an hour's prime-time special.

However, a quite separate story might give us pause. The Confederate spy Belle Boyd had married a Union officer.[5] While she was in exile in London, her husband ventured back over here and got thrown into assorted unpleasant prisons as a deserter. Belle wrote to the President. It was not a supplication, it was practically an order: "I think it would be well for you and me to come to some definite understanding," she snapped. She told him she was about to publish her memoirs in England and they were full of "atrocious circumstances respecting your government . . . which would open the eyes of Europe." If he'll turn her husband loose, she'll cross out those parts. If not, Lincoln will be jolly sorry.

The morning after the President got the letter, quite abruptly, the bewildered husband was a free man. Furthermore, her letter wasn't in the official files but turned up in 1947 in the previously-sealed private papers. Now, we could assume that he just wanted to

---

[5] She hoped to convert him.

protect some beloved Cabinet member or hide some unofficial policy, or we could assume she must have known some pretty spicy stuff about him. Alas, Belle kept her word and cheated us out of details we need to know.

Suppression of such presidential facts is now a felony, but Herndon and Boyd are beyond special prosecutors now.

If you know where Herndon's secret notebooks are, you'd better hand them over.

Lincoln married Mary Todd in 1842, when he was thirty-three. They'd been engaged earlier, but he'd broken it off, and then went quite distracted with brooding and confusion, and had second thoughts, and third thoughts, and finally went through with it, still brooding. They say that while he was getting dressed for the wedding a little boy at the boardinghouse asked him where he was going and he said, "To hell, I suppose." Nine months and four days later their son Robert was born.

Abe's forebodings turned out to be well-founded, but he would have had them in any case. He always had forebodings. He called it "hypo," short for hypochondria, and was rather proud of it.[6]

Mary was a Southern belle who liked shopping and flirting and having hysterics. Sometimes she had migraines too. Sometimes she felt as if hammers were knocking nails into her head and hot wires were being pulled through her eyes. (Abe called her "Mother" around the house, which never helps.)

Americans like to think Lincoln was just a country boy hanging around the farm splitting rails when we all got together and went and carried him off on our shoulders to be President. It's a

---

[6] His favorite song was a merry little ditty called "Twenty Years Ago," about this fellow standing around in a graveyard where all his friends are buried.

pretty thought, but actually he was a terrific pol and always running for something or other. Herndon said, "Politics were his life, newspapers his food, and his great ambition his motive power."

When he got to Congress he kept the House in stitches. A reporter wrote, "His awkward gesticulations, the ludicrous management of his voice, and the comical expression of his countenance, all conspired to make his hearers laugh at the mere anticipation of the joke." Stand-up comedy was born.

He was always a great one for jokes and stories. He used *Joe Miller's Joke Book* so hard it fell apart, and wasn't above telling the same joke over and over and over.[7] Like Reagan later, he had a story for everything. Ask him a question and he'd say it reminded him of the story about the Irishman, or the farmer, or the little boy with the raccoon. This could be pretty maddening if you just wanted a simple yes or no.[8]

Your teacher wanted you to remember the Lincoln-Douglas debates, and you do remember they had something to do with the Slavery Question, but you may feel they involved the presidency somehow. They didn't. Lincoln and Stephen Douglas were running for a Senate seat, and Lincoln lost in spite of all those nifty speeches and saying "A house divided against itself cannot stand," though actually Matthew 12:25 said it first. This left him at leisure to run for President and fulfill his destiny as our national hero and an ornament on every classroom wall. The debates had been terrific publicity, with people trudging in from miles around. Fans said Lincoln "stood like some solitary pine on the lonely summit."[9]

---

[7] I hear some of them were pretty raunchy.

[8] It gave him a good out. Later he could always say you misunderstood, and the story about the farmer didn't mean yes, it meant no.

[9] Others said he looked like a baboon.

The Republican national convention was a zoo. Lincoln wisely stayed home and pretended not to know what his henchmen were up to. They were running around promising delegates the moon, that's what they were up to. They packed the house with the noisiest claque on record by printing counterfeit seat-tickets and giving them to all the people who could shout the loudest.[10] This didn't leave any seats for William Seward's supporters and even if they'd been there you couldn't have heard them. It was deafening. Then they brought in some fence rails and said Lincoln had split them himself, and the cheers were heard in four counties. Cows ran distracted and small birds dropped dead.

After that it was plain sailing.[11] The Democrats nominated Douglas, and eleven slave states walked out and nominated Breckinridge of Kentucky, Buchanan's Vice President, and split the party, so the Republicans had it made.[12]

Many people thought Lincoln would get killed before he was inaugurated. Some felt it would be for the best, actually, while others felt he should just turn down the job, but he didn't, and he and Mary moved into the White House with Tad, who was seven, and Willie, who was ten.[13]

In his inaugural address he said he had no problem with slavery in the states that already had it, or with the Fugitive Slave Act either, but that nobody should secede because secession was illegal.

---

[10] They gave them some free drinks too, to limber up their lungs.

[11] Mary had always had a funny feeling Lincoln would be President, but then, most of Mary's feelings were funny.

[12] This was silly of the slave states, since they would have liked Douglas better than Lincoln. Nobody ever stops to think.

[13] Robert was off at college and little Eddie was dead.

Naturally the Abolitionists called this waffling and the South said it meant war.

The poet Longfellow got so excited he said Lincoln was "a colossus holding up his burning heart in his hand to light up the sea of life." The *New York Herald,* on the other hand, gave the administration a month and then called it "cowardly, mean, and vicious" and Abe "incompetent, ignorant, and desperate," and urged the people to rise up and overthrow the government.

On to Fort Sumter.

Sumter was a Federal post right there in the water off Charleston, and you know those South Carolinians, always getting their knickers in a twist about something. Some folks, even old Fuss and Feathers Scott, thought it would be smart just to close down the fort and say to hell with it, and maybe they were right.

Anderson, the man in charge out there, said he was going to run out of bacon by April fifteenth and the government had better send some more because nobody in Charleston would sell him so much as a slice of bread. The governor of South Carolina told him, "Let your President attempt to reinforce Sumter, and the tocsin of war will be sounded from every hilltop and valley in the South."

General Pierre Beauregard and most of Charleston with nothing better to do stood around on shore and kept a close eye on the place. On April eleventh, Beauregard told Anderson to pick up and pack out. Anderson said he really couldn't, but his men would be starved out in a few days anyway. Beauregard sent back saying if he'd fix an exact time for his surrender then he, Beauregard, wouldn't blow the place into next Tuesday, but otherwise . . . Anderson sent back saying he'd surrender at noon sharp on the fifteenth, after they ate the last bacon. This wasn't good enough, so Beauregard sent back saying he had the honor of notifying Anderson he was going to start shooting in exactly an hour, and he did.[14]

All the guns in the area pounded away all day and all the next night. The relief ships showed up in the middle of it with more bacon, but who had time to cook? The shelling went on for thirty-three hours and Beauregard pitched over three thousand rounds of assorted hardware at the place. This was hideously noisy and disagreeable but not very dangerous. Only one man in the fort got killed, when one of his own cannon blew up.[15]

So Anderson got on a relief ship and went away, the Confederate flag went up, the rest of the South seceded, and there, finally, was the Civil War, which you already know about. Maybe you can't tell First Manassas from Second Bull Run, or even from Spotsylvania, but you remember who won and that's the main thing about wars.

Lincoln never had any fun being President because of the Civil War the whole time. It was all ready to roll when he took office, and five days after it was over he was dead as a duck. He had the war, the whole war, and nothing but the war.

He really did want to free the slaves, because he was that kind of a guy, but he had the border states to worry about, and besides, freeing slaves wasn't as urgent a call to arms as you might think. Many potential soldiers simply couldn't care less. So he said the war was to save the Union, and that was a big hit. People got all steamed up about saving the Union and rushed right out to volun-

---

[14] It was half-past four in the morning, but nobody could sleep anyway.
[15] Artillery at that time tended to be more lethal in back than in front.

teer. This is apt to baffle the modern schoolchild, who wonders what was so special about the Union anyway, and if the South didn't want to stick around, then who needed them, and whose business was it anyway? And why was it such a swell idea for us to break off from England and such a lousy idea for the South to break off from the North?

Questions like this do nobody any good.

Meanwhile Lincoln brooded a lot and had nightmares.[16] He saw ghosts too. Modern ophthalmologists say this was due to hyperopia, possibly connected with anisometropia, muscle imbalance, and astigmatism. On the other hand, they may have been real ghosts. Sometimes when he looked in the mirror he saw two of him, one face its usual swarthy color and the other white as a sheet. He told Mary about it and she said it meant he'd be elected to a second term but wouldn't live to finish it.[17]

The question was raised as to whether Mary might be a Southern spy, since most of her family was fighting on the other side. It isn't very likely. She couldn't even keep her temper, much less a secret.[18]

In 1862 young Willie died of typhoid but went on visiting his mother every night anyway, standing at the foot of her bed and smiling. Sometimes he brought little Eddie with him, the one who'd died back in Springfield. It was a great comfort to her. So were seances and shopping. She bought three hundred pairs of gloves in four months. Whenever she felt low in her mind, she bought some

---

[16] He kept thinking somebody was going to assassinate him.

[17] Home life with the Lincolns was a laugh a minute.

[18] Later the question was also raised as to whether she had all her marbles. Her son Robert had her locked up for a while, but she got out.

more expensive clothes, but she was afraid to wear them because Abe would be cross. After all, there was a war on. She had boxes and boxes of them hidden away in closets, and owed over twenty-seven thousand dollars she hadn't told him about.

On New Year's day, 1863, Abe signed the Emancipation Proclamation saying all the slave were free. They weren't any such thing, of course, but his heart was in the right place, even if it did make workers in the Northern cities mad as hornets thinking of the future competition.

Then he got elected for a second term by telling everyone the story about the farmer—or the Dutchman, I forget which—who advised against changing horses while crossing a stream.

The war went on and on, and then finally it was over. (See GRANT.)

In the long run the Civil War was the right thing to do because it answered the Slavery Question, so people could ask each other something else for a change, and gave birth to *Gone With the Wind* and some rattling fine songs. On the flip side, it made the most awful mess all over the place, and nobody left to milk the cows or marry the girls. You can't have everything.

Lincoln was our only President to be assassinated in a theater. People carry on about John Wilkes Booth as if he were some kind of amazing accident, like Krakatoa, but actually all sorts of people had been itching to shoot Lincoln since they first laid eyes on him. He'd had his hat shot off twice and kept a file folder of death threats as thick as your arm. It was only a matter of time.[19]

After the funeral many grieving mourners ransacked the White House for souvenirs, some of which took several men to carry.

---

[19] With the fancy new guns we've got now, he'd have been toast in a week.

When you've lost a beloved President, it's nice to have a sofa to remember him by.

Lincoln's second Vice President was Andrew Johnson, because they'd thought a running-mate from Tennessee would balance the ticket or bring in some Democrats or something. It wasn't their brightest idea.

ANDREW JOHNSON

★ ★ ★

1865–1869

THOUGH JAMES BUCHANAN is a popular choice for the worst President ever, many would vote for Andrew Johnson. In the luck-and-timing business, there's not much to choose between them. Buchanan couldn't stop the Civil War, which was wicked of him; it was won[1] on Lincoln's watch, shooting him to the top of the President list; then Johnson got stuck with the mess it left behind, plunging him to the bottom.

Andrew Johnson should not be confused with Andrew Jackson. He didn't have Jackson's charm, or anyone else's either.[2] Before television, an alarming number of charmless people sneaked into the Oval Office.

Like Jackson, Johnson believed in the common man and kept telling everyone how common he was himself, and he was. His father was a gravedigger and odd-job man who died when Andy was three, and his mother took in washing and scrubbed floors in a tavern, and when he was twelve she indentured him to a tailor. He learned to tail all right, but he hated being indentured, so he ran away.[3] He tried to set up in business for himself in places like Carthage, North Carolina, but he couldn't get any customers. There was nothing wrong with his suits, it was just that people in Carthage didn't have much use for suits. When he was eighteen he

---

[1] Or lost, depending on where you lived.

[2] The White House staff called him "The Grim Presence."

[3] His master offered a ten-dollar reward for his capture and return, but there were no takers. Andy always carried a gun, even in bed.

married a nice girl named Eliza who taught him to read and write and do simple arithmetic, and after that there was no stopping him.

He moved to Greeneville, Tennessee, where people had never even heard of suits, and discovered politics. By the time he was twenty he was an alderman, and at twenty-two he was mayor of Greeneville.[4] Then he went off to the state legislature, and to Congress, and back home to be governor, making extremely noisy speeches about the common man all the way.

When he was campaigning for re-election as governor, he heard someone was planning to take a shot at him, so he stood up and whacked his revolver down on the table and said, "Fellow citizens, I have been informed that part of the business to be transacted on the present occasion is the assassination of the individual who has the honor of addressing you . . . Therefore, if any man has come here tonight for the purpose indicated, I do not say to let him speak, but let him shoot."

Nobody did. Later some of them were sorry, and said they would have done it, only they thought somebody else was supposed to.

Johnson got re-elected governor and by this time he was doing pretty well and had eight slaves, but he still made all his own clothes. It was the only way to be sure they were made properly, and besides it was soothing and took his mind off the cares of office. He even made a suit for the governor of Kentucky and sent it over as a gift, and the governor of Kentucky was tickled pink.

In 1857 he went to the Senate, and pretty soon there was all that secession business. When Tennessee seceded in '61 he said *he* wasn't seceding, and stayed right there in the Senate while all the

---

[4] He was the only candidate in a suit.

other Southern senators went home.[5] In '62 Tennessee got occupied by Union troops and Lincoln sent him over to be military governor.

Then in '64 he turned up on the ticket with Lincoln. Lincoln was a Republican and Johnson was a Democrat, but he was a War Democrat and they'd sort of joined the Republicans. They called it the National Union Party.[6]

At the inauguration Johnson was all of a twitter about getting sworn in, and he braced himself with a little nip or, according to witnesses, two full glasses of nip. He turned up for the ceremonies drunk as a hooty-owl and tried to say a few words and the bystanders had to wrestle him down into his seat and shut him up.

After that people took to calling him "Andy the Sot," but I can't find any evidence that he got pickled as a regular habit. One little slip and they jump all over you.

Johnson and Lincoln weren't each other's kind of guy. While Johnson was Vice President, Lincoln never once called him to ask what he thought of the war or the weather or to tell him the story about the Irish farmer and the cow, but then he wasn't Vice President for very long and Lincoln was a busy man.[7]

Since nobody'd planned on Lincoln getting shot, Johnson took over rather abruptly.[8] Congress wasn't in session, so he took it on himself to forgive the South for the war and appoint some governors, and they quickly elected some congressmen and hustled them

---

[5] He was all for the Union, and besides he was poor white trash and proud of it. He hated the Southern gentry like poison. He hated all gentry like poison. He was sorry to have missed the French Revolution.

[6] The New York World called it "two ignorant, boorish, third-rate backwoods lawyers."

[7] No use telling Johnson jokes anyway. He never thought anything was funny.

[8] A man named Atzerodt was supposed to kill him too, the night Lincoln was shot, but he got cold feet. Hard to find a really reliable assassin.

up to Washington. Then the real congressmen came back and they wouldn't let the Southerners come in and sit down, or even use the rest rooms. The Radical Republicans were in charge and they wanted to stay in charge, and they had blood in their eye. They said the Southern states weren't even states any more, just conquered territories, and had to be under military rule and get punished for a long, long time and nobody who'd seceded could ever get elected to anything at all. Many earnestly believed that all white male Southerners over age fourteen should be hanged for treason with no questions asked.

It was clear right away that Congress and Johnson weren't going to make a great team. After the congressional elections in '66, the Radical Republicans had enough votes to override Johnson's vetoes, which they enjoyed hugely, and passed the Reconstruction Bills.

The old abolitionist Thaddeus Stevens was the fiercest. He thought hell wasn't hot enough for the rebels. He said, "The punishment of traitors has been wholly ignored by a treacherous Executive and a sluggish Congress. To this issue I desire to devote the small remnant of my life." He wanted to make sure all the freed black men voted, so they'd be running the South and could *really* give their ex-masters something to cry about and fix their feet for seceding.

Johnson thought the states should decide for themselves about black men voting, which was the wrong thing to think and makes him an evil President as well as a bad one. It's always been wrong not to make sure men can vote, though quite right to make sure women can't, which is beside the point and morally quite different, as anyone can see. Johnson also wondered who, if the ex-rebels couldn't even run for dog-catcher, was going to fill all the public of-fices down there. He was clearly soft on the South.[9]

There'd been a lot of confusion all along about what was to be done with the blacks, and were they citizens now, or what? Even Lincoln had been confused. At first he'd thought they should all be sent home to Africa, and then later he figured they should go col-onize Central America, even though it was already chock-full of Central Americans.

It was a messy time. Seward was still Secretary of State, and he bought Alaska, or "Seward's Folly," for seven million and change, because some people will do anything to get a laugh, and it was funny enough but didn't solve the problems.

Andy got blamed for everything. Just to be spiteful, Congress cooked up the Tenure of Office Act, saying the President couldn't do anything without Senate approval, including and especially fire anyone. So Andy jumped up and fired Stanton, the Secretary of War, and tried to replace him with Grant, but Grant wouldn't play ball and Stanton barricaded the office door with heavy furniture and wouldn't leave.

Congress decided to impeach Johnson for getting too big for his britches, and disagreeing with the Rads, and not being able to see a joke. They even said he'd helped to kill Lincoln, which was silly. He'd been in bed with a bad cold that night.

Johnson said, "Let them impeach and be damned!" and wouldn't even attend the proceedings. He sent some lawyers, who tried to think of nice things to say about him, like "He is a man of

---

[9] He did think Jeff Davis should go to jail, and he wanted to hang Lee but Grant talked him out of it.

few ideas, but they are right and true, and he would suffer death sooner than yield up or violate one of them."

Thaddeus Stevens retorted, "He is surrounded, hampered, tangled in his own wickedness. Unfortunate, unhappy man, behold your doom!"

Well, they talked it back and forth for two months and nothing else got done, and finally he squeaked through, acquitted by just one vote, with the majority voting for conviction.

The trial cleared the air some, and people cheered up and the Johnsons gave parties and everyone came.

Eliza Johnson never felt very well and sat in her small south bedroom knitting and wishing she were back in Tennessee, but their daughter Martha did the honors. She was a good housekeeper and covered the carpet with a dropcloth for very large receptions.[10] She bought two Jersey cows, and came down to the dairy at dawn every morning in a fresh clean apron to do the dairy chores. There were five grandchildren in the White House and they needed a lot of milk.

After Johnson wasn't President anymore, he went back to Washington as a senator, and the other senators were distant but polite and never mentioned the little unpleasantness about impeachment.

Historians agree that Thaddeus Stevens was the hero of the administration for standing up for black men's rights while Johnson waffled. Just the same I'd like to see old Thaddeus make a suit. I bet he couldn't even sew on a button.

---

[10] Everything had tobacco stains all over again and bugs were living in the upholstery, in addition to the permanent White House residents like black ants, rats, mice, and buffalo moths.

ULYSSES S. GRANT

★ ★ ★

1869–1877

BACK DURING THE war, Grant went to Washington so Lincoln could officially put him in charge of it, and author Richard Henry Dana was hanging around the lobby of the Willard Hotel[1] and saw him. He wrote, "He had no gait, no station, no manner, rough, light-brown whiskers, rather a scrubby look. He had a cigar in his mouth, and rather the look of a man who did, or once did, take a little too much to drink . . . a slightly seedy look, as if he was out of office on half pay, nothing to do but hang around, a clear blue eye and a look of resolution, as if he could not be trifled with, and an entire indifference to the crowd around him. He does not march, nor quite walk, but pitches along as if the next step would bring him on his nose."

Later that day the general had to say a few words at a reception, and blushed all over and couldn't read his own notes.

Several respected authorities claim there's no evidence whatever that Grant ever touched a drop of whiskey. Well, I wasn't there myself, but his dear friends spent as much time worrying about his drinking, and writing to each other about it, as his enemies spent tattling to Lincoln about it, so I don't think we can rule out the possibility.[2] Halstead, who was a bit of a rat, told Lincoln that

---

[1] Everybody who was anybody hung out in the lobby of the Willard. They still do. It's Washington central.
[2] Lincoln liked to say he wished he knew what brand Grant drank so he could send a few barrels to his other generals. He said it often.

Grant was "a poor stick sober and he is most of the time more than half drunk, and much of the time idiotically drunk."[3]

What do the authorities mean, no evidence? Do they want me to break into his Tomb and take a blood sample? We do know that he *quit* drinking for long periods, and it's a foolish waste of time to quit doing something you weren't doing to begin with. Folks said he'd been sober for ever so long before his best friend, McPherson, was killed near Atlanta, and then he fell off the wagon and got blazing roaring drunk and cried till the tears ran down and soaked his whiskers. (This isn't what you'd call evidence, of course. It's just what folks said.)

Anyway he won the war, and besides, when he was in the White House he hardly drank at all[4] and it's none of the respected authorities' business or mine either.

Grant and James Garfield both claimed to be descended from William the Conqueror by way of his daughter Gundred. This is all very well except that Gundred was William's stepdaughter. Her real father was a man named Mr. Gerbod who never amounted to a hill of beans.

When Grant went to West Point a clerical error changed his name from Hiram Ulysses to Ulysses S. He was glad, because his original monogram embarrassed him.[5] Some people make a big deal out of him graduating twenty-first in a class of thirty-nine, and completely forget to mention that while he was there he jumped a horse over a hurdle six feet six inches high, which was a record and for all I know it still is. How would *some* people like to jump over

---

[3] McClure said he was drunk at Shiloh. Everyone with any sense was drunk at Shiloh.
[4] An English lady visitor waxed quite contemptuous about him drinking tea at dinner.
[5] He was easily embarrassed. He was so embarrassed at Appomattox he almost forgot to mention the surrender.

a six-foot six-inch hurdle? Anyway, he never wanted to be regular Army. He wanted to teach math and ride horses, but you can't mess around with destiny.

He fought in the Mexican War under Scott and Taylor and impressed even the Mexicans by riding for more ammo, under fire, hanging down the side of his horse like a Comanche. When the war was over he got posted to some really boring places on the West Coast where he couldn't take his wife and kids and there was nothing to do in the evenings but get drunk.[6] Then he either resigned or got asked to resign, depending on whom you believe, and went back to his wife in Missouri. His father-in-law gave him eighty acres and he built a house and called it "Hardscrabble" and failed at farming. Then he tried to sell real estate and failed at that, so he moved to Galena, Illinois, and tried to sell hides to shoemakers, and he'd probably be there still except for the Civil War.

Maybe he wasn't a gentleman like Lee but he was a real bulldog of a general[7] and the North was lucky to have him because a lot of the Union generals didn't care for fighting at all and just sat in their tents playing pinochle and sending excuses.

He said he was going to take Vicksburg and he did. The Confederate troops there said they'd hold out until they'd eaten the last rat, and after they'd eaten the last rat they came filing out to surrender looking so mangy that Grant paroled the whole bunch. He figured they were sick of war and just wanted to go home.[8] Anyway, getting Vicksburg cleared the whole Mississippi for the North,

---

[6] Or, if the respected authorities insist, not get drunk.

[7] He said, "The art of war is simple enough. Find out where your enemy is. Get at him as soon as you can. Strike at him as hard as you can, and keep moving on." Easy for *him* to say.

[8] Imagine his surprise when he met a lot of them later at Missionary Ridge.

and Lincoln said, "The Father of Waters again goes unvexed to the sea," which was fancy talk for Lincoln.

Grant ran the war so well—with help from Sherman and Sheridan—that even while it was still going on people asked him to be President. They said he could call himself "The People's Candidate," but he said, "I aspire to only one public office. When this war is over I mean to run for mayor of Galena and if elected I intend to have the sidewalk fixed up between my house and the depot." Alas, it was not to be.

We all know that nice picture of him at Appomattox, slouching around with his shirt unbuttoned looking embarrassed.[9] He told Lee his men could take their horses home with them for spring plowing, and he passed out rations for them, and when the Union troops started to cheer he shut them up, saying "The war is over, the rebels are our countrymen again."

It was one of those high points in a person's life. He should have stopped right there, but how was he to know? A basic rule of democracy is that the general who won the war gets to be President, even if he can't tell Washington from Nebraska and doesn't know which party he likes best.

The Republicans got to Grant first, as soon as we were finished with Johnson.[10] His campaign slogan was "Let us have peace" and he beat the Democrat Horatio Seymour so hard nobody's heard from him since.

Mrs. Grant, who was a good wife and nice lady and perfectly sane, liked the White House and enjoyed being hostess. It made a

---

[9] He'd been a big fan of Lee's since West Point days.
[10] The other generals went west to subdue the Sioux and take out their frustration on Crazy Horse, Sitting Bull, etc.

change from Army life and was much more fun than Galena, Illinois. She said it was "a constant feast of cleverness and wit," and gave a party for King Kalakaua of Hawaii. The food was said to be good but heavy; Grant's meat had to be cooked till it was practically black because he hated the sight of blood. (While off at the wars, he'd breakfast every morning on a cucumber soaked in vinegar, but she soon put a stop to that.) Their five children were still young and private family dinners were merry, with the President rolling little pellets out of his bread and flinging them at Nellie and Jessie, usually missing but offering an apologetic kiss when he scored a hit. Summers they went to their beach house with all the relatives.

Julie was a fine First Lady, but Grant had trouble being First Man. It's specialized work and some of us are better at it than others. I hear he'd never even read the Constitution.[11] He handed out jobs to people he thought were his friends, even if they knew less about the work than he did, and when he accidentally hired someone good he got nervous and fired him later.

As far as the South was concerned, he couldn't please anyone. Who could? He believed in amnesty for the Confederate leaders, which made the Radicals mad, and in black civil rights, which made the Confederate leaders mad. He sent troops to protect the blacks from the Ku Klux Klan and overthrew the elected governments, and the Carpetbaggers took over and made *everyone* mad.

It was so much more complicated than war that he got quite testy and snappish. Then the scandals started. I mean, these were scandals that *were* scandals. Industrial-strength scandals. The Golden

---

[11] Unlike the rest of us, who gather the family around every evening and read it aloud after dinner.

Age of scandals. Harding never even came close. The anti-Grant faction claims he was right in there grabbing bribes with the best of them, while the pro-Grant people say he was too dumb to know a bribe if he found one in his bed, and of course it wasn't his fault what James Fish and Jay Gould almost did to the gold market, but just the same, he *was* the President.

Right in the middle of the mess he ran for re-election. His opponent, Horace Greeley, was editor of the *New York Tribune* and some people said he looked just like the Mad Hatter. Others said no, with his shaven face and tufty white whiskers under his chin, he looked like an albino gibbon. He believed in eating vegetables and graham crackers and changing the country's name to "Columbia."[12] The vote was so decisive that Greeley almost immediately went insane, or even more insane than usual, and died.

Then there was the Crédit Mobilier scandal, about railroad stocks, and Vice President Schuyler Cofax had both hands in that one.[13] Then there was the Whiskey Ring, about tax cheats, and Grant's private secretary had to do some explaining. Rich folks bought whole state legislatures as if they were candy bars, and the railroad barons bought Wisconsin, Minnesota, and California. Some of Grant's favorite officials got so rich they had to leave the country. He was always sorry to see them go. He let the Secretary of War resign suddenly so as not to get impeached.

Personally, I don't think Grant made a nickel himself. All right, so Congress doubled his salary and he didn't say no,[14] but he didn't

---

[12] Also running was the famous clairvoyant and free-love advocate Victoria Woodhull, with the ex-slave Frederick Douglass for Vice President. It was an idea whose time had not come.

[13] Come to think of it, Garfield never really explained what *he* was doing that day.

[14] *You'd* have said no, of course.

know shucks about money and later got swindled out of every cent he owned. What was really happening was a New Age dawning.

We'd spent about fifty years warming up for the Civil War, and having it, and getting over it, and now it was time to move on to the next big thing, which was all about money, and business and industrial types getting hugely, amazingly rich and the working stiffs getting fretful about it. Grant just got caught out on the leading edge.

In different times he might have done just fine. He wasn't dumb. He said he hoped that one of these days "the nations of the earth will agree upon some sort of congress which will take cognizance of international questions of difficulty, and whose decisions will be as binding as the decisions of the Supreme Court are upon us." It was a pretty thought, and still is.[15]

Of course Henry Adams called him commonplace and simpleminded. There's always an Adams carping on the sidelines. He said the very *existence* of Grant disproved the theory of evolution. He said, "The progress of evolution from President Washington to President Grant was alone enough to upset Darwin."

After he'd been swindled out of his money and was dying of throat cancer,[16] Grant wrote his memoirs, trying to earn a few dollars to leave his family. Four days after he finished them he died. Mark Twain published them. They were good memoirs. They were a lot more exciting than Henry Adams's memoirs.

---

[15] And Wilson told us it was all *his* idea.
[16] He'd always smoked twenty cigars a day, and gnawed on the butts.

RUTHERFORD B. HAYES

★ ★ ★

1877–1881

THE LAST TIME I was in the Hall of Presidents at the National Portrait Gallery, I couldn't find Rutherford B. Hayes.

I suppose they were running short of wall space and figured that if they had to leave someone out, it might as well be Rutherford B. Hayes.[1]

In a manner of speaking he was scarcely President at all. Samuel Tilden won the popular vote hands down, and then there was a spot of hanky-panky in the Electoral College, with some states sending in two sets of ballots, and committees and inquiries and votes found in wastebaskets, which were the primitive equivalent of shredders, and finally, for reasons not entirely clear, they gave all the disputed votes to Hayes and he won by one. This was a good thing, as by now the inauguration was only two days off and Rutherford and Lucy were already on the train to Washington, and it would have been a shame to have made the trip for nothing.[2]

All you remember about the Hayeses is that they didn't serve anything fun to drink, so Mrs. Hayes was called "Lemonade Lucy" and the usual Washington wags went around saying that at her parties the water flowed like wine. This leads you to think of her as a prune, but she wasn't, she was sweet. It wasn't her fault that the dresses of the time looked more like lampshades. She had a wide, kind, generous face and five well-brought-up children, and she'd

---

[1] It's also possible that there was so little demand for the commodity at the time that nobody painted one. Painters have to eat too, you know.
[2] Just to be on the safe side, he took the oath of office a day early.

been to college, a White House first. She started the custom of the Easter Monday egg-rolling on the south lawn, and a charming custom it is too. She grew roses and lilies in Harriet Lane's conservatory, as Rutherford was exceptionally fond of a nice flower. In the evenings she gathered the family and various Cabinet members and congressmen in the Yellow Oval Room and served water, while Secretary of Interior Carl Schurz tickled the ivories and everyone sang items of a spiritual nature like "There is a Land of Pure Delight" and the ghost of Dolley Madison wept in the wings.

Some say that not serving wine was all Rutherford's idea anyway, since he'd been a big wheel in the temperance movement in his youth and his speeches at the Sons of Temperance meetings were widely admired by people attending Sons of Temperance meetings. Others say that the Hayeses started out serving the customary refreshments but changed their minds after something regrettable happened at a party they gave for a couple of Russian grand dukes.[3] Still others maintain that before his election, Rutherford enjoyed an occasional glass but gave it up to set a good example for the country. We do know that at the inaugural dinner there were six wine glasses by each plate, and they can't *all* have been full of water.

The matter of wine at dinner versus no wine at dinner is the most memorable aspect of President Hayes, unless you count the talk about him and his sister, which you really shouldn't. Probably it was nothing but talk anyway, and it's *nice* for a young man to be fond of his sister. She was said to be a real knockout, but not very stable. In any event, they put her away in a quiet place and Rutherford married Lucy, and we should consider the subject closed.

---

[3] I'm sorry I don't have the details for you. It must have been some party. You know those grand dukes.

Rutherford B. Hayes rejoiced in an unblemished public record dating clear from his early school days, when he won all the spelling bees. He often boasted about this later, claiming that not one in a thousand could spell him down. He went on to graduate from Harvard Law, and go to Congress, and get elected three times as governor of Ohio, and become a valued member of the Literary Club of Cincinnati. He was wounded over and over in the Civil War. He believed in integrity in government, and even tossed Chester Arthur out of his job at the New York Customs House for hiring more friends than were needed for the available chores. His motto was, "He serves his party best who serves his country best."[4]

Henry Adams said, "He is a third-rate nonentity whose only recommendation is that he is obnoxious to no one."[5]

Hayes had such long gray whiskers that they dipped in his soup unless he drew them to one side like a curtain. His decisive actions in the White House included laying out a croquet lawn and installing a telephone. He believed in a quiet life, and couldn't understand why the Indians and the striking railroad workers didn't believe in a quiet life too.

The Indians persisted in making trouble on the western plains and providing useful employment for the Army, which kept busy herding them from malarial swamps to desolate salt-pans and back again and shooting at them when they tried to get back home where it was nicer, or at least they remembered it as being nicer. The Indians complicated things by shooting at each other a lot too and refusing to live peacefully next door to their traditional ene-

---

[4] Just the same, some people were homesick for Grant. Being a terrific speller isn't everything.
[5] The Adamses felt that not being obnoxious to people was a sign of mental deficiency and moral flabbiness.

mies. They didn't figure out about solidarity until it was much too late.[6] Hayes said they could be citizens if they'd calm down and stop being tribes, but even when they were citizens they kept right on freezing and starving and dying of malaria, and what's a President to do?

The strikers were much more trouble because they weren't out in the Dakotas, they were in Baltimore, Pittsburgh, Philadelphia, Chicago, Cincinnati, St. Louis, and other populous locations. They wanted the railroads to pay them more money, but the people who owned the railroads felt that the less money they paid the workers, the more they got to keep for themselves. By this time the Gatling gun had been invented, and a number of people got hurt.

Hayes was afraid there was going to be a workers' revolution, and gathered in the troops to defend Washington and called his Cabinet into permanent session so they could all sit around the table drinking water and wondering what to do.

An unsettling feature of the strikes was the sudden appearance of a lot of women no one had ever seen before, shaking their fists and looting stores and shouting about starvation wages. Most Americans had barely noticed women for a hundred years, and now you could hardly walk down the street without hearing some. Even respectable women started having opinions, and taking up education, socialism, divorce, suffrage, good works, private clubs, cutting their hair, breaking whiskey bottles, and deciding not to get married.

It was all very upsetting and many people thought it meant the end of civilization as we know it, not foreseeing that soon the middle class would show up and take over and calm everyone down.

---

[6] If they'd learned earlier, you and I would be living on the rez at this very moment, making patchwork quilts and pewter candlesticks to sell to Indian tourists.

Rutherford B. Hayes didn't run for a second term because he wanted to go back to Spiegel Grove, Ohio, and devote his days to prison reform and the education of black youths in the South. No one missed him very much, and after a few years they could hardly remember what he looked like.

I'm afraid I really don't have any more to say on the subject. I've already said far too much, and if you want to know more you'll have to go look it up for yourself. When you find something exciting, give me a call.

JAMES GARFIELD

★ ★ ★

1881–1881

GARFIELD WAS TALL and handsome and genial and scholarly. He believed that strikers had a right to strike and black men a right to vote, and might have been a historically Good President if he'd stuck around long enough. (I hope you've forgotten the Crédit Mobilier scandal, because that was years ago and you don't want to hold a grudge.[1])

Garfield was born quite correctly in a log cabin, and graduated first in his class at Williams, and taught Latin and Greek at Hiram College. He wrote poetry too, they say, though none of it springs to my mind at the moment. He was the first left-handed President and one of his best parlor tricks was writing Latin with one hand and Greek with the other at the same time. Everyone mentions this, so I'm sure it's true, though you'd think a person would need two heads as well as two hands. It would be mean-spirited to ask just who was watching while he did it; we have to assume that all his guests could lean over his shoulder and actually read the simultaneous passages of Homer and Cicero unrolling from his pens, or at least distinguish Greek letters from ink-spatters. Just because some of *my* guests don't read Greek doesn't mean Garfield's didn't. Education has gone sadly downhill.

He studied law, and fought at Shiloh and Chickamauga and got made a major general, and went to Congress repeatedly.

---

[1] You also want to forget that five-thousand-dollar present from the street-paving people. Garfield himself said there was nothing wrong with taking it, and if he didn't think so, why should you?

His wife, Lucretia, was a scholar too. She wasn't half as handsome as he was, but she was a good wife and polite to his mother, who followed them around everywhere and told her how to bring up the children and cook James's eggs the way he liked them.

In 1880 he was elected to the Senate, but his career there was nipped in the bud because he turned up as President instead. He happened to be at the convention with some delegates, and the Republicans had split themselves into Stalwarts, Grant lovers who wanted to run Grant's buddy, Roscoe Conkling, and the Half-Breeds, who liked James Blaine better.[2] After thirty-six ballots they picked on Garfield instead, because there he was standing around looking tall and handsome and genial and scholarly. The Half-Breeds figured he'd do, and gave him Conkling's buddy Chester Arthur as a running mate to keep the Stalwarts happy.[3] Arthur was an awful sleaze and many people tried to vote for Garfield without Arthur, but it didn't work. It never does.

Garfield beat Winfield Hancock and moved into the White House with Lucretia, five children aged eight to seventeen, and his mother. He was nervous about it. He said, "I am bidding goodbye to a private life and to a long series of happy years which I fear terminate in 1880."[4]

He made Blaine Secretary of State, and this made the Stalwarts mad. Every time he gave a job to a Half-Breed, the Stalwarts gathered around in little knots muttering darkly. Day after day he worked his way down the list of jobs. As previously noted, dealing out jobs was what Presidents did back then, and it took a long

---

[2] Pay attention.
[3] Are you taking notes?
[4] He had premonitions, like Lincoln.

time. Some Presidents died before finishing. I don't mean Cabinet posts, I mean staffing every two-bit post office and customs shed in the country, and you wouldn't believe the hordes of deserving politicos who jammed themselves into the White House looking for work. You could hardly breathe. Contemporary observers said you didn't even *want* to breathe. The poor man was working hard and wanted to be fair, but people kept yelling at him and snatching at his clothes and trying to trip him on his way to breakfast, and he couldn't sleep nights. He said they were "wholly without mercy." He said, "Some civil service reform will come by necessity after the wearisome years of wasted Presidents have paved the way for it."

Finally it was July second and everyone took a break. Garfield was off to his twenty-fifth reunion at Williams, doubtless looking forward to telling his classmates what he was doing these days, the way people do at reunions, and then going to join his family at the Jersey shore. In the train station Charles Guiteau shot him in the back.

Guiteau was one of the job-hunters. He'd wanted to be the American consul in Paris and he'd wanted it badly, which is under-standable since it was a fine job and still is, but we can't *all* be the American consul in Paris. Guiteau was a Stalwart. When the police grabbed him, he yelled, "I am a Stalwart of the Stalwarts! I did it and I want to be arrested. Arthur is President now!"[5] In his coat pocket they found a wrinkled old copy of the *New York Herald* with an article about how Garfield gave all the good jobs to Half-Breeds and left the Stalwarts to sort mail and run errands. He'd underlined

---

[5] It didn't do him any good, though, because Arthur didn't send him to Paris either. His ghost hung around the District Jail for decades, complaining.

some of the fiercest bits and it seemed to have gone to his head somewhat.

Everyone thought Garfield was a goner, and Arthur was already testing the mattresses and deciding which furniture to get rid of, but at four in the morning the President was actually quite chipper and telling funny stories.

The doctors rallied round and tried everything they could lay hands on to dig for the bullet. The bullet was minding its own business and not bothering anyone, comfortably lodged behind the pancreas out of harm's way, but the doctors couldn't rest till they'd excavated.

Dr. Bliss hauled in the big Nelaton Probe and shoved it into the wound and twisted it around and around, looking for a pathway that felt like a bullet track. It made some interesting tracks of its own, and got wedged in the broken bits of a rib and had to be wrenched back out, but it didn't find any bullet. Then Bliss poked around with his fingers for a while, and called more doctors in from all over the country to poke with their fingers too, and pretty soon Garfield was a maze of secret passageways, but the bullet stayed put.

Then Alexander Graham Bell had a better idea. He was so pleased with his telephone that he thought it could do *anything,* and he rigged up a receiver with a primary and secondary coil that he said would hum when it got near the bullet. He brought it around, and they rubbed it all over Garfield, and once they did hear it hum, or anyway, they thought they did.[6] Bell showed the

---

[6] Some claim it was confused by the metal bedsprings. Others say it wouldn't have known a bedspring from a bluebell and might as well have been a dowsing rod, though much later the Army did use something similar for finding land mines.

doctors where to go in and dig ever deeper and wider holes, and they did, but still no luck.[7]

All this time it was summer in Washington with no air-conditioning. In an engraving of the bedside scene Garfield's mother is lurking nearby with a palm-leaf fan, but believe me, palm leaves are no match for summer in Washington, even when your insides *aren't* full of unsterilized doctors and burrowing probes. In September the unfortunate man asked to go to the Jersey shore for a breath of air, and they took him on a special train. They laid the tracks clear to the door of the hotel and pushed the car along them and carried him in.

For ten days or so he really did feel better, as people tend to do once they get out of Washington, but then he died.

He was only fifty. It was a scandalous waste of a perfectly serviceable tall, handsome, genial, scholarly President who could write Greek and Latin with both hands at once.

---

[7] The autopsy found it a good ten inches from where Bell said it was.

CHESTER A. ARTHUR

★ ★ ★

1881–1885

NOBODY KNOWS WHAT got into Chester Arthur. He'd always been considered a political bottom-feeder from the darkest, siltiest depths and seemed perfectly happy that way. He was the contented tool of Senator Roscoe Conkling, the man to know if you wanted a job in New York, and he'd never run for public office, since you didn't need to do anything that strenuous if you knew Roscoe Conkling.[1] (See GARFIELD.)

Arthur wasn't even a Civil War veteran like everyone else. As Conkling's friend, he'd spent the war cozy as a worm in an apple being quartermaster general for New York. Besides, though he always said he was born in Vermont, rumor had it that his mother, unmindful of the future, had strayed over the line into Canada before she went into labor, meaning he couldn't be President anyway.

Nobody except Roscoe Conkling wanted him to be. All summer everyone prayed hysterically for Garfield's health. Rutherford B. Hayes wrote in his diary that Garfield's death would be a national calamity: "Arthur for President! Conkling the power behind the throne, superior to the throne!" *The Nation* referred to Arthur's political origins as "a mess of filth."

Maybe his feelings were hurt. He spent eighty days hanging around waiting and reading the papers and listening to people pray for Garfield, and maybe he took it to heart and repented. He had

---

[1] Conkling was one of the chums Grant shouldn't have taken up with. Army life doesn't prepare a person for Conklings.

Bright's disease too, though he never let on about it, and maybe that helped.

Whatever happened, he turned into an acceptable and honest President and scarcely gave Conkling the time of day. Everyone was surprised, especially Conkling.[2] Furthermore, he supported the Pendleton act of '83, which said that people could take civil service exams for a lot of jobs and then keep the jobs no matter who got elected, freeing up future Presidents to do something besides appoint postmasters.

This made all the key people perfectly wild, since handing out jobs had been a great way to make friends, and get presents, and votes, and surprising envelopes full of money, and pay folks for favors past and future, as nobody knew better than Chester Arthur.

His old friends thought he'd lost his mind.

Arthur was a widower, his wife Nell having died the year before.[3] He was considered a handsome dog, which goes to show how styles change, and sported the most amazing tuffets of grayish woolly mustachios and side-whiskers, as if he'd been trying to eat a sheep without peeling it. He was also one of our nattiest dressers since Van Buren and his New York tailor had to hire extra help just to keep up with the White House orders. Sometimes he called for twenty-five coats at a clip.

The first thing he did in the White House was redecorate. He called the place "a badly-kept barracks" and went to live with Sen-

---

[2] He was more than surprised. He was beside himself.

[3] By this time you may think that presidential connections were unhealthy for women, but actually most American women in the nineteenth century were sick most of the time, and died often. No one knows why. It may have had something to do with childbirth, which wasn't a respectable medical field at the time.

ator Jones of Nevada and sent for Louis Comfort Tiffany to fix things up. Twenty-four wagon-loads of leaky cuspidors, battered hair mattresses, priceless antiques, and moth-eaten carpets got hauled off and sold at auction, and Tiffany went to work. Everything that could have fringes on it had fringes on it, and everything else was painted gold. As far as the eye could see there was red velvet and plush and floral embroidery, decorated screens, friezes, sconces, cabbage-rose wallpaper, and enormous painted urns. It was simply gorgeous.

Then he moved in and started giving the grandest possible dinner parties, at which everyone ate and drank as much as they could pack in for two or three hours. Arthur's cheeks got quite rosy and stayed that way.

One school of thought calls him a terrible flirt, while another says nonsense, he grieved constantly for his lost Nell. The latter cite as evidence that he had the servants put fresh flowers daily beside her photograph, but I'm not sure that signifies. He had fresh flowers put daily on every flat surface in the house. He grew over a hundred different kinds of roses in the conservatory and sent to New York for some truly breathtaking floral centerpieces for his dinners.

Besides, if he was so faithful and grief-stricken, how do they explain Pepita's daughter?

Pepita, who preferred to be described as a dancing girl, was such a dear friend of the second Lord Sackville that they had seven children together. One of the daughters, Victoria, went to Washington to be her father's hostess at the British Legation. Queen Victoria, who wasn't the prude you think she was, said it was all right with her if it was all right with Washington, and Washington said *it* didn't see anything wrong with the idea.[4] She was only nineteen and a real peach and charmed everyone, including Chester Arthur. According to herself, he proposed, and she "burst out laughing and said, 'Mr. President, you have a son older than me, and you are as old as my father.'"[5]

The White House issued a formal denial of the whole story, as who wouldn't?

When Arthur's name was mentioned at the Republican convention, no cheers went up. Politicos were still pretty ticked about the Pendleton Act and not getting to pass out jobs, and they liked Blaine better anyway. Arthur didn't pursue the matter. His Bright's disease was creeping up on him,[6] and he'd had a fine time while it lasted, with all that good food and wine and pretty ladies, and enough suits and coats to last several lifetimes.

Not to mention the shock he'd given Roscoe Conkling, which must have been good for many a quiet chuckle under the sheep's-wool.

---

[4] Lionel Sackville-West was rather a stick and Washington felt that *anyone* would improve his parties. He was described as having "an unusual power of silence."

[5] This left her free to marry her cousin, the third Lord Sackville, and produce Vita Sackville-West, famous chum of Virginia Woolf and all that crowd.

[6] We now know there's no such thing as Bright's disease, but whatever it was, it was creeping up on him.

GROVER CLEVELAND

PART I

★ ★ ★

1885–1889

GROVER CLEVELAND WAS elected back in the dark days before television, back even before we learned that Presidents ought to be charming, physically toothsome, and fit as fiddles. He was none of the above. He weighed nearly three hundred pounds and wore an immense walrus mustache with bits of corned beef and cabbage in it. The orator Robert Ingersoll said he could "slip his collar off over his head without unbuttoning it," which gives you an idea of his neck, and he had a high squeaky voice and some unrefined personal habits. I've heard that when he was practicing law in Buffalo he couldn't be bothered to go down the hall and relieved himself through his office window, and once a passerby sued.

People called him "the Beast of Buffalo." He was a bachelor, and no wonder.

He was a conscientious public servant, though. On two occasions while he was sheriff of Erie County, malefactors were sentenced to hang, and Grover adjusted the noose around their necks himself, tightened the rope, and sprang the trapdoor. He was your hands-on type executive and made sure things were done right.

After that he was a reform mayor for Buffalo, and then a reform governor of New York, and became a popular hero by vetoing the five-cent trolley fare. Before you knew it he was campaigning for President, buying beer for all comers in every bar in town.

It was an exciting campaign. The Republican James Blaine, who had finally got himself on the ticket, was an ingratiating fellow, only it seems that while he was in Congress there'd been a little something about some land grants and some railroads and some dear friends of his that didn't look good, though perhaps there was no real harm in it. On the other hand, Grover had fathered a child whose mother was an alcoholic prostitute named Marie Halpin.[1] Pretty soon the Republicans were singing "Ma, Ma, where's my Pa?"[2]

The Democrats sang back,

> "Blaine, Blaine, James G. Blaine,
> Continental liar from the state of Maine!"

Many old folks feel that some of the glow has faded from recent American political contests. Nobody sings about the candidates anymore.

There were only about a hundred thousand votes between them, and it was two days before the authorities would say who won. If television had been around, the dashing Mr. Blaine would have taken it in a walk, and maybe things would have been worse. Or maybe not.

Grover gave a popular inaugural address saying he believed in Washington's Farewell Address and the Monroe Doctrine, civil service reform, fair play for Indians, and no extra wives for Mormons.[3]

His sister Rose, teacher, lecturer, Greek scholar, and feminist au-

---

[1] Some say no, she was a maker of shirt-collars. Well, maybe as a sideline.
[2] Senator Vest of Missouri replied, "What of it? We did not enter our man in this race as a gelding."
[3] Many people felt this meant he was a liberal and in favor of the working man, but they weren't listening closely.

thor, came to the White House to be hostess. She was bored by the official parties[4] and went back home after Grover married his ward.

Frances Folsom was twenty-one and beautiful. He was forty-nine and Grover Cleveland. She was the daughter of Grover's late law partner and he'd helped buy her baby carriage and acted as her guardian ever since her father died when she was eleven. Some say he'd been in love with her mother. He called her "Frank." She called him "Uncle Cleve."

By this time paparazzi had been invented, and hordes of assorted shutterbugs and reporters followed them on their honeymoon in Maryland and listened at keyholes and peered in the window through spyglasses. Grover was furious, but Frank may have liked it. She was gregarious and energetic and a natural-born celebrity. So many people squeezed into her parties that sometimes hysterics and fainting broke out. She shook as many as nine thousand hands at receptions and had to have her arms massaged afterwards, but she didn't care. She liked it.

A visitor said her parties were "gorgeous, gay, and giddy," and "the dear people come by the thousands. Of all classes, ages, and sizes, of all colors, sexes, and conditions, they formed long lines reaching from the White House door . . . to the War Department."

The railroad baron Jay Gould is on record as telling Grover, "I feel sure that the vast business interests of the country will be safe in your hands," and he was right. Grover had said he wouldn't do any special favors for big business, but they didn't need any favors, they just needed to be left alone.

He didn't believe in mollycoddling the public. He cut federal

---

[4] It was mutual.

expenses by cutting pensions and aid programs. When some Texas farmers went bust in a drought and came whining to him for money to buy seed, he said, "The lesson should be constantly reinforced that though the people should support the Government, the Government should not support the people."

In the '88 campaign the Republicans behaved badly and said Grover beat his wife. They said he chased her out of the house into a storm. She issued a formal denial, saying "I can wish the women of my country no greater blessing than that their homes and lives may be as happy, and their husbands may be as kind, attentive, considerate, and affectionate as mine," but not all that many people believed her. Some thought he just *looked* like a wife-beater.

Then the Republicans sent a phony letter to the British minister, who was still Sackville-West, asking him which candidate he liked. Sackville-West said "Cleveland," and the Republicans ran out and told the Irish that the English were for Cleveland, so the Irish all voted for Harrison instead.

Grover wasn't sorry to leave the White House and go back to corporate law and making a tidy fortune on Wall Street, but Frank was. She told the servants to take good care of the place because she'd be back in exactly four years.

Cleveland was the only President to serve two disconnected terms and count as two Presidents, each section weighing a little more than Andrew Jackson and nearly twice as much as Madison, with Harrison wedged uncomfortably between them.

BENJAMIN HARRISON

★ ★ ★

1889–1893

BENJAMIN HARRISON WAS the grandson of William Henry Harrison, and I suppose that explains it, though it's hard to see why it should be an advantage. We have no hard evidence that William Henry would have been any more effective alive than he was dead.[1] Still, William Henry had at least been the hero of Tippecanoe and his grandson wasn't the hero of anything. A wicked cartoonist drew Benjamin, who was only five foot six, dwarfed and engulfed by his grandfather's hat.

Benjamin bought a lot of his votes, though not quite enough. Cleveland got a hundred thousand more in the popular count, but Harrison got New York and Indiana and that's what matters. After the election he found out his campaign people had sold all the Cabinet posts for cash to finance the campaign, so he didn't have anyone to appoint and just sat there looking foolish.

He wore a long flowing beard to make himself look taller, and this worked out pretty well in his portraits though not in person. Back home, he used to superintend a Sunday school, when he wasn't busy being defeated in local elections, and teach a men's Bible class. Cigars were his only other interest in life. If you asked him about cigars he brightened right up. Otherwise he didn't. Unkind people called him "The White House Iceberg" and said he had a handshake like a wilted petunia.

---

[1] Some people get the Harrisons mixed up, but manage to lead fairly normal lives just the same.

His wife, Caroline, was very fond of orchids and painted pictures of orchids on all the dinner plates and cups and saucers. She hated the White House because it was full of people all the time, tramping back and forth to see her husband, ruining the carpets, and distracting her from painting orchids. She kept submitting architectural plans to Congress for new, improved White Houses, some of them as big as Pittsburgh and much fancier. Congress just laughed and refused to build any more White Houses. In 1892 she died.

Harrison did many useful things as President, such as greatly improving the filing system and working out a method for classifying government data, but this failed to excite the public. The reporters and photographers got so bored with the senior Harrisons that they took up Baby McKee, their grandson, instead. He was a towheaded little boy with a little cart pulled by a little goat named His Whiskers, and for four years the American public knew more about him than they did about their own families. White House spokespersons said Baby McKee and the President were constant companions, but actually they rarely met except for photographic purposes.[2]

Presently the English financial house of Baring failed, and this was more significant than you might think and the whole world sank into financial mourning. People were unemployed, and the Socialists and Anarchists poured out from wherever Socialists and Anarchists wait when there's no depression. Harrison didn't know *what* to do, but neither did anyone else.

During Harrison's administration the Dakotas, Montana, Idaho,

---

[2] Harrison didn't have anything against children, but he never knew what to say to them. Baby McKee wasn't even interested in cigars yet.

and Washington became states. Some people cite this as evidence of executive leadership, but I'm not sure about that. Sooner or later they would have become states even without Harrison, if just to fill in the holes in the map.

Harrison's most decisive action was having the White House wired for electricity, which was a progressive step even if it did show the stains on the carpets. Unfortunately the whole family was terrified of the stuff and wouldn't touch the switches for fear of getting fried. They left the lights burning when they went to bed and the servants turned them off in the morning.

Teddy Roosevelt called Harrison "a cold-blooded, narrow-minded, prejudiced, obstinate, timid old psalm-singing Indianapolis politician."[3] Someone said he had "no bowels." Someone else said if he served another term it would be "four more years in a dripping cave."

He was the first President to watch a professional baseball game. Cincinnati beat Washington 7–4 in the eleventh.

Later, in 1897, he wrote a book called "This Country of Ours," and the *Ladies' Home Journal* ran it in installments and Scribner's published it as a book. It seems to be out of print. I guess that's about it. . . .

---

[3] And that's only what he said in public.

GROVER CLEVELAND

PART II

★ ★ ★

1893–1897

CLEVELAND II WAS for gold and the McKinley Tariff, and the Democratic platform was for silver and no McKinley Tariff, but he ran as a Democrat anyway, and won, and walked smack into a walloping depression, with millions unemployed.[1] If there was one thing that got Grover's goat, it was people being unemployed, because it was bad for business and probably all their own fault.

To make matters worse, even people who did have perfectly good jobs in the mines or the steel mills or on the railroads complained about making three dollars for a ten-hour day[2] and went on strike. Sometimes Grover had to be quite firm with them, and send in Pinkertons, federal troops, the militia, special deputies, etc., to keep them from breaking up things that didn't belong to them, like locomotives. Some strikers resorted to unfair tactics, like Mother Jones and her army of three thousand miners' wives with brooms and mops, all screeching and banging on buckets and frightening the scabs and the mine mules. Hotheads like Emma Goldman made speeches about strikes until they had to throw her in jail to keep her quiet.[3]

Cleveland didn't intend to be a lovable President. He told the public not to ask him any favors. If people agreed with him, he

---

[1] No, it wasn't the same as Harrison's depression. This was the *next* one.
[2] Remember, in 1893 you could buy a lot more with three dollars, but some people are never satisfied.
[3] She enjoyed it, and a good thing, because she never did keep quiet and spent a lot more time behind bars.

agreed with them right back, but otherwise he said, "If they wanted a fight, he would give them one." He had uniformed guards to keep people out of the White House, and a journalist said that getting news from the place was accomplished "much after the fashion in which highwaymen rob a stage coach."

Things brightened up briefly with the Chicago World's Columbian Exposition, which was a grand fair and a huge success. Cleveland opened it with a stirring speech about how all these fine things on display proved we were the greatest nation in the world and could teach the rest of them a thing or two about freedom and enterprise. George Ferris reinvented the wheel for the fair. Harry Houdini was there, escaping from various traps. Henry Adams was there, and spent a long time staring at steam engines and dynamos.[4]

Then the fair closed and everyone went back to being depressed. There were thousands of tramps wandering all over the place, because in those days the homeless didn't settle down on sidewalks and in train stations, they walked around frightening little old ladies. People expected Congress to do something, but Congress just kept fiddling with tariffs.

In the spring of '94 a little fellow named Jacob Coxey got some people together to march on Washington and ask about jobs, even though Cleveland had told everyone not to come whining to the government. Coxey called it "a petition in boots." About four hundred of them started out from Massilon, Ohio, accompanied by a six-piece band and forty reporters. Coxey's wife had a baby, and he named it Legal Tender and brought it along. The weather was terrible, but they kept on slogging. By the time they hit Pennsylvania

---

[4] Later he wrote about them interminably. He thought they Meant Something, but they probably don't.

Avenue there were possibly thousands of reporters and it was a major media event, with Coxey's daughter Mame leading them on a white horse, dressed as Peace. Grover called the cops, who broke a lot of heads and put Coxey in jail for carrying a sign and walking on the grass, and that was the end of that.

Cleveland knew a thing or two about keeping malcontents in their place. He sent more troops to break up the Pullman strike, and put Eugene V. Debs in jail for starting it. The *New York Times* applauded, calling Debs "an enemy of the human race," but the Socialists were pretty disgruntled.[5]

A determined doctor managed to heave Grover's mustache aside long enough to look in his mouth and find a tumor. Grover didn't want to worry the stock market, so on July 1, 1893, he sneaked off and had secret surgery in the dead of night, on the yacht *Oneida* moored in the East River, and never told a soul. With a lot of his jaw gone he had trouble talking, so a dentist made him a rubber jaw that fattened his jowls back to their familiar bulge and fixed his voice as good as ever, which wasn't great. When he spoke to Congress in August they never noticed, and the story didn't break until he'd been dead for years. He hadn't helped the stock market, though. It was already worried, and it stayed worried.

If you still need to know more about that tumor, the dentist, Dr. Kasson Gibson, kept it for a souvenir, and it wound up in the Mutter Museum in Philadelphia, where you can visit it anytime, right next to John Wilkes Booth's thorax and some urinary stones of Chief Justice Marshall's. It's not much to look at, though.

Conservative historians consider Cleveland the most distin-

---

[5] Socialists, if you've noticed, are almost never gruntled.

guished President between Lincoln and Teddy Roosevelt. When pressed to explain, they say he was honest, which seems to astonish them, and saved the country from protective tariffs and dumping the gold standard, heaven forbid.[6]

Historians don't care if you look like a walrus and beat your wife and piss out the window. They just care about history.

Contemporary opinions may vary. On March 4, 1897, the *San Francisco Examiner* exulted "the sky is blue, the birds sing, and joy is unconfined. It is the last day of the Cleveland administration."

---

[6] Please don't worry about the gold standard. Other people are worrying about it for you.

WILLIAM McKINLEY

★ ★ ★

1897–1901

McKINLEY WAS ASSASSINATED by an anarchist. Plenty of Presidents were just *asking* to be assassinated, but not McKinley. He was a nice man, and it's a darned shame, because very few nice men get to be President. It just never occurs to them. Nobody would have heard of McKinley if Mark Hanna hadn't needed a really nice President.

Mark Hanna had made enough money selling groceries and running mines to buy Ohio, which he did, and appointed McKinley governor of it, to keep things perking along for his businesses and everyone else's. Hanna loved business more than anything, and he knew McKinley loved it too because he'd spent fourteen years in Congress jacking up the tariffs to make things cozier for business. He was a staunch Republican.[1]

In 1896 Hanna decided McKinley should be President, so the whole country could be like Ohio. He told everyone to vote for McKinley, while McKinley sat home on his front porch and smiled. The Democrat was William Jennings Bryan the Boy Orator, who made his famous speech saying that gold was disgusting and mankind shouldn't be crucified on a cross of it. This sounded terrific[2] but since your basic voter didn't understand it any better than you do, he voted for McKinley, who hadn't said anything.

---

[1] Nobody knows why Democrats, Socialists, Federalists, etc., are never staunch, but that's the way it is. Only Republicans can be staunch.
[2] Everything Bryan said sounded terrific.

All Washington marveled at how nice McKinley was.[3] His wife, Ada, had lost two infant daughters and hadn't been quite herself since. Some White House wives lurked in their rooms when they should have come down and joined the party; Ada came down and joined the party when she should have lurked in her room. She had her good days and her bad days. She went in for phlebitis and epileptic fits and nobody wanted to sit next to her at dinner, so McKinley sat beside her himself. He took very good care of her, and when she had a seizure during state receptions, he hurried to her side and flung a napkin over her face so nobody would notice.[4]

I suppose you're thinking, if McKinley was such a sweetheart, how do you explain the Spanish-American War, and us being an empire all of a sudden, and taking all those islands from Spain?

Well, it's a long story, but it wasn't *McKinley's* fault. It all began back in Cleveland's time, with some local uprisings in Cuba, which belonged to Spain. Highminded people thought we should hustle right down and help the Cubans, and business types thought we should hustle right down and protect American business interests, but Cleveland kept the lid on it for a while.

Still, some people went on complaining that Spain was being mean to Cuba, and we hadn't had a good war in ages and were all sitting around getting rusty. Then it seems there was this battleship, the *Maine,* that had stopped off in Havana Harbor for a rum-and-Coke, and on February 15, 1898, it happened to blow up. It was quite a blast, and 266 sailors got killed. This is a lot of sailors. You

---

[3] Teddy Roosevelt said, "McKinley has no more backbone than a chocolate eclair," but Teddy really only admired people who shot tigers, and charged up San Juan Hill, and were named Teddy Roosevelt.

[4] Well, that's what I'm told. Maybe they were just pretending not to notice.

can't pretend not to notice that many sailors getting blown sky-high.

McKinley said it was probably some kind of accident,[5] but Teddy Roosevelt said Spain had done it and it was an act of war.[6] Some people thought Cuba did it to make Spain look bad, and some thought certain American newspaper publishers did it to make headlines and sell newspapers.[7] Whatever happened, it certainly did blow up.

Spain felt just terrible about it, and the Queen of Spain and the Pope and other influentials said they'd do *anything* if we'd stop being angry, and besides, the new governor-general of Cuba was much kindlier than the old one, and the Cubans had all quieted down and the troubles were over.

This would have been fine with McKinley, but it wasn't fine with Congress, or with Teddy either. They kept nagging at McKinley until he burst into tears and said, all right, then, let's have a war.[8]

John Long was the real Secretary of the Navy, but he couldn't do anything with his assistant, who was jumping out of his skin with excitement. Long threw up his hands and went to take a nap, and Teddy sent Admiral Dewey to the Philippines, which also belonged to Spain, besides being a swell place for us to park our Navy in the future, not to mention all the trade we could open up in the

---

[5] Later a commission of inspectors concluded it was due to "an external cause." That ruled out the microwave.

[6] He was Assistant Secretary of the Navy and as far as I know nobody asked him, but he was always hyperactive.

[7] Personally, I think Teddy did it. It could get awfully quiet just sitting around being an assistant secretary.

[8] According to a friend, he "broke down and wept as I have never seen anyone weep in my life. His whole body was shaken with convulsive sobs." I *told* you he was nice.

neighborhood. When Dewey got to Manila Bay, he said, "You may fire when ready, Gridley," and sank the Spanish fleet.[9]

Then Teddy made sure the Navy had plenty of guns, sent out a call to enlist more seamen, and resigned. He ordered an extra-splendid uniform from Brooks Brothers and started organizing the Rough Riders. He could hardly wait.

The Spanish-American War was the shortest war on record at the time, being long before Granada and the Gulf Wars, and lasted from April till August. We lost three hundred and seventy-nine men fighting, plus 5,083 from the usual other causes like drinking the water, and won all the islands. We paid Spain twenty million for the Philippines, and they threw in Guam[10] for good measure, and we took Puerto Rico, and gave Cuba to itself on condition that it install indoor toilets and let us keep our Navy there. Then we decided we'd better have Hawaii too. Teddy said we needed it to defend our Philippines, and the Senate Foreign Relations Committee said we deserved it because our feelings toward it were like "the love of a father for his children."

McKinley prayed hard for guidance, and God told him he should accept the Philippines as a personal gift from Himself. Rudyard Kipling, who knew a thing or two about empires, sent McKinley a rather doleful warning—

> *"Take up the White Man's burden—*
> *Send forth the best ye breed—*
> *Go bind your sons to exile*
> *To serve your captives' need."*

---

[9] It was terribly fragile. Just a few little holes and down it went.
[10] *Guam?*

—but if God has personally given you some islands, you can't just mark them "return to sender" and give them back. He made a speech saying, "We cannot shirk the obligations of the victory if we would, and we would not if we could." We couldn't just set a lot of brown people adrift on their own, getting into who knows what mischief, running through stop signs and ripping the tags off their mattresses. It was plainly our duty to civilize them, and sell them things, and convert them to Christianity. (They'd been Catholics for centuries, but McKinley was a homebody and not quite clear about foreign lands.)[11]

The Filipinos didn't want to be ours, because they didn't know it was for their own good, so McKinley had to send troops and spend several years on what he called "benevolent assimilation." Some historians think it was too bad about the thousands of Filipinos who got killed being assimilated, and the torture and concentration camps and so on, but nobody doubts that McKinley was completely sincere and only trying to help.

In 1900 it was time to run for re-election. The Vice President, Garrett Hobart, had died along the way, so we needed a new one, and wouldn't you know Teddy Roosevelt showed up at the convention in his Rough Riders hat and all hell broke loose? It made McKinley itch all over just to be in the same room with Teddy, but as usual nobody paid any attention to what McKinley wanted. If you're nice, people just walk all over you. Besides, Teddy had been crashing around being governor of New York, and Boss Platt, who was in charge of New York, wanted him out of there before he broke something.

---

[11] Early on, he'd asked a friend where the Philippines were, but the friend didn't know either.

William James called the team "a combination of slime and grit, soap and sand." Teddy ran around making hundreds of speeches about prosperity and the Full Dinner Pail. McKinley just smiled. The Democrats dragged out William Jennings Bryan again, who was still calling himself the Boy Orator though he was fully forty years old, and still whining about the cross of gold.

McKinley was re-elected, and he was just as nice the second time around and mellower about tariffs. He smiled and nodded and always wore a clean white vest, which he changed several times a day, with a red carnation in his buttonhole. (He was usually smoking a cigar too, but he hid it from the photographers.)

In September, 1901, he went to the Pan American Exposition in Buffalo. As he bent down to give a little girl his red carnation he was shot at close range by a fellow named Czolgosz.[12] Czolgosz had been brooding about this and that, the way anarchists do, and bought a gun from a Sears Roebuck catalog and told a friend he was going to shoot a priest with it, just to show people. The friend said not to bother, there were so many priests that nobody would notice, so he shot McKinley instead and everyone noticed.[13]

Czolgosz's explanation was, "I am an anarchist. I don't believe in marriage. I believe in free love."

McKinley was nice even when shot, and immediately gasped to his secretary, "My wife—be careful, Cortelyou, how you tell her!" and added that nobody was to hurt poor Czolgosz.

The doctors hadn't learned a thing from the Garfield episode and spent a week excavating McKinley in search of the bullet, and

---

[12] Pronounced "Czolgosz."

[13] Many people are pretty sure that Emma Goldman was the friend and behind the whole thing and made the arrangements, but if so, she was carefully somewhere else at the time.

then he died. I've been told he died singing "Nearer My God to Thee," and I've been trying to believe it. Some days I almost do.

It has been suggested that McKinley and Garfield were really the same person, since they were both Republicans from Ohio, both had been congressmen and senators, both died in September from gunshot wounds and doctors, and both had eight letters in their last names.

There is no truth in this theory and I'm sorry I even brought it up. Besides, Garfield had whiskers and was fully six inches taller than McKinley.

THEODORE ROOSEVELT

★ ★ ★

1901–1909

WE KNOW MORE about Teddy Roosevelt than we do about most Presidents, because he's more fun to remember, and he invented national parks and the Teddy bear. He always had a wonderful time doing exciting things and making sure they got written up in all the papers. Everyone loved him except the industrial barons[1] and Mark Hanna, who had no sense of humor and called him "that damned cowboy."

The high point of the Spanish-American War had been Teddy leading the Rough Riders and whole squadrons of reporters up San Juan Hill. It was a historic moment, and nobody cared a bit that it wasn't San Juan Hill at all but a small mound in the neighborhood called Kettle Hill. A few staunch historians insist that Kettle Hill was a good way to *get* to San Juan Hill, and it was certainly close by, because Teddy himself said in his memoirs that it offered "a splendid view of the charge on the San Juan blockhouse." Other historians say he was just plain lost[2] and by the time he found the right hill it was all over, with a mere five thousand American troops routing the five hundred defending Spaniards.

Nobody even cared that in the confusion the Rough Riders had left their horses behind in Tampa and had to charge up hills on foot, which isn't half as stirring unless it's Teddy doing it, chanting, "Rough, rough, we're the stuff! We want to fight and can't get

---

[1] They thought he was a liberal. He often sounded like one.
[2] He couldn't see very well, even with his glasses.

enough! Whoopee!"[3] He trudged up the wrong hill with such flair and dash that he ended up the most important person in the world. Style counts.

Teddy did not shoot McKinley. Everyone saw Czolgosz do it, and it's just as well he did because otherwise Teddy might have done something foolish.[4] At the funeral he could hardly keep from crowing.[5]

He moved into the White House with his nice quiet wife, Edith, and their children, who took after their father. By actual count there were only six of them, but in full cry they sounded like dozens. They were allowed to come down to dinner with important guests, and interrupt and bang on the table with their forks and spoons.[6] They understood their responsibility to the press and public and were always doing fun things like taking their pony upstairs in the elevator, roller-skating in the halls, and sliding down the grand staircase on trays swiped from the pantry, while the staff reminisced wistfully about the two sweet little Cleveland girls. They kept badgers, raccoons, cats, dogs, birds, guinea pigs, snakes, a kangaroo rat, a bear, and the pony, Algonquin. They brought in friends to help them throw spitballs at the portraits of Presidents past.

Alice was the oldest and very pretty but a cutup too. Her father said, "I can do one of two things. I can be President of the United States, or I can control Alice." It was a great relief to her parents

---

[3] He stole a locomotive too, either to make up for the missing horses or just for fun.
[4] Being Vice President can be even duller than being Assistant Secretary of the Navy.
[5] Lincoln Steffans wrote, "His joy showed in every word and movement," and a few days later he "laughed with glee at the power and place that had come to him."
[6] Teddy's gray cat, Slippers, came to dinner too but had impeccable manners.

when she married Representative Nicholas Longworth of Ohio.[7] They thought marriage would calm her down. It didn't. She went on being a famous Washington cutup pretty much forever, and said many awful, famous things about famous people and everyone wanted to sit next to her so they could tell everyone the next morning what she'd said. Half the cracks we read on T-shirts to this day were Alice's.

The reformers expected Teddy to be a reformer, because he'd been trying to reform New York while he was governor there, which was why Boss Platt made him Vice President. Now he said that he was President of all the people, and he could certainly see both sides of these labor/capital squabbles. Certainly he was going to squash the "malefactors of great wealth" as promised, but he believed that people who own mines and mills have rights the same as the rest of us slobs, though he wished they didn't have to make such mean, dirty money, instead of already having lots of nice, clean money like the Roosevelts.[8]

Not that he was against labor unions. He just didn't want them slowing down production with strikes. He stepped into the coal strike in 1902 and said he'd jolly well send in the Army to run the mines if both sides didn't come to an agreement on the double. And he dug up the moldering Sherman Anti-Trust Act and brought suit against forty-four major corporations. And he invented the Square Deal, whereby if a brick fell on you at work, the company should do something nice for your widow, and people who make medicines should stop putting poisonous or addictive ingredients in them,

---

[7] It was a swell wedding. She borrowed a sword from a bystander and whacked up the cake with it.

[8] The Roosevelts had had money for so long they'd forgotten where it came from. It just sort of ran in the family, like politics and asthma.

or if they did, they should mention it on the label. He even made it illegal to sell spoiled meat.

Unless you were a major corporation, he was the greatest possible fun to have in the White House and people could hardly wait to open their newspapers in the morning to see what he'd been doing. He invited prizefighters to dinner and staged jujitsu and Chinese wrestling matches in the East Room. He was a pioneer fitness addict and loved boxing, wrestling, tennis, fencing, carrying a big stick, running around and around the Monument Grounds, playing cowboys and Indians with his children, and killing animals.

He thought fitness was so important that he invented the Rock Creek Test. He took his aides and staff and prospective Cabinet members and new ambassadors to Rock Creek Park for a workout of running, scrambling, wading, swimming, and climbing. The object was to proceed in a straight line through or over everything in the way, including small buildings. Anyone who drowned or broke his neck or sat down and cried was a weakling and unfit for his post.

The new French ambassador reported that "it is important to walk straight into a river, or mudhole, and avoid with a feeling of horror paths and bridges." He passed. The new British ambassador failed dismally. He got stuck halfway up a rock and Teddy had to haul him to the top by his collar, and afterwards kept writing to London saying the man was totally useless and ought to be recalled.

One day Teddy realized it would be simpler and faster if we could take a boat cross-country from the Atlantic to the Pacific instead of sailing clear around Patagonia. Since it would be too much work to dig a trench clear across the United States, the smart place to dig was across a part of Colombia where the continent is only fifty miles wide. He asked Colombia about buying the area, but they dithered around and wanted too much money.[9] Then he realized that the people living in this narrow place were probably sick of belonging to Colombia and just dying to be independent and if they were independent they could rent us a strip for our canal. So he sent some warships down there to protect their right to have a revolution if they should happen to want one, and after some prodding they did. (It was sad that a Chinese laundryman and somebody's dog got killed in the uprising, but remember they died in the cause of liberty.) As soon as we'd freed the natives from the oppressive yoke of Bogotá, we named the place the Republic of Panama and broke out our shovels. The Colombians were sore as a boil, but it's not as if they'd been real people, like Europeans.

Teddy was as fond of nature as cannibals are of missionaries, and he didn't just go backpacking through it either. He charged right in and shot it between the eyes and had it stuffed and mounted. When Gifford Pinchot, a man who knew a few things about trees, complained that the lumber companies were chopping them down left and right, Teddy was upset. He was afraid the outdoors would disappear and he'd be reduced to popping at squirrels in the Rose Garden. He and Pinchot decided to tell the lumber companies to go easy, and only cut down the large, commercially valuable trees and leave us some of the rest. They called this "Conservation," and the word caught on. Teddy put a hundred and ninety-four million acres in the National Park system, and called a Conservation Conference in Washington, where people got up and talked about pre-

---

[9] Teddy said, "You could no more make a deal with the Colombian rulers than you could nail currant jelly to the wall."

serving our natural resources so we could go on making money out of them for years. Pinchot said this was "a turning point in human history."

When it came time for re-election, nobody wanted to run against Teddy and the best Democrats could come up with was a man named Alton B. Parker, a kind of human sleeping pill. He'd been an appeals-court judge in New York state, and when you'd said that, you'd said it all. His press agent, a desperate man, sent out bulletins on what he usually ate for lunch.[10]

During his second term Teddy became seriously involved in reforming English spelling and in straightening out some European problems. He won a Nobel prize for helping with the Russo-Japanese peace negotiations.[11] He tried to get Germany, France, and England to stop sharpening their swords and glaring at each other, which was quite futile and always had been, but at least he tried. Highly civilized places that had always considered us a bunch of hooligans in coonskin caps began to eye us with new respect.[12] Nothing came of the spelling reform, however.

When his second term was up he appointed Taft to be the next President and said he was going to retire quietly to shoot animals in Africa, with plenty of reporters and a full film crew to make a movie about him and a magazine contract to write about it all.

He said, "No President has ever enjoyed himself as much as I."

Even back in those golden days, typesetters weren't infallible. After McKinley's assassination the newspapers covered Teddy's

---

[10] "Thin soup, tea without milk or sugar, fruit and custard or pumpkin pie."

[11] When someone suggested he follow this up with a worldwide disarmament conference, he was horrified. He still kept his Rough Riders suit pressed and ready to go.

[12] Maybe they admired the way we got our hands on Panama. It *was* pretty slick.

swearing-in, and in the excitement of the moment somebody reached for a "b" instead of an "o." Next morning New Yorkers read that "for sheer democratic dignity, nothing could exceed the moment when, surrounded by his Cabinet and a few distinguished citizens, Mr. Roosevelt took his simple bath, as President of the United States."

The story was picked up abroad, so that the world too could read about this quaint but oddly moving American ritual.

WILLIAM HOWARD TAFT

★ ★ ★

1909–1913

WILLIAM HOWARD TAFT was the world's largest President. He was bigger than Grover Cleveland I and II put together, and when he sat down at his desk he could hardly reach it. He got wedged in the White House bathtub and had to call for help, after which they built him a special one, and groups of workmen had their picture taken in it, lounging around together.

A newspaper reporter said he looked "like an American bison—a gentle, kind one."[1] Indeed, there's a photograph of him when he was governor of the Philippines, sitting on a water buffalo, and the resemblance is striking. He is correctly dressed as befits a governor and wears a Panama hat and carries a riding crop, and the pyramidal line of spreading mass from his hat to the feet of the buffalo is artistically satisfying. He doesn't look as if this was a joke, or a photo opportunity. He looks like a man about to go somewhere on a water buffalo.[2]

Plenty of candidates go all coy and say they don't really care one way or the other about being President, they can take it or leave it, but Taft *really* didn't want to be President. He said politics made him sick. He said all his life all he wanted was to be a Supreme Court justice. His wife, Nellie, had other plans. When she was an impressionable young thing of seventeen she'd spent a week in the White

---

[1] This is how you can tell him from Cleveland. Cleveland looked like a walrus, which is quite a different animal.

[2] What did you expect, roller skates?

House as a guest of the Hayeses, and she'd loved every minute. Then and there she vowed she'd only marry a man who could be President and take her back to her dream house. Compared to being First Lady, she thought judicial life would be pretty tame,[3] and she led him down Pennsylvania Avenue like an ox to the slaughter.

Taft had been Teddy Roosevelt's Secretary of War after he got back from the Philippines, and Teddy said sure, he could be on the Supreme Court if he wanted to. Then Nellie jumped in a cab and ran round to the White House for a private chat. She told Teddy how much nicer it would be if Taft could be President instead. So Teddy said okay, and Taft was President.[4]

The *Washington Post* congratulated Nellie rather pointedly.

A terrific blizzard blew in the night before the inauguration, and Taft looked out the window and said, "Even the elements do protest." He was hoping it would snow so hard the whole thing would be called off permanently, but the elements had better sense than to mess with Nellie and it stopped.

Taft hated being President so much that he fell asleep whenever he wasn't playing golf. Nellie sat next to him at important conferences and jabbed him in the ribs to wake him up from time to time. Sometimes she answered questions for him, because she knew what he would have said if he'd been awake for the questions.

Unfortunately, Nellie had a stroke early on, and while she was off the job his mind wandered more and more. Senator Dolliver called him an amiable man surrounded by men who knew exactly what they wanted. What they wanted was land, and timber, and

---

[3] "An awful groove," she called it, which was slang for pretty tame.
[4] William Jennings Bryan the Boy Orator lost, but he was used to it by this time and just shrugged.

oil, and coal. While Taft was napping his Secretary of the Interior tried to give Alaska to a pal of his, who thought it would be a good place to dig up some coal. Pinchot, TR's old forestry friend, squealed like a stuck pig and kicked up such a row about it that Taft had to fire him from the Forest Service.

Well, people thought that wasn't what Teddy would have done. They thought maybe Taft was a friend of malefactors and a foe of trees.[5] They were disappointed in him.

When Nellie got better she resumed her duties and bought a cow to graze on the White House lawn and bring fresh milk to the kitchen. (Some say the cow was named Pauline Wayne and some say Mooly-Wooly. My personal feeling is that Pauline Wayne was her formal, registered name, and Mooly-Wooly was what Nellie called her in moments of uncontrollable affection.) Then she sent for three thousand cherry trees from Japan, but they were all diseased and had to be burned, so she sent for three thousand more and planted them in strategic spots to cause April traffic jams for generations yet unborn.

None of this solved the unions and Socialists and the painful misunderstandings that kept cropping up between workers and their rightful employers. Socialism was all the whirl, and people like Mable Dodge gave terrific parties in honor of it, where everyone made passionate speeches about the workers and then passed the peyote and turned into Egyptian mummies or forest birds or whatever.

Taft simply didn't know what to make of it.

He tried being the first President to throw out the opening ball of the baseball season, and Walter Johnson was so inspired that he

---

[5] He wasn't. He was just sleepy.

pitched a one-hitter for the Senators against the Philadelphia Athletics for a final score of 3–0, but it didn't help.

The truth was that Taft wasn't half as much fun as Teddy and people were tired of him almost before he'd unpacked. The only reason they bought newspapers now was to find out what Teddy was doing in Africa.

He was doing plenty. Scarcely anything taller than a rabbit was left in the land. Skeptics wondered how he could shoot so many animals with the terrible eyes he had on him, and it was quietly explained that when he pointed his gun at a lion, various other people pointed their guns at it too, and either way that lion was in trouble.[6] From time to time he left the hired help behind to stuff elephants and went on triumphal tours around Europe. The citizens lined the streets and cheered themselves hoarse as if Teddy were President of the world.

Back home, people looked forward to the next election.

For the Democrats, there was a liberal sort of fellow named Bob La Follette who'd been doing liberal things in Wisconsin, but he drank too much brandy the night of the Periodical Publishers dinner and got wound up and spoke all night long, and people lost interest in him shortly before the sun came up. At the same dinner, a horse-faced intellectual named Woodrow Wilson, who used to be president of Princeton, spoke so briefly that everyone liked him better.[7]

Then Teddy came back from Africa with a whole mountain of dead lions and many exhausted reporters. He'd changed his mind about Taft. He said Taft "meant well, but he meant well feebly."[8] So

---

[6] Ernest Hemingway was around twenty years old at the time. An impressionable age.
[7] People hate listening to speeches after dinner. Why doesn't anyone realize this?
[8] By Teddy, "feebly" was a four-letter word.

the Republican Party split, with the Conservatives saying they'd sooner vote for the dead lions than for Teddy, and the Progressives saying they'd vote for *anything* rather than Taft. Teddy called the Progressives the Bull Moose Party, because that was what he said he felt like, and charged around campaigning. In Milwaukee somebody shot him but he paid no attention and went on with the speech, bleeding all down his front.[9]

Taft wasn't very good at campaigning. When some reporters asked him what could be done about unemployment, he said, "God knows."

The conservative Republicans voted for him anyway and the progressive Republicans voted for Teddy and everyone else voted for Wilson.

So Teddy packed up his reporters and went off to kill whatever it is people killed in Brazil, and in 1921 Harding made Taft the Chief Justice of the Supreme Court. He was very good at it and very, very happy. He said, "The truth is that in my present life I don't remember that I ever was President."[10] He even got salty with Nellie and gave all her Faith Baldwin novels away to the Salvation Army.

So she went upstairs and threw all his law books out the window.

Later, during rush hour, the magnificent chief-judicial rear could be seen looming over New Hampshire Avenue as Taft rummaged in the hemlock hedge dragging out damp copies of the *Supreme Court Reporter.* Playing with Nellie, you never got to keep all the marbles.

---

[9] Campaigning against Teddy could break your heart.
[10] By this time lots of people didn't.

WOODROW WILSON

★ ★ ★

1913–1921

WOODROW WILSON WAS very good and pure and thought everyone else could be good and pure too if they'd just follow his Fourteen-Point Plan for a perfect world.[1] That way there'd never be any more wars, and all the countries would bring their little troubles to his League of Nations and live happily ever after.

Historians say he was a great genius because nobody had ever thought of the League of Nations before, but this is probably not true. It's the kind of thing small children think up all the time, and their parents tell them to hush. Even Grant had thought of it.

Wilson was so right about everything that he never had to ask anyone's advice, because it couldn't be half as right as his own. He only talked things over with his wives. *They* thought all his policies were simply lovely.

He was just crazy about his first wife, and when she died he went quite distracted and sat by her body for days, wringing his hands. His friends feared for his reason, so they introduced him to Edith Galt, and right away he was just crazy about her too and married her almost immediately. He really needed a wife. You can't imagine how inconvenient it is to keep asking the presidential aides to stroke your brow when you have a headache or join you for your crackers and milk.[2]

As a general rule, Wilson much preferred women to men, and

---

[1] This established a commanding four-point lead over Moses, who gave up in despair.
[2] He drank a lot of milk. This can be a bad sign.

all his best friends were women. They were so much more admiring and sympathetic than men, and never argued or interrupted. He hoped they'd never manage to get the vote, as voting would quite spoil their charm.

Wilson had been a professor, and president of Princeton, and governor of New Jersey, and was widely respected for being an intellectual and very, very serious. He was serious because he had two rotten teeth right smack in the middle of where his smile would be if he smiled. In private, though, with plenty of admiring women around, he unbent and recited funny limericks and did impersonations and, I'm told, often cranked up the phonograph and danced a merry jig. (This is not a thought you want to dwell on.) He also like to read aloud to people and tell dialect stories in Cabinet meetings.[3]

William Allen White said shaking hands with Wilson was like shaking "a ten-cent pickled mackerel wrapped in brown paper."

That second wife, Edith, was one tough cookie. She'd only been to school for two years and didn't know beans about affairs of state, but Wilson discussed them with her anyway. He ignored his advisors entirely and stopped even saying "good morning" to his Cabinet, and he and Edith held policy meetings over many a glass of milk.[4]

He got elected the first time because of Teddy and his Bull Mooses[5] and the second time because he'd kept us out of the war in Europe. Then he decided we should join the war anyway. He

---

[3] Professors and dentists get like that. They think people listen to them because they *want* to listen to them.

[4] She didn't like his advisors, or his Cabinet either, and never gave official dinners. She thought it was much nicer with just the two of them.

[5] Not to mention Taft.

cried buckets about it, but how else could he show the Europeans how to be good and pure and follow the Fourteen Points? Europe had been getting pretty sick of the war and thinking they might even call it off, but as soon as we got there it perked up again.

I don't recommend trying to understand World War I unless you plan to make a career out of it, and I don't recommend that either. As we all know, it consisted of opposing teams facing each other from trenches, waiting for someone to poke his head up and get shot. From time to time small planes looking like wire butterflies chased each other around the sky until one of them went down in flames. This was fun to watch but had no discernible effect on the war. Mostly it was trenches. I don't know whose idea they were to start with, but four years later, when the war was over, the trenches were pretty much where they were in the beginning. There were more of them, because whenever things went badly the generals ordered everyone to fall out and dig more trenches, but geographically they'd hardly moved. Nobody complained. Nobody wanted to be the killjoy who said, "Hey, you know this trench idea? What if we tried something else for a change?" After all, the trenches were there, and digging them had been hard work, and they couldn't just walk off and leave them for someone to fall in and break a leg.[6]

Edith Wilson buckled right down to the war effort and bought a flock of sheep to graze on the White House lawn.[7] When she had them sheared, their wool fetched a thousand dollars a pound at

---

[6] In the next war we had foxholes instead, which were like trenches only shorter. They didn't work either. If you scrunched down, people couldn't shoot at you, but they could drop things on you. I don't know what the answer is.

[7] I can't find out what happened to Nellie Taft's cow.

auction, because they were the Presidential sheep, and famous. She gave the money to the Red Cross. Sometimes she even sewed pajamas for the Red Cross, and it was just delighted.

Finally the war was over and everyone came down with the flu. It was a lot worse than the trenches.

Woodrow and Edith went to the Versailles Peace Conference in person, to make sure the other winners were as kind and good as we were. A reporter said Wilson was "like a virgin in a brothel, calling sturdily for a glass of lemonade." Our allies liked his League of Nations scheme but they didn't think much of his other Points, especially the smarmy "Peace Without Vengeance" bit. They told each other he was a class-A ninny and gave Germany the full rack-and-thumbscrews, bread-and-water treatment.

Wilson felt just awful about it. He was a wreck, but then, he'd always been a wreck. He had such terrible nervous indigestion that he'd bought his own stomach pump and carried it with him wherever he went.[8]

As soon as he got back from Versailles he went on a tour to preach about the League of Nations all over the country, but people didn't want to hear about it. They wanted to know what he was going to do about inflation and unemployment. He went right on talking about the League of Nations. He had a one-track mind.

Then he had a stroke and came back to the White House, and Edith put him in the bedroom and slammed the door. She stood outside it to make sure nobody talked to him. She didn't want anyone asking him questions, or finding out how sick he was. She just stood there for months, shaking her head "no."[9]

---

[8] Everyone's favorite dinner guest.
[9] She was directly descended from Pocahontas.

People worried. They thought maybe the President was dead in there, or permanently unconscious, or a raving drooling loony. Passersby suddenly noticed the bars on the White House windows. They'd been put there to keep Teddy's kids from throwing each other through the panes, but now they started to look sinister. You can see how they would.

Wilson did sign some official papers, or at least Edith took some papers into the bedroom and brought them back signed, and who am I to raise an eyebrow? Eyebrows were raised, certainly, but they weren't mine. She transferred the Secretary of Agriculture to Treasury, and when the Secretary of the Interior quit she picked out a new one. She said it was what her husband would have wanted.

After four or five months of this, Secretary of State Lansing suggested that Wilson might turn over his duties to the Vice President, and the next day he was reading the help-wanteds.[10] Well, it wasn't a very bright idea. The Vice President was that fellow Thomas Marshall who said, "What this country needs is a good five-cent cigar," and meant every word of it. When people asked him about taking over the Presidency, he cried, "I can't even think about it!" When they tried to get him to do some work, he said he wasn't being paid to be President and went out and played golf.

The *London Daily Mail* wrote, "Although Washington tongues are wagging vigorously no suggestion is heard that Mrs. Wilson is not proving a capable 'President.'" Others referred to the Petticoat Government, the Regency, and the Presidentress. Edith just folded her arms and stood there.

The Senate wouldn't ratify the Treaty of Versailles, so we could join Wilson's League of Nations, unless he made some changes.

---

[10] She never could stand the fellow.

Edith went and asked him, and came back and said, no, he wouldn't make any changes, so the Senate didn't, and we didn't.[11]

By spring he could limp around and talk a little, though he didn't make much sense, and Edith let him out from time to time. His grasp on reality hadn't improved and he really thought the Democrats were going to nominate him for a third term. There wasn't enough left of him to nominate. Instead they picked a man named Cox, who was never heard from again, with a running-mate named Frank Roosevelt, who was.

Wilson was so disappointed he used words even Edith didn't know he knew.

Teddy Roosevelt said Wilson was "an utterly selfish and cold-blooded politician always," but Wilson didn't think he was selfish. He said he'd been sent here to carry out the teachings of Jesus Christ. He didn't say Who sent him, but we can guess.

---

[11] Maybe the League would have made out better if we'd joined, but I don't know. We joined the United Nations, didn't we?

WARREN G. HARDING

★ ★ ★

1921–1923

MOSTLY THE DEMOCRATIC process works about as well as could be expected, but every so often it stirs up something from the soft bottom of the gene pool, and everyone goes "Yecch! What is it?" and then acts all injured innocence, as if they'd never marked a ballot in all their born days. Some of these unidentifiable objects were originally Vice Presidents, so the public's not entirely to blame, but Harding was elected on his own with what the *New York Times* called "gigantic majorities . . . unprecedented in American politics."[1]

Harding owed everything to his wife and friends. He started out trying to teach in a one-room schoolhouse, which he said was the hardest job he ever had, and only lasted one semester. Then he tried selling insurance, and then he wrote for the Marion, Ohio, *Democratic Mirror* for a while before they fired him.[2] Then he bought the bankrupt *Marion Star* and tried running that, and married Florence. Florence was five years older than he was and had an idea or two of her own.[3]

He was handsome and friendly, though, and he happened to catch the eye of a man named Harry Daugherty. Ohio had changed hands again and now belonged to Daugherty, who carried it around in his pocket. He had a lot of important connections, like Standard Oil, and a lot of high-maintenance friends who called

---

[1] It was the first election women voted in. They needed more practice.
[2] Small wonder. The poet e.e. cummings said Harding was "the only man, woman or child / to write a simple declarative sentence / with seven grammatical errors."
[3] He called her "The Duchess."

themselves the Ohio Gang. He needed a President of his very own, and when he saw Harding he said to himself, "Jeez, put some proper clothes on this hick and get him a decent haircut, he'd look *exactly* like a President." So he and Florence got together and sent Harding to Washington to start out as a senator.

Well, he just loved it. It was the very thing. He missed half the roll calls and had affairs with pretty ladies and enjoyed himself enormously, so when Daugherty came and suggested he move on to bigger and better things, Harding said no, he didn't want to be President, he wanted to stay in the Senate and play. Then Daugherty went to Florence, and Florence went to work.[4] Nobody knows what she did to him, but pretty soon there was Harding wandering around in the original smoke-filled room, slightly drunk and looking bewildered.[5]

The nomination startled some people. It startled the *New York Times,* which called Harding's Senate record "faint and colorless" and added, "We must go back to Franklin Pierce if we would seek a President who measures down to his political stature."

Harding campaigned be telling everyone they could quit thinking about foreigners and their foreign problems and get back to normalcy. There's no such word, but people knew what he meant and voted for him in droves.

After the election, I'm told that Florence said, "Well, Warren Harding, I have got you the Presidency, what are you going to do with it?" and Harding said, "May God help me, for I need it." (No,

---

[4] A fortune-teller had told her he was going to be President. She was just giving Destiny a hand.
[5] His father once said to him, "If you were a girl, Warren, you'd be in the family way all the time. You can't say 'no.'"

I haven't the faintest idea how we know this. Were they bellowing at each other across the Mall? Was the bedroom bugged?)

Anyway, Florence was pleased as punch.[6] On inauguration day she threw open the gates and invited everyone in, and sightseers swarmed all over ripping souvenirs off the trees and bushes.[7] She loved being First Lady and shook almost as many hands as Frances Cleveland. She tried to keep a close eye on her husband so he wouldn't do anything he'd regret or say something dumber than usual, and even rewrote all his speeches for him. He read them without noticing the difference.

She was learning fast. Harding wasn't. Some people just aren't equipped for learning much. He said to his secretary, "Jud, you have a college education, haven't you? I don't know what to do or where to turn . . . Somewhere there must be a book that tells all about it . . . But I don't know where that book is, and maybe I couldn't read it if I found it. . . . My God, but this is a hell of a place for a man like me to be in!"

He did have consolation, though. When it got too much for him, he'd go to the little green house on K Street and hang out with Daugherty's Ohio Gang. He wasn't always sure what they were up to, but he did know they were his buddies, and it made him feel warm all over to have his buddies around. Sometimes he played poker with them all night, trying to forget. He said, "Oftentimes I don't seem to grasp that I am President." Then his buddies, who did grasp it, gave him a hug and let him win the pot. They didn't mind when he picked his teeth after meals or chewed tobacco, or

---

[6] So was Daugherty.
[7] I can't find out what happened to Edith Wilson's sheep.

when he ran out of chewing tobacco and slit open a cigarette and chewed its insides instead.

Sometimes the Gang dropped by the White House, and Florence served drinks upstairs in the private quarters. There wasn't any wine on the dinner table because of Prohibition, but you couldn't exactly entertain the Ohio Gang on decaf.

She liked to have Warren home where she could keep an eye on him, but occasionally he slipped out anyway.[8] Often she didn't quite know where he was, which was most provoking.

He should have stuck with the ladies and stayed away from the poker players, who kept asking him for little favors. He was always happy to help out, because he was an amiable, kind-hearted fellow and fond of children and dogs and his buddies. He should never have made Charley Forbes head of the Veterans' Administration, because Charley stole the veterans' money and went to prison, but how was Harding to know?

The Teapot Dome was another honest mistake. It consisted of a whole lot of oil underneath Wyoming, and it was supposed to be Federal oil, waiting there until the Navy needed it. Harding had made his buddy Albert Fall Secretary of the Interior, and when Albert said he was the very man to watch over this oil, Harding told him to go ahead and watch. No one was more surprised than Harding when Fall turned around and sold the stuff.

Accidents like that kept happening. It's really depressing when so many of your friends start committing suicide and going to jail that you can hardly scratch up a decent poker game, so he and Florence decided to take a nice long train trip across the country, all

---

[8] A certain Nan Britton claimed he was the father of her daughter, but the jury decided not to go there.

the way to Alaska, which is as far as it goes. They figured if they smiled and waved a lot along the way, people wouldn't notice the string of scandals crackling and sputtering back home. Harding kept walking up and down the train asking reporters and the hired help what *they'd* do if all *their* friends turned out to be a bunch of bums.

Along about Seattle, he was feeling a bit under the weather, so they detoured to San Francisco to rest. Presently he was feeling ever so much better, and Florence was reading to him in his room, and he just up and died.

There is not a shred of evidence that she poisoned him, and I don't see how you can be so mean. Five days later, when she got off the train in Washington, anyone could see she was not carrying a half-empty bottle of prussic acid. It's true she didn't let anyone do an autopsy, but plenty of people think autopsies are nasty, even people who've hardly poisoned anyone at all. And yes, she was cool as a cucumber at the funeral, but maybe she was all torn up inside. And she was overheard talking to his body in the coffin, saying "No one can hurt you now, Warren," but surely there's nothing sinister in *that?*

Yes, maybe he would have been impeached if he'd come home alive, but then again, maybe he wouldn't have been.[9] And yes, she did grab up and burn all his papers and letters, but she was just tidying up. She wouldn't have wanted the Coolidges peeking at them. If there was one thing Florence hated—and there was—it was Coolidges.

Besides, all the doctors agreed that Harding died of a stroke, or pneumonia, or apoplexy, or a blood clot, or food poisoning.

---

[9] And maybe I'm the real Anastasia Romanov.

Florence gave his dog, Laddie Boy,[10] to the servants and washed her hands of the whole affair, but the scandals kept popping up like toadstools all over town. It got so the Harding administration was what people meant when they said "corruption" or "sleaze" or "ugh."

Harding said, "I am not fit for this office and never should have been here." Teddy Roosevelt's daughter Alice said, "Harding was not a bad man. He was just a slob."

Florence didn't say anything.

---

[10] Some authorities believe Laddie Boy was a Scottie; others, a Collie. In his pictures he looks kind of like an Airedale. I had a dog like that once myself.

CALVIN COOLIDGE

★ ★ ★

1923–1929

CALVIN COOLIDGE WAS born in Vermont and weaned on a pickle.[1] He never said much of anything to anyone, so when he did say something, like "The business of America is business," it sounded deep, or anyway a lot deeper than if he'd always been chattering away about this and that, and people wrote long articles considering what it meant.

Many people felt he could hardly be worse than Harding, but there were dissenting opinions. Oswald Harrison Villard of the *New York Evening Post* wrote, "And now the Presidency sinks low indeed. I doubt if it has ever fallen into the hands of a man so cold, so narrow, so reactionary, so uninspiring, so unenlightened, or who has done less to earn it than Calvin Coolidge."

When Harding died, Coolidge was visiting his father on his farm in Vermont. His father was a notary public, and he found the Presidential oath of office in some book he had lying around and swore Cal in by the light of a kerosene lamp at a quarter of three in the morning in the family dining room. Then Cal went back to bed, as he was a firm believer in getting plenty of sleep.

This was completely unofficial, of course, since a notary in Vermont can only swear in people who plan to be working in Vermont, and they might as well have stayed in bed, but for a public relations ploy you couldn't beat it, especially the kerosene lamp. It was the most colorful moment of his whole administration.

---

[1] Well, that's what Teddy Roosevelt's daughter Alice said, but she wasn't there and may have been guessing.

Cal wasn't named "Calvin" for nothing. He believed in the Spartan life and not throwing good money away. In the White House he prowled around in his nightshirt with his skinny bare legs sticking out and kept checking the pantry to make sure nobody was buying food. The chef said he couldn't cook without groceries and quit.

Before and after his Washington career the Coolidges lived simply in half a rented double house in Northhampton, Massachusetts, and Grace made do.[2]

Those who were allowed to catch a glimpse of her said Grace was a perfectly charming lady with a pet raccoon named Rebecca that she carried around with her. Nobody could figure out why she married him. He said it was because he "outsat everyone else," but marrying Silent Cal just because you couldn't get him out of your living room seems like an extreme solution.

Grace really loved life in Washington because sometimes she was allowed to have visitors or go to dinner parties. Cal didn't let her visit with anyone important, like Cabinet wives, because he thought she wasn't all that bright, but he couldn't keep her locked up entirely. Of course she had to have her husband with her when she went out, but many of the guests hardly noticed him. He just stared at his plate, and sometimes at his watch. His idea of entertainment was to make selected congressmen eat breakfast with him at eight-thirty in the morning, an hour when many selected congressmen weren't at their sharpest, those being more leisurely times. The recipe he gave the kitchen for their breakfast was four pecks of

---

[2] It was wonderful what she could whip up with a little salted water and an onion.

whole wheat mixed with one peck of whole rye, boiled until it was just soft enough to chew.[3]

At one of the congressional breakfasts everyone watched while Cal poured some coffee into his saucer and added a splash of milk. Several guests respectfully did the same, and then Cal put the saucer down on the floor for his dog. The others didn't know what to do with theirs, but they didn't mind because it gave them a Coolidge story to tell. (It might have been his idea of a joke. Sometimes it was hard to know.)

Queen Marie of Romania came for a state visit. She was a famous party person and adored going to visit people, but Cal only let her stay for an hour and forty-five minutes, including all those ceremonial greetings, and dinner and dessert and coffee, and then finding everyone's coats, and the ceremonial farewells. It was probably a world record.

You might think Calvin Coolidge wasn't a playful President, but you'd be dead wrong. He had his fun-loving side, and liked to push all the buttons on his desk at once and watch his aides come running. Once, on a fishing trip, he made his Secret Service agent put the worm on his hook for him, and then at the strategic moment he gave the line a quick jerk and impaled the man's thumb. And there was an alarm bell in the White House he could ring whenever he wanted to peek through the curtains and watch the guards and policemen go bananas all over the place.

He had his sensual side too and loved to eat his boiled wheat-and-rye in bed while people rubbed Vaseline into his hair. He had

---

[3] This was very healthful and modern and just what we now know we should eat, but back then folks were so ignorant they thought it was horse feed.

that very fine, thin, reddish hair with no staying power and his forehead was slowly getting bigger and bigger. This was one of his major concerns while in office. There was a portrait of John Adams in the Red Room that he hated because John was pretty bald. He couldn't help seeing it from his chair at the dinner table and it bothered him more and more until he finally got Ike Hoover, the chief usher, to smear turpentine on Adams' shiny scalp until it looked furry, and then he liked it better.

In the summer of '24 Calvin Jr., who was sixteen, got a blister on his toe playing lawn tennis and died of blood poisoning. Coolidge was said to be dreadfully upset about it, though it was hard to tell when he was dreadfully upset and when he wasn't.[4]

He ran for re-election, if "ran" isn't too strong a word, on the slogan "Keep Cool and Keep Coolidge," which the public correctly understood was not a cigarette ad but meant that everyone was rich and happy and having a wonderful time and it was all because of Cal. Naturally they voted for him instead of the Democrat John Davis or the Progressive Bob La Folette, who were trying to tell them everyone *wasn't* rich and happy.[5]

Coolidge believed that business and Wall Street knew what was best for themselves and as long as everyone was happy, why bother them? William Allen White called him "an economic fatalist with a God-given inertia. He knew nothing and refused to learn." Will Rogers asked him how he stayed so healthy, when being President had gotten Wilson so wrought up it made him ill, and Coolidge said, "By avoiding the big problems."[6]

---

[4] George Creel said he was "distinguishable from the furniture only when he moved."
[5] This is not a good thing to tell people. They don't want to hear about it.
[6] He took long naps and that helped too.

Folks thought he must be in the office working hard because they never saw him out doing anything else, like pitching horse-shoes, but he didn't like work any better than horseshoes. One of his Secret Service men—not the one with the fishhook in his thumb—felt that Coolidge should have some sort of hobby or interest in life, or at least get some exercise, and had an electric horse installed in one of the bedrooms. Sometimes Coolidge got on it and it bounced him around. Sometimes he let the Secret Service fellow take turns with him. It was fun, sort of.

Some people think nothing much happened during the Coolidge administration, but it only seems that way. Leopold and Loeb kidnapped and killed little Bobby Franks. Ma Ferguson was elected governor of Texas. Bootleggers bootlegged. King Tut's tomb was opened. Ford threw caution to the winds and started painting cars green and maroon as well as black. John Scopes was convicted of teaching evolution. Gertrude Ederle swam the English Channel and Lindbergh flew to Paris. "The Jazz Singer" was released. Sacco and Vanzetti were executed. Ten people died of heart attacks while listening to the Dempsey-Tunney fight on the radio. Babe Ruth kept hitting home runs and "Show Boat" opened. Al Capone went to jail and the first Mickey Mouse cartoon appeared. The Valentine's Day massacre took out fourteen of Bugs Moran's boys. Everyone sang "Ain't We Got Fun" and danced indecent dances and pretended to be Scott and Zelda.[7]

A notion has taken root recently that the personal style and amusements of the First Couple set the tone for the whole country. Hah.

---

[7] Everyone except the Coolidges, that is.

In August, 1927, Coolidge was in Rapid City, South Dakota, which was his idea of a great place to go on vacation, and called a press conference at the local high school. The reporters, who were already quite unhinged from hanging around Rapid City watching the dust blow back and forth and waiting for something to happen, all filed past him in a long line and he handed each one a folded slip of paper like a fortune-cookie fortune. Each piece of paper said, "I do not choose to run for President in nineteen twenty-eight." He spelled out the year so that the message came to twelve words.[8] The *New York Times* reporter said, "It is believed that the President will say nothing more," and he never did, so everyone buckled down to figure out what he meant by it. They asked his wife, and all his aides and advisors, but they didn't know either. Analysts thought the word "choose" was peculiar, and "run" was open to question too. One group felt he wanted to be drafted, and another felt that he wouldn't mind *being* President as long as he didn't have to run.

It turned out he just meant "no."

When they asked him to sum up his administration in a farewell speech, he said, "Goodbye, I have had a very enjoyable time in Washington."

It wasn't exactly a memorable Presidency, but what happened next was so much worse that everyone looked back wistfully on those happy golden years when whatsisname was in the White House.

When he died in 1933, Dorothy Parker said, "How can they tell?"

---

[8] People were always tallying up Coolidge's words like that. Mostly they could use their fingers.

HERBERT HOOVER

★ ★ ★

1929–1933

HERBERT HOOVER HAD a very exciting life but you'd never know it. Some people manage to stay boring wherever they are and whatever's happening. He even looked boring. He had a pudgy baby-face and parted his hair in the middle, and there are no pictures of him smiling.[1] He was a Quaker and always worked hard and kept his files tidy.

With even the most ordinary luck he might have made a perfectly decent President. Is it his fault that "Hooverville" means a town built out of flattened paint cans and "Hoover blankets" are newspapers stuffed into your clothes? This is not a nice way to go down in history, and it's a shame, that's what it is.

Hoover was orphaned at the age of nine, and schoolchildren were told that he picked potato bugs off the potato plants for a penny a hundred. The schoolchildren were allowed to assume that he was buying stale bread with the pennies, but actually he was saving up to buy fireworks. When he had enough fireworks, he quit with the bugs. Later he studied mining and managed gold mines in Australia and married Lou and went to China as chief engineer of the Chinese Imperial Bureau of Mines. Lou learned Chinese and became an expert on Chinese vases.[2] After that they lived in En-

---

[1] Wilson wouldn't smile either, but on him it looked intellectual. On Hoover it just looked cross.

[2] The Chinese are famous for vases, available in an assortment of styles called Dynasties. Every time a new Dynasty came along, they figured this would be the one that made it all worthwhile, and fired up the kiln again. There were vases *everywhere*. Their wives got sick of dusting them.

gland, Australia, New Zealand, Burma, and Russia, but they never got any more exciting. When they found a book about mines called *De Re Metallica,* written in 1556 by Georgius Agricola, they spent five years translating it from Latin into English. They thought it would sound better in English, but it didn't.

During the Boxer Rebellion in China, Hoover had been in charge of distributing food, and he found this so exhilarating that he went on distributing food all over during and after World War I. Everywhere you looked, there was Hoover holding out a can of beans. Soon he became a household word for food, mines, and traveling, so Harding and Coolidge made him Secretary of Commerce, which is about as boring as it gets.

He ran for President by telling people the country was so rich and happy that "the slogan of progress is changing from the full dinner pail to the full garage." The Democrat, Al (The Happy Warrior) Smith, was a Catholic and got left in a crumpled heap gasping in the dust by the roadside.[3] At his inauguration Hoover said, "In no nation are the fruits of accomplishment so secure." Well, nobody's right all the time.

In October the stock market crashed and everything else kind of caved in after it. This was called the Great Depression, because it went on and on, unlike previous samples which had always stopped after a while.

There are many complex theories about the Depression, but Coolidge, who was writing a newspaper column at the time, put it most neatly. He wrote, "When more and more people are thrown out of work, unemployment results."

---

[3] He'd been four times governor of New York and even *they* wouldn't vote for him. Talk about gratitude.

Hoover told everyone what to do when they were out of work and out of money. They should move in with their neighbors and relatives and open a line of credit at some gullible grocery store. When the neighbors and relatives got their mortgages foreclosed and the grocery store went out of business, the cities and states should do something. They didn't have any money either, because nobody was paying taxes, but somehow they should hire people for civic projects, like picking up newspapers and orange peels in the parks. Under no circumstances should the Federal government step in, because it was none of its business, and Federal handouts lead to waste and corruption, and besides, the whole thing was only a "temporary halt in the prosperity of a great people."[4]

The Hoovers gave nice parties for their personal friends, none of whom were a bit depressed. These they graciously paid for themselves, and the guests all admired Lou's many Chinese vases and pretended they'd stayed up all night reading *De Re Metallica*. Other than that, the Hoovers were paranoid about their privacy. They stopped the long-standing custom of the New Year's open house and wouldn't tell reporters what they were doing.

Somehow people did learn that they had a small dog named Piney, a large dog named Snowflake, and a German shepherd named Tut who hated Hoover and growled whenever he saw him.

Lou was almost uncontrollably interested in the Girl Scouts and filled the place with little girls in green uniforms selling cookies. At Christmas, everyone wanted to know what was going on in the White House, so an intrepid Associated Press reporter dressed

---

[4] He could tell it was nothing serious, because he still had four million pre-inflation dollars from his engineering company.

herself as a Girl Scout and crashed the party, lip-synching the carols while memorizing the decorations and refreshments.

The Hoovers didn't like the White House staff lurking around either, and they all had orders to stay out of sight. If he or Lou came into a room and there was a servant in it dusting or whatever, that servant was supposed to jump into a closet and hide until the coast was clear. Sometimes there was no room for the coats and jackets because of all the servants crouching in there in the dark and mashing the galoshes.

When people kept badgering Hoover about the Depression, he said, "Prosperity cannot be restored by raids upon the public treasury," and went to his fishing camp on the Rapidan in the Blue Ridge Mountains.[5]

Everyone who wasn't starving went around saying, "Well, it isn't as if anyone is actually starving." This wasn't strictly true. People were starving, but they did it so gradually that they didn't get much publicity, and they came down with the various ailments you get from living on flour-and-water paste. People from the farms went to the cities to look for work and people from the cities went to farms to look for food, and other people went nowhere in particular, mostly by boxcar. Resourceful types managed to get thrown in jail, where it was warmer, or set fire to forests so they could hire on for three dollars a day as emergency firefighters.

Hoover said in his memoirs that selling apples on street corners had nothing to do with the Depression but was just a fine business to be in. "Many persons left their jobs for the more profitable one of selling apples," he explained. This was foolish of them, since sell-

---

[5] Fishing is a good hobby for Presidents. It's peaceful and relaxing and gets the reporters and Secret Service agents all wet and muddy and lost.

ing apples was a mug's game compared to shining shoes. A shoe-shine kit cost less than a box of apples and it was a permanent investment, unlike apples, which go away after you've sold them. The *New York Times* went outside to count the shoe-shiners on one block of West Forty-third Street, and there were nineteen of them, ranging in age from sixteen to seventy. It was the Golden Age of shiny shoes.

In the summer of 1932, some twenty thousand veterans marched on Washington wanting their bonuses ahead of time, and hung around pitching tents and trampling the grass and wouldn't leave until Hoover sent General Douglas MacArthur with some cavalry and infantry and some tanks and bayonets and tear gas, and a box of matches for the tents. A couple of veterans accidentally got killed, and the rest were persuaded to leave town. The *Times* said, "Few knew whither to go," but they went anyway. Hoover said they probably weren't veterans at all, just Communists.

He tried to distract people by making "The Star-Spangled Banner" our national anthem, but only the chosen few who could hit that high note near the end were distracted. In fact, folks were getting so undistractable that he was forced to sign the Emergency Relief Act to lend the states three hundred million dollars for soup ingredients. This went against his deepest convictions, but he needn't have worried, as the thing got so tangled in red tape that only a tenth of it actually got lent.[6]

Biographers try to explain Herbert Hoover by saying he was an orphan and couldn't help it. This is nonsense. Plenty of orphans grow up perfectly normal.

After Hoover stopped being President, he went on being Hoover

---

[6] When asked about it, the officials in charge just smiled and changed the subject.

for a long time, distributing cans of beans and serving on worthy committees and making speeches about how Roosevelt was wrecking everything. He gave all his government salaries away to charity, and after a while some people forgave him for the Great Depression. "A conscientious public servant," they called him, stifling a yawn.

Others always bore a grudge.

In 1963 he wrote a book called *Fishing for Fun and to Wash Your Soul*. It's out of print so I don't know whether it was any more exciting than *De Re Metallica*. Probably not.

FRANKLIN DELANO ROOSEVELT

★ ★ ★

1933–1945

ROOSEVELT WAS PRESIDENT for so long that by the time he died, everyone under twenty thought "President" was his first name and wondered what we were going to call the next man.

Roosevelt, a distant cousin of Teddy's, was a gentleman from a family with money so old that it didn't crackle anymore, it whispered. The name was originally "van Roosevelt," so you could see they'd been around a while. The Delanos came out of the same drawer. Nobody with a background like that can get elected in a proper democracy, so the Great Campaign Manager up there arranged to give him polio in 1921, when he was thirty-nine. His legs were crippled, so he had to scoot around in a wheelchair or clump along on eight-pound leg braces with a cane and someone to lean on. The historian Paul Conklin wrote, "Polio made the aristocratic Roosevelt into an underdog. For him it replaced the log cabin."

In a wheelchair he didn't look half so tall and snooty, and besides, you're supposed to be nice to the crippled and admire their pluck. You could hardly accuse him of fooling around with women either; it would be morbid. The poor fellow couldn't even use his *legs,* for heaven's sake.

As far as we know, he didn't fool around with a *lot* of women.[1] First there was Lucy Mercer, his wife's secretary, and I've heard he thought about divorcing Eleanor and marrying her until his mother

---

[1] I don't put much stock in that wartime gossip about Princess Martha of Norway, do you?

threatened to cut off his allowance and he changed his mind.[2] Then there was his own secretary, Missy LeHand, but that hardly counts because it lasted twenty years and heavens, they were just like some old married couple and slept in adjoining bedrooms, in case he wanted to dictate a letter in the night.[3] After Missy died, he took up with Lucy again, so you can see what a faithful fellow he really was. Lucy was with him at Warm Springs when he died, but she beetled off the premises before Eleanor and the reporters showed up.[4]

Anyway, we've had Presidents who couldn't be trusted alone with a lady *armadillo,* and I think we should change the subject.

At college Roosevelt was pretty extracurricular and his GPA showed it, but he did write various stirring articles about football and school spirit for the *Harvard Crimson*. At. Columbia Law he was bored to tears and flunked some subjects and dropped out, but he passed the New York bar anyway. Democratic leaders took an interest in him because his name sounded familiar[5] and he had enough money to run for the State Senate from the wrong place. They talked him into being the Democratic candidate in Dutchess County, which was like running for Pope in Israel, but he rode around shaking hands in such a very bright red touring car that everyone noticed him and he won. Then in 1912 he said such nice

---

[2] She just never liked his friends. She'd dragged him away on a cruise to take his mind off Eleanor, and was mad as a wet hen when it didn't work.

[3] This was all right with Eleanor, apparently. She wasn't home much, and she had a friend or two of her own, but we needn't go into that.

[4] His son Elliott wrote a book about it all. Don't kids say the darndest things?

[5] Teddy was only a fifth cousin but he was Eleanor's uncle, and President when he gave her away at the wedding. All eyes were upon him, which is right where he felt all eyes belonged. His daughter Alice said he wanted to be the bride at every wedding and the corpse at every funeral.

things about Wilson[6] that Wilson made him Assistant Secretary of the Navy, just like Teddy only without the Spanish-American War. Then he got plowed under with Cox in the Harding election, picked himself up and went on to be governor of New York a couple of times, and by 1932 everyone knew his name even if they couldn't pronounce it.

When he got nominated for President, the *New York Times* ran a front-page box explaining about his name. They said it was Dutch and pronounced "Rose-velt" in two syllables. You'd think folks would have noticed by now, with Teddy being the most famous person in the world for so long, but they hadn't, and they still didn't. Democrats called him "Rose-a-velt" and Republicans called him "Rooze-uh-veld" or sometimes "Rosenfeld," claiming he was secretly Jewish, which he wasn't.[7]

He campaigned against Hoover by saying he'd cut government spending and hand out lots of government money, which he seemed to think was no problem. He said, "If you've spent a year in bed trying to wiggle your big toe, than anything else seems easy." He said there was going to be a whole New Deal, and folks figured it couldn't be much worse than the Old Deal, even if he had filched the phrase from Mark Twain. His supporters kept singing "Happy Days Are Here Again," a ditty that subsequent candidates keep recycling with varying degrees of success. He buried Hoover 472–52.

There's nothing like a fresh President when you've been feeling down in the mouth, and here was this one in a long flowing cape

---

[6] In return, Wilson called him "a handsome young giant." Well, really.

[7] Strict conservatives never called him anything but "That Man" and ordered the servants to scissor any mention of him out of the morning papers before carrying them into the breakfast room with their tatters fluttering.

like Superman, grinning like a horse-collar with a cigarette holder jammed in his teeth[8] and that big booming laugh, and besides, he's crippled, and you think *you've* got troubles? He told people that the only thing they had to fear was fear itself, which was an over-statement and left out a few odds and ends but cheered folks up anyway.

He'd promised action, and right away there was action. He was the one who started this "first hundred days" contest, where re-porters keep asking new Presidents what *they've* done in *their* first hundred days, and plenty of them haven't even unpacked yet or fig-ured out where the bathrooms are. Roosevelt closed the banks down for four days to stop people taking their money out and hid-ing it under the couch cushions, and repealed Prohibition so he could mix his friends a nice martini in the Oval Study, and put a woman in the Cabinet as Secretary of Labor, and stirred up a whole snowstorm of legislation and federal agencies with letters instead of names, like the TVA, the NRA, the PWA, the RFC, the AAA, and the CCC, so nobody knew who was doing what. He set Brain Trusters to running back and forth in the hallways, and Eleanor running around everywhere else and reporting back to him.[9]

Soon the previously unemployed were swarming all over the country getting paid by the government for useful works, like building long stone walls along deserted stretches of highway, photographing sharecroppers, and planting endless rows of tree seedlings, some of which survived, on every hillside. Eleanor crawled

---

[8] In recent times, his jauntily cocked cigarette has been air-brushed out of the photo-graphs so as not to set a bad example.
[9] She logged forty thousand miles in the first year and that was just a warm-up. Her Secret Service code name was "Rover."

through the coal mines and came out very dirty saying the miners had a right to complain and organize and strike. There was always something going on, and you know how this cheers people up even while they're stirring the flour-and-water paste for lunch.

Sometimes they wrote fan letters to Roosevelt's black Scottish terrier, Fala, the dog who stood at attention for the national anthem. Fala got lots more fan mail than his boss did.

In the evening they could listen to Roosevelt's Fireside Chats on the radio. Everyone did. The novelist Saul Bellow said that if you walked down the street on a pleasant evening when people's windows were open—and back then, people opened their windows on pleasant evenings—you could walk for blocks and blocks without missing a word of the Fireside Chat. Everyone knew that everyone else was listening, and that made them feel cozy.

The conservatives did not feel cozy. They grew quite hysterical and told each other the end of the world was at hand. Social Security had been the last straw. Any fool could see that those people who still had jobs would quit them at once and just sit around waiting to be sixty-five and collect, and besides, Germany had started the idea in the 1880s and England had had it since 1911, making it repulsively un-American.

In 1936 the Republicans ran Alf Landon, calling him "The Kansas Coolidge."[10] Their slogan was "Save America from Socialism," and their platform was all about how unconstitutional Roosevelt was and how "even the integrity and authority of the Supreme Court have been flaunted."[11]

---

[10] Talk about charisma.

[11] If you've got 'em, flaunt 'em, I always say.

Landon carried Maine and Vermont, giving birth to the encouraging thought for future candidates, "As Maine goes, so goes Vermont."

By 1940 John Garner was tired of being Vice President while Roosevelt got all the attention, and Roosevelt wanted the totally radical Henry Wallace instead. The convention wanted someone just the teeniest bit more politically normal, but Eleanor rushed unexpectedly to the podium and made a speech for Wallace that blew them away and he was in.[12]

The Republicans said that not only was Roosevelt still a Socialist and a traitor to his class, he was helping Britain fight Hitler, and if we didn't watch out we'd end up fighting him too, and maybe Hitler wasn't the pleasantest fellow in the world but at least he wasn't soft on Communism like some people they knew. Their candidate was Wendell Willkie, who'd been a Democrat until he noticed the New Deal eating into his business profits and saw the error of his ways.

Political verses and insults had been shrinking down to slogans, due to Ford's discovery of the automobile bumper, and Willkie's slogan was "No Man is Good Three Times." We're not sure quite what he meant. The Democrats replied, "Better a Third-Termer than a Third-Rater." Willkie carried some midwestern states.

This brings us to December 7, 1941, the "date which will live in infamy," though it seems too bad to blame it on the calendar when it was the Japanese who dropped those bombs without even telling us first. Roosevelt called a joint session of Congress, and

---

[12] People got so sick of Eleanor jokes that up until quite recently, subsequent First Ladies kept their chins tucked into their collarbones and stuck to roadside daffodils and children's reading lessons.

Congress agreed to go to war, 82–0 in the Senate and 388–1 in the House.[13]

War turned out to be just what the doctor ordered to put a stop to the Depression, and everyone quit planting rows of little trees and rushed off to enlist and make tanks and guns and pay taxes again, and the economy was back in Biscuit City.

World Wars I and II should not be confused with each other, even though many of the same teams were playing. The second one was easier to understand because it had Hitler, who invaded Poland and committed many Nazi atrocities too nasty to mention and wasn't a nice person at all. The first war had more trenches but the second one had more bombs. Bombs were so much more interesting to photograph than trenches that the newsreel was born. It was a little like the television news only it was a week old and cost money to watch.

The players to remember from World War II are Hitler, Hirohito, Mussolini, Churchill, Stalin, De Gaulle, and Roosevelt—who was *still* President.[14] There were machine guns on the White House roof and a bomb shelter in the basement and a gas mask dangling from the Presidential wheelchair, but Roosevelt's Scottie, Fala, who had grown quite portly bumming goodies from the staff, still went with him everywhere and his Fireside Chats still went out over the radio, mellow as ever. Eleanor was still busy. They called her "Public Energy Number One" and she was running through Secret Service agents the way you and I go through a box of Kleenex.

---

[13] Miss Jeannette Rankin (R., Mont.) hadn't changed her mind since she voted against the other war in 1917. All the other congresspersons hissed and booed, but she took no notice.

[14] Come to think of it, it wouldn't hurt to remember General Eisenhower too. You'll see why later.

In 1944 everyone was so used to Roosevelt being President that they hardly noticed Thomas Dewey, governor of New York, running against him by calling him an invalid and a Communist, which wasn't exactly new stuff but they'd been so busy down at Republican headquarters they hadn't had time to find anything fresher. Besides, there was a war on, and it was going pretty well as wars go, so who needed a new President?

Vice President Wallace was still totally radical, so Roosevelt agreed to tone things down a bit and substituted a Missouri senator named Harry S Truman. Nobody knew much about him but it didn't matter, as Roosevelt was clearly going to be President forever and ever.

Actually, he hadn't been feeling quite the thing lately, but he did want to stick it out and help fix the peace arrangements and make sure the colonial empires stopped being colonial empires and the United Nations happened. He thought he'd do better at this than Wilson had, but he died on April 12, 1945.

Even his worst enemies were surprised. They'd thought he was permanent. He almost was.

HARRY S¹ TRUMAN

★ ★ ★

1945–1953

---

¹ The "S" didn't stand for his middle name. It *was* his middle name.

EVERYONE WAS SO startled to learn that Roosevelt wasn't President anymore that it took them a while to adjust. As Admiral Leahy, White House chief of staff, put it, "Who the hell is Harry Truman?"

People said he was just a *little* man.[2] The union leader Al Whitney called him a ribbon clerk. Everyone thought he wouldn't be any more successful as President than he'd been at anything else, which was scary.

He was surprised himself. He'd been Vice President for only eighty-three days, and the two times he'd run into Roosevelt, Roosevelt forgot to tell him what was happening, or how the war was going, or anything useful. At his first press conference he told the reporters, "Boys, if you ever pray, pray for me now."

He was the son of a Missouri farmer and mule-trader, and he wanted to be a professional musician when he grew up. Nothing came of this. He had thick glasses and was no good at games. After high school he worked as a railroad timekeeper, mailroom clerk, bank clerk, farmer, postmaster, and road overseer. Then he tried being a partner in a lead mine and an oil-prospecting firm, but those didn't pan out either.

Pretty soon he was thirty-three and still living at home and reading the help-wanteds, so he figured what the hell and enlisted in World War I. He was better at that. The men called him "Cap-

---

[2] Roosevelt was six foot two when he stood up and Truman was only five nine. He barely came up to de Gaulle's collarbone, even with his big hat on.

tain Harry" and he learned some bad language and felt a lot taller and braver, but then the war was over and he was back home in Missouri playing Chopin till all hours and reading the help-wanteds again. He went partners in a haberdashery shop, but he wore such awful sport shirts and ties that people were embarrassed to shop there and it went bankrupt.

Well, he did know somebody who knew Big Tom Pendergast, the Democratic boss of Kansas City, and pretty soon he was a Jackson County judge, which made a nice change from selling ties, but after the next election he found himself out on the street again, selling memberships in the Kansas City Automobile Club. Then he went partners in a Missouri state bank, and I'll give you three guesses what happened to that bank. Finally Pendergast[3] pulled some more strings and Harry went off to the Senate—the *United States* Senate—and stayed ten years.

The Senate is set up so that it can't go bankrupt no matter who gets into it, and Missourians were greatly relieved that whatever Harry got mixed up in, it would be in Washington and not in Missouri, as long as they kept sending him back there. Little did they know.

In the White House the Trumans were so unpretentious—except for moving in with three pianos—that it was almost pretentious of them. They weren't used to having a staff underfoot and didn't know what to do with them, and vice versa. Harry got up at five-thirty every morning and took a brisk walk around town. (Once a couple of malcontents took a shot at him, but he shrugged it off and went on with his walk.)

---

[3] This was *before* he went to jail for tax evasion and bribes.

He and Bess had been sweethearts since fifth grade and set an example of domestic devotion for married couples everywhere. She'd once been a basketball star, and it was said she could whistle through her teeth, but those days were over. She flatly refused to give interviews or press conferences and was only rarely visible, wearing clothes so unpretentious people couldn't figure out where she'd found them.

Their daughter Margaret played the pianos and sang. Sometimes she sang in public, which gave rise to an unfortunate incident when the *Washington Post* music critic, Paul Hume, suggested that she take up some quite different and preferably silent hobby, and Harry wrote to him saying that if he ever met Hume, then he, Hume, would "need a new nose and perhaps a supporter below." This was considered un-Presidential and artistically pigheaded, since Hume's views were supported by other music critics.[4]

Truman didn't get much chance to study up gradually. It was one of those busy seasons in the White House. In his first four months the war with Germany ended, and the atom bomb got dropped, and the war with Japan ended, and the United Nations geared up. It was a zoo. Harry put a sign on his desk saying "The buck stops here," so people kept coming to him with their problems, like whether to nuke Japan and what to do about Communism, and kept him hopping. Even his nights were restless, because Abe Lincoln's ghost kept prowling around the second-floor corridors looking tall and gloomy. Several other people saw it too. Some found it ominous.

---

[4] Later she did take his advice and wrote books instead, and her reviews improved somewhat.

Harry wrote himself a memo, in case he forgot, saying the White House was a great white jail and "Why in hell does anybody want to be head of state? Damned if I know." Later he got used to it, though, and quite enjoyed it. He gave the very first White House telecast, telling the elite few with television sets about his Food Conservation Program and not eating meat on Tuesdays. He recommended soybeans instead, and people tried making meat loaf and hamburgers out of them but they lacked a certain something. He sent the real meat to Europe.

Various historians hold that the Marshall Plan was actually Truman's idea, but he knew how Congress felt about him and where they'd tell him to stuff it if he suggested it himself, so he handed it over to his Secretary of State, George C. Marshall, to be *his* idea, because everyone loved George. The idea was, the war had left much of Europe quite flattened, since this newfangled business of dropping bombs is much messier than the old custom of armies lining up on the battlefields to shoot at each other. People in Europe were cold and hungry and cross and surrounded by rubble, even the ones who'd won the war, and in danger of thinking un-American thoughts. By sending them food and building materials and so on, we could make them feel grateful, open up profitable future markets for ourselves, and keep their minds off Communism.

Whoever thought of it first, it was a fine plan, and worked. Soybean meat loaf never caught on, though.

Truman got so cocky that in 1947 he built a balcony behind the pillars of the south portico, and you should have heard Washington holler. You'd think he'd painted the place green. It wasn't the last of their surprises, though, because by fall Harry noticed that his bathtub was getting lower and lower, and then a chandelier in the Blue Room took to trembling during receptions, and a leg of

Margaret's grand piano punched a hole in the dining room ceiling, and the great staircase started to sway, and the whole family prudently moved across the street to Blair House.

A committee came to check out the place, and then scampered hastily outside again. It seemed the footings were just eight feet deep, in squishy clay, and only a natural feeling of respect had kept the building upright since we'd stuck on that heavy third floor in 1927. For a while it looked as if the whole pile of rubble should be given a gentle push and allowed to fall down, which would have been cheaper in the long run, but sentimentalists prevailed and we propped up the outside walls and built a whole new inside, while the Trumans stayed in Blair House.

By now it was time to decide whether Harry was going to get elected on his own in 1948, or even nominated. Various key Democrats who weren't from Missouri thought he should go back to Missouri, and the Republicans went around saying "To err is Truman" and thought themselves frightfully funny. The Democrats asked everyone in town if they'd like to run for President instead of Truman, but they all said sorry, they were busy.[5]

The Progressives went off and ran Henry Wallace instead, and the Southern Democrats said they were really Dixiecrats and ran Strom Thurmond of South Carolina, who was still grumbling about states' rights and threatening to fire on Fort Sumter. The Republicans got Thomas Dewey again. He was still wearing that absurd little black mustache that Teddy Roosevelt's daughter Alice said made him look like the bridegroom doll on a wedding cake, but for some reason everyone thought he'd win anyway and started

---

[5] Both parties wanted General Eisenhower, but he was out on the golf course and couldn't be reached.

calling him "President Dewey." This made them look pretty silly later, though not as silly as the *Chicago Tribune* running that "Dewey Elected" headline in the early editions. But I'm getting ahead of my story.

Truman was the only person in the whole country who thought he was going to win.[6] He packed up Bess and Margaret and went on a whistle-stop campaign to four hundred towns and cities, and told people there was going to be a Fair Deal, and it wasn't *his* fault the Republican Congress was a bunch of you-know-whats. Folks took to shouting, "Give 'em hell, Harry!" so naturally his language got more and more colorful. He could really fry a person's ears off, that Harry.

As you may have already guessed, when he woke up the next morning he was still President and everyone was embarrassed, except possibly his mother-in-law. Apparently some people had voted for him because he was spunky and just plain folks, while others simply couldn't bring themselves to vote for a man with a ridiculous little black mustache.

He invited the journalists and pollsters to dinner to eat crow.

Well, now that we didn't have Hitler to worry about, we took to worrying about Communism. Roosevelt had never lost any sleep over it and thought the Russians were okay, but Truman was all for something called "containment." This meant that Communists had to stay bottled up in Russia where they belonged, but we could go anywhere because we were the good guys. We put NATO together to make sure they stayed bottled. This wasn't good enough for certain people, though, who felt only extermination would an-

---

[6] His mother-in-law, a dreadful woman who insisted on living with them, told everyone Dewey was a sure thing.

swer the Communist problem. They felt the whole "peace" business was a trap so the Commies could catch us with our guns un-
loaded.

Then Senator Joseph McCarthy (R., Wisc.) jumped up and said
they weren't staying bottled at all, and they were all over *this* country, disguised as people, and he had lists and *lists* of them that he'd
show us, only he'd left them in the pocket of his other suit. The
House UnAmerican Activities Committee said *they* had over a
million names of dangerous pinkos, some of whom had planted
hidden messages about "peace" in movies, history books, plays,
folk songs, "Dick Tracy," "Prince Valiant," and the minutes of the
Audubon Society meetings. Communism seeped through the country like a deadly odorless gas, poisoning our schools and libraries
and little children in their sleep.

Everyone had to sign loyalty oaths that they weren't planning
to overthrow the government, or, if they were, they had to report
to their local FBI office and register and get fingerprinted. The Mc-
Carran Act provided for concentration camps in which to bottle
them. Nervous types took to jumping out of high windows rather
than explain themselves to the Committee, which proved they'd
been up to no good.

Truman thought it was all poppycock. He called the House
Un-American Activities Committee an un-American activity and
said, "All this howl about organizations a fellow belongs to gives
me a pain in the neck."[7]

In 1950 there was a local dust-up in Korea. Some say our buddies, the South Koreans, may have started it, with a little coaching

---

[7] Right away his own name popped onto a lot of lists. Nixon said he'd "covered up
this Communist conspiracy and attempted to halt its exposure."

from their American advisors, but it was the North Koreans who were the bad guys because they were Communists. We sent General MacArthur over to contain them. Truman said it wasn't a *war*, exactly, just a police action, so not to worry. When we charged clear up to the Chinese border, the Chinese, who were also Communists by now, got excited and sent their troops in.

MacArthur wanted to invade China, which is always a foolish thing to do. Others have tried it in the past. It's too big, and there are too many Chinese. The troops start in all right at the edge, but they take a wrong turn somewhere west of Wuhan and nobody ever sees them again. Their descendants look Chinese.

Truman sent MacArthur his pink slip and told him to drop it and come home.[8] This was unpopular, since many believed that the sooner we went to war and exterminated all the Communists everywhere, the better.[9] For starters, we put Julius and Ethel Rosenberg in the electric chair for stealing atomic secrets for the Russians. Scientists found this a terrific giggle, since there weren't any atomic secrets and never had been, and any fool with a spoonful of uranium could cook up an atom bomb in the kitchen. After a while a lot of foreign countries started doing just that, with no help at all from the Rosenbergs. Our feelings were hurt. Whose bomb was it, anyway?

I forget how the Korea business ended. I'm not sure it did end, but after a while it sort of stopped, leaving things much the same as before.

Truman said he'd done his damndest and didn't want to be

---

[8] He said he did it because MacArthur was insubordinate, not because he was "a dumb son-of-a-bitch," though he was.

[9] The Russians felt the same way about us. This was called the Cold War, and bumper stickers appeared saying "Better Dead than Red" and people sat around trying to read in stuffy bomb shelters in their backyards.

President anymore, which was just as well. The Republicans said he stood for "Korea, Communism, and Corruption," and many Democrats agreed, though some later decided he'd really been better at being President than at selling shirts and ties.

Some historians think he really shouldn't have dropped those things on Japan.

They say it was childish and irresponsible and Japan was all ready to surrender anyway, and some critics go so far as to call it the most heinous[10] decision ever made by an American President. Truman himself felt quite cheerful about it. After all, we were fighting a war, and it was a bomb, wasn't it? What were we supposed to do with the thing if not drop it, put place-mats on it and call it a tea table? When the atomic scientists themselves moaned and repented the whole thing, Truman said, "This kind of sniveling makes me sick."

Right or wrong, the bomb didn't go away afterwards. It waxed fruitful, and multiplied, and strengthened. History now came to an end and the modern world began. No one has quite decided whether this is a good thing or not.

---

[10] This is a word critics love to use, especially if they know how to pronounce it, but they usually save it for folks like Hitler.

DWIGHT DAVID EISENHOWER

★ ★ ★

1953–1961

EISENHOWER, KNOWN AS Ike, was President for eight years and nothing much happened. This was just fine with most people, and it was fine with Ike too. He'd been busy as a beaver with the war and considered the Presidency a well-deserved retirement. He was fond of golf, bridge, and canasta.

Ike didn't look much like a general. He had a round bald head and a cheerful smile and looked like a happy doorknob.[1] He came from Abilene, Kansas, and graduated from West Point sixty-first in a class of a hundred and sixty-four, which was better than Grant, anyway. He won the war in Europe while MacArthur was winning the war in the Pacific, and having him in the White House made everyone feel safe: nobody would mess with us, not while he was in charge.

His wife's name was Mamie and they were a devoted couple like the Trumans, only not much like the Trumans.

He was confused but kindly and he didn't know diddley about politics. He'd never been much of one for voting. He said, "Nothing in the international or domestic situation especially qualifies for the most important office in the world a man whose adult life has been spent in the military forces."

When the Republicans finally tracked him down on the golf course and asked him to run for President anyway, he said he'd do

---

[1] MacArthur, now, *there* was a general who looked like a general. He tried to get nominated in '48 and '52 but nothing came of it. You can look too much like a general.

it only if *both* parties wanted him. They explained that this isn't the way it works, so Adlai Stevenson ran against him.

Stevenson was governor of Illinois and an intellectual. The word "egghead" immediately came into widespread use, meaning someone so impractical he can hardly tie his shoes but who thinks he's smarter than you are because he knows a bunch of fancy words. Stevenson lost badly.[2]

Eisenhower's campaign slogan was "I like Ike." What was not to like? The most exciting thing about the campaign was Nixon. He was going to be Vice President and was already famous for exposing disguised Communists, particularly the ones running for office against him. Then some nosy parkers wanted to hear what he'd done with a bunch of money people had given him. Indignant clamor got clamored, and Ike wouldn't say anything. He just smiled. So Nixon had to spend seventy-five thousand dollars of the National Committee's money for television time, which was cheaper then, so he could make his Checkers speech. I can't find out who wrote it but it was a corker, and everyone cried and hugged, and Ike and Dick won in a landslide.[3]

Military Presidents make a nice change because the ruthlessness needed to win wars and be top general is quite different from the ruthlessness needed to win elections and be top politician. Probably Washington and Taylor and Grant and Eisenhower walked into office with a different mindset, having fought their way up through Yorktown and Buena Vista and Shiloh and Normandy instead of through state-house wrangling and Congressional cross-

---

[2] Next time he lost worse.
[3] Okay, so it wasn't *very* exciting, but it seemed exciting at the time. It was a quiet time.

fire. They bring a kind of innocence. This, at least in Grant's case, can be a dreadful drawback.

The inside of the White House was back in business and Mamie had most of it painted pink. She like pink carnations too. In the evenings she and Ike liked to watch television, or have some folks over for bridge. They'd moved thirty times in thirty-six years and it was nice just to sit around for a change.

Not that their private life was lax. Far from it. Mamie looked harmless enough and never got out of bed before noon, but she could pitch a first-class fit if things weren't done just right. Commanding generals and their families get accustomed to a lot more spit-and-polish and domestic yes-sirs than failed haberdashers from Missouri, and the White House staff had to shape up fast. It had to get bigger fast too, since Ike was used to a whole Army ready to hand. Luckily he'd brought along his old valet, Sergeant Moaney, to help him get dressed in the morning. On Moaney's day off, though, the staff had to fill in for him, and his substitute staggered back to the kitchen all agog, because it was part of the drill to crouch down and hold the Presidential underpants open so he could step gracefully into them.

John Foster Dulles was Secretary of State, and he tried to make things more exciting but Ike wouldn't let him. Dulles wanted to free the Eastern European countries from the Russians. He wanted, he said, to "unleash" the forces of poor old Chiang Kai-Shek from where he'd been vegetating and picking his cuticles on Taiwan, and go free Red China from the Red Chinese and give it back to Chiang. He believed in the domino theory, related to the containment theory, and explained it to Ike, how if one country went Communist, then all the neighbors and then *their* neighbors would go Communist too, because, though any idiot could see it was a stupid, nasty, evil, useless idea, it was strangely irresistible. Anyone living next door to Communism would fall under its spell.

Dulles was interested in the new hydrogen bomb for some industrial-strength Communist-containing. Ike just smiled. He never felt at home with those newfangled weapons, the ones he called "nucular." He was a guns-and-tanks man himself.

Since any good general knows transport is half the battle, he set up America's interstate highway system, so his guns and tanks could dash quickly from place to place repelling invasions. This system has proved so effective that, since we built it, not a single enemy has invaded us on foot. It's also perhaps our most enduring Presidential legacy and changed the hearts and minds and habits of Americans forever.

To use the new highways to the fullest, we built ever swifter and more powerful cars in which to drive all over the United States without seeing anything except other cars and trucks the size of Kansas bearing down on us at the speed of light. Towns were replaced by shopping malls in the middle of howling nowhere, and other towns that had once supported themselves with speeding tickets levied on out-of-staters never saw another out-of-state tag and went bankrupt. People grew up and grew old without ever having ridden on a train, or even seeing one. It was a whole new landscape.

One of the coziest things about Ike was that he never worried much. When people handed him worrying papers to read, he just smiled and handed them right back. He didn't even worry about Senator McCarthy. He pretended there wasn't any Senator McCarthy. He just blinked and got in his helicopter and went out to Burning Tree to play a few holes before dinner. He figured if he paid no attention McCarthy would just go away, and presently the

Senate got fed up and censured the gentleman from Wisconsin and he did go away, sputtering and fumbling with his lists and still needing a shave, so Ike was right not to worry.

In 1957 the Russians sent up the Sputnik satellite, and in 1959 Castro took over Cuba. When it was too rainy for golf, Ike did some oil painting, but he never got very good at it.[4] When the rain stopped he went out and putted a few on his putting green at the edge of the White House lawn. The squirrels there gave him a hard time and he tried to have them all trapped and taken somewhere else, but there are always fresh supplies of squirrels. You can't get rid of *all* the squirrels and it's foolish to even try.

Everyone liked Ike so much that he would have been a cinch for a third term and maybe even more, except that the Republicans had been afraid Roosevelt might come back from the dead and keep being President, so they'd passed the Twenty-second Amendment saying you only got two turns. Didn't they just kick themselves too.

---

[4] Frankly, he was even worse than Churchill.

JOHN FITZGERALD KENNEDY

★ ★ ★

1961–1963

THE KENNEDY ADMINISTRATION was so short that some historians call it an interlude instead. Fans called it Camelot, after King Arthur's headquarters, also a famous center for knights-errant, highfalutin ideals, parties, and romantic canoodling in the corridors. King Arthur had it easier, though. He may have had Guinevere, but he didn't have Congress.

Jack Kennedy got pushed into politics as a second-string substitute for his brother Joe Jr., the family jewel, who was killed in the war, and don't think Joe Sr. let Jack forget it for a minute. Joe Jr. had always been better and bigger and stronger than Jack.[1] When they were kids he pounded Jack to a pulp, and later danced off with his dates whenever he'd a mind to.

Sometimes, when he was President, Jack got a feeling Joe Jr. had come back disguised as Russia and was threatening to beat him up and steal his toys. This made him touchy and led to enterprises like the Cuban Missile Crisis and the Bay of Pigs, giving rise to the word "brinkmanship" and competitions like the Space Race. Jack hated coming in second. His father always told him that it wasn't how you played the game, it was whether you won or lost, and if you lost you got sent to bed without supper.[2]

Jack always thought Joe Jr. would be President and he'd be a writer, and he *was* a writer. His senior thesis at Harvard was pub-

---

[1] Jack was such a sickly child that his family said if a mosquito got a drop of his blood, it was curtains for that mosquito.

[2] If you were beating Jack at checkers, he'd tip the board over and pretend it was an accident.

lished as *Why England Slept* and made the bestseller list. So did *Profiles in Courage,* and it won a Pulitzer too.[3] But nobody said no to Joe Sr. and when he sent Jack to bat for Joe Jr., off he went to Congress when he was only twenty-nine and looked about twelve.

It was no contest. He was famously handsome and charming and a genuine war hero too. When his PT-109 got rammed and sunk, his back, which had been dicey for years anyway, was seriously smashed, but he hauled out all ten survivors and swam them to an island miles away, all the time towing a wounded man with his teeth in the fellow's life preserver. Top that. Besides, both his grandfathers had been Irish Democratic bosses in Boston and Honey Fitz had been mayor too.

As soon as Jack was old enough he moved up to the Senate. A highlight of that campaign was the night when he and his brothers Bobby and Teddy all stood on a table at the G&G Deli and sang "Heart of My Heart." Who could resist?

Came the Democratic convention of 1960. Skeptics said no Catholic could ever get elected[4] and remember the pasting Al Smith took in 1928, and why not have Lyndon Johnson, the Senate majority leader, instead? But Jack made it on the first ballot and said Lyndon could be his running mate. In his acceptance speech he told people there were New Frontiers all over—science, space, peace, war, ignorance, poverty, etc., etc.—and we had to pitch in and do something about them. Nobody paid much mind until the debates.

---

[3] The disgruntled say someone else wrote them for him, but they always say that. They say that about Shakespeare.

[4] While he was President many insisted that he was digging a tunnel from the White House basement straight to the Vatican. This would have been expensive and impractical. Couldn't he just pick up the phone?

Kennedy and Nixon argued with each other on television programs specially arranged for the purpose, which was a novelty, and Nixon fans claim their boy lost the election because of his makeup man. They said that with the right makeup man, Nixon could have been *every bit as sexy as Kennedy.* Nixon always needed a shave, out of respect for his old mentor and fellow Commie-spotter Senator McCarthy, who always needed a shave too. The makeup man tried to cover the stubble with a special heavy-duty face powder that made him look badly embalmed,[5] and the lighting did sinister things to his eye-sockets. One historian said, "He looked for all the world like a man with shaving and perspiration problems, glumly waiting for the commercial to tell him how not to offend."

The debates were mostly over what to do about a couple of islands off the coast of Taiwan.[6] This may have seemed more urgent then than it does now. Kennedy won the debates, but the election dragged on into the next morning and was such a close squeak it didn't give him any clout with Congress.

Robert Frost wrote a special poem for the inauguration, but the winter sunlight was so bright and squinty he couldn't read it. This was just as well. It was awful slop. Kennedy's speech was a zinger, though, and the recording later sold millions as a 45-rpm single. He said, "Ask not what your country can do for you; ask what you can do for your country."

Countless Americans had slipped away from their offices to the nearest pub to watch it on television, and when they heard this they rushed out onto the sidewalk with their beer mugs slopping over their knuckles and peered up and down the street looking for

---

[5] As of this writing, there is still no real substitute for a shave.
[6] I'd tell you their names, but you'd only forget.

something to do for their country. There wasn't anything in sight, so they went back to their offices.[7]

Ernest Hemingway said, "It is a good thing to have a brave man as our President in times as tough as these are."

A senator said, "He seems to combine the best qualities of Elvis Presley and Franklin D. Roosevelt."

John Steinbeck said, "What a joy that literacy is no longer prima-facie evidence of treason."

An unidentified Kennedy aide said, "This administration is going to do for sex what the last one did for golf."

Kennedy had a photogenic wife named Jackie who could speak French and ride horses, and two photogenic children named Caroline and John-John, and he didn't break any lenses himself, even in bathing trunks. In nice weather they all joined hundreds of other tanned and fit Kennedys at the family compound in Hyannisport and made the guests play football. The Kennedys played a hardnose game.[8] Important guests staggered home exhausted and frightened, saying to watch out for the women because even eight months pregnant they're faster than you are. It was kind of like Teddy Roosevelt chasing the ambassadors through Rock Creek Park, only there were so many more Kennedys. They were everywhere, even in the Cabinet, and non-Kennedys started feeling paranoid and outnumbered.

In the White House Jackie found things had gotten terribly unsophisticated under the Trumans and Eisenhowers, so she hired a French chef and dusted off the punch bowls of state, and had mu-

---

[7] Later it turned out they could go fight in Vietnam.
[8] Jack was serious about fitness. He told everyone on his staff to lose five pounds or leave.

sic and dancing in the East Room, and Nobel prizewinners, and performances of Shakespeare. She called in a Fine Arts Committee and fixed the place up with antiques and some better-looking pictures. She rummaged around and found a sofa of Dolley Madison's and that carved oak desk Queen Victoria sent to Rutherford B. Hayes, and kept pushing the stuff around till she got it just right. Then she went on television and showed all of us. It looked fine.

The Kennedys had a Welsh terrier named Charlie, and Caroline had a pony name Macaroni, who followed visitors around the lawn, and two hamsters named Bluebell and Marybelle. Nikita Krushchev gave them a dog named Pushinka, offspring of Strelka, the first dog in orbit. It had to have its ears probed for possible electronic bugs. Joe Sr. gave them a German shepherd named Clipper. When reporters asked Jackie what she was going to feed it, she said, "Reporters."

Intellectuals thought it was exciting that we were finally getting some intellectuals around here. Jack hired a performing troupe of Rhodes scholars and Phi Beta Kappas to help run things. He read newspapers to find out what was happening, unlike some previous incumbents, and tore through four morning papers in fifteen minutes flat, even with the children racing around underfoot. He could read two thousand words a minute.

He and some other Kennedys thought up the Peace Corps, under which earnest Americans went off to the Third World to teach it useful skills like English and digging latrines.[9] He tried to do all sorts of good things for his New Frontier, like Medicare, and aid to education, and a civil rights bill, but nothing much happened except that he single-handedly destroyed the men's hat industry by re-

---

[9] Many of them wound up marrying each other, and were twice as earnest afterward.

fusing to wear a hat. Congress just stuck its fingers in its ears and ignored him.

He had better luck in other countries, where people found him and Jackie far more dashing than previous samples of American leadership, even if he did do some scatty things in Cuba. In France he introduced himself as "the man who accompanied Jackie Kennedy to Paris." In West Berlin he said he was a Berliner too, and he said it in German. The crowds just ate it up.

His daughter, Caroline, called him Silly Daddy. His son John-John called him Foo-Foo Head. Jackie called him Bunny. Some of his friends called him Jack the Zipper—they didn't explain why.

In Dallas, on November 22, 1963, three hours before he was shot, he said, "If anybody really wanted to shoot the President . . . it is not a very difficult job . . . Get on a high building some day with a telescopic rifle and there is nothing anyone can do to defend against such an attempt."[10]

Afterward the Warren Commission went back and forth over the whole thing, with the aid of some home movies taken by a helpful fellow named Zapruder, who'd remembered to bring his camera, and decided Lee Harvey Oswald shot him from the Texas School Book Depository. Others disagreed and dragged up complicated questions about the number of bullets and which directions they were traveling through Kennedy and Governor Connally, who was sitting next to him, and in a twinkling who-shot-Kennedy became a leading industry accounting for a significant percentage of the GNP. Suspects included, but were not limited to, Oswald, who

---

[10] Collectors of the strange and marvelous are potty about this and keep marveling over it. I don't see what's so special about it. He may have said it every time he went outdoors. Who wouldn't?

got shot by Jack Ruby before he could say anything; the FBI; the CIA; the Mafia; the Fair Play for Cuba Committee; Jack Ruby, who shot Oswald before he could say anything; a Mr. Clay Shaw; Vice President Johnson; and an unidentified man in a sort of police uniform who was walking across the grassy knoll.[11]

Some people said there was no mystery about it, it was simply Fate, and we should have known, because Lincoln was elected in 1860 and had seven letters in his last name and got shot on a Friday, so naturally Kennedy, elected in 1960 with seven letters in his last name, was going to get shot on a Friday too. They still believe this.

Three years later, eighteen of the key witnesses were dead, including two suicides. Somebody with nothing better to do figured that the odds against this mortality rate were one hundred thousand trillion to one, give or take a couple.

Jackie stayed up all night and made the funeral arrangements and refused to change her clothes. She was wearing a pink suit that was all spattered with blood and brains but she wouldn't take it off, and for three days she was our first national heroine since Betsy Ross.[12]

At the funeral, drums were drummed all day and little John-John saluted the casket, and everyone cried, even foreigners. Even anchormen.

For a few minutes there, Kennedy had persuaded us that we were all of us stylish and witty, merry in heart and terrific in bed, and really *good* people besides. Special people. After he was killed

---

[11] People heard so much about the grassy knoll they thought it was a suspect too.
[12] Later people were furious that she didn't go on forever being our national heroine, but she felt three days had been plenty. It's hard work.

we realized we were just the same old money-grubbing us we'd always been, and we were a terrible disappointment to ourselves for a while.

Of course, if he hadn't been killed, we'd have realized it sooner or later anyway. These moments never last.

LYNDON BAINES JOHNSON

★ ★ ★

1963–1969

WHEN THE SHOTS rang out in Dallas,[1] a Secret Service agent knocked Johnson down to the floor of the car and lay on top of him as a shield—an awkward maneuver since Johnson was six foot three and had to be folded up and stuffed onto the floor—and when they untangled their arms and legs and sat up again Johnson was President.

He was the only President ever sworn in on an airplane in Texas, and his first words were, "Now, let's get airborne." After he got back to Washington, Congress felt so guilty about Kennedy that it passed all those bills he'd set his heart on, about Medicare and education and letting black people eat in restaurants and have real jobs.

Johnson started up the Department of Transportation, something the Founding Fathers had overlooked because of not having any. He added Housing and Urban Development and gave it to Robert Weaver as the first black in the Cabinet. He put the black Thurgood Marshall on the Supreme Court too. The black writer Ralph Ellison said, "Perhaps President Johnson will have to settle for being recognized as the greatest American President for the poor and for Negroes."

He isn't. He's recognized as the villain of the Vietnam War. Pity about that.

What Johnson really wanted was to be king of something he called The Great Society, where nobody would be hungry or angry

---

[1] This is the recognized universal description of the occasion.

or uneducated and people would like each other and sing hymns to Johnson all day. He had big plans for it, only he had trouble getting that Vietnam business out of his hair.

The North Vietnamese were Communists and the South Vietnamese weren't. After John Foster Dulles had explained the domino theory to Eisenhower, they agreed that America should do everything necessary, including bloodshed, to keep the southern half on our side of the ideological wall. Then Kennedy came along, and he hedged and dodged about committing ourselves to the thing. Then Johnson inherited it.

He said, "Just like the Alamo, somebody damned well needed to go to their aid. Well, by God, I'm going to Vietnam's aid."

It wasn't very much like the Alamo. Hardly at all, really. It was bigger, for one thing, and full of North and South Vietnamese shooting each other in swamps, and Ho Chi Minh, and places with funny names like Num Dong. Besides, the Alamo was over in ten days and the war in Vietnam had already been going on for ten years and showed no signs of fatigue.

So every time he tried to think about his Great Society, there was Vietnam whining around his ears[2] like a mosquito in the bedroom. It was a great nuisance and it got worse too.

When Johnson was born in Stonewall, Texas, his granddaddy said, "He'll be a United States senator some day." The responsibility so weighed on his parents that it took them three months to think of a name for him, and then the best they could come up with was "Lyndon." He was often called LBJ, after his LBJ Ranch in the

---

[2] He had the largest ears of any American President. They looked like the giant tree-fungi from hell and made the cartoonists very, very happy.

Texas Pedernales.[3] He had his wife and daughters answer to Lady Bird, Lynda Bird, and Luci Baines, so they could all have the same initials as the ranch.

Lyndon knew the alphabet by the time he was two and was reading up a storm at four. He graduated from high school at fifteen as president of the class, because the other six kids didn't want to be president and he did.[4] After Southwest Texas State College he taught public speaking for a while and then went to Washington as secretary to Congressman Kleberg. Roosevelt took a shine to him and made him the Texas straw boss of the National Youth Administration, administrating youths, and pretty soon he turned up in Congress. In '41 he was the first congressman to enlist, and just had time to grab a Silver Star before Roosevelt told all the congressmen in uniform to quit playing soldier and come home and get back to work. In '49 he went to the Senate, just as his granddaddy said he would, and he was majority leader when Kennedy whistled for him.

In the matter of luck and timing, being Vice President when Kennedy got shot pretty much used it all up. The luck stopped there.

In the beginning, though, he had a whooping great time being President, and handed out ten-gallon hats to visitors. In 1964 he walked into the Democratic convention and everybody there stood up and burst into "Hello, Lyndon," to something like the tune to "Hello, Dolly," and it was the most dismal racket you ever heard but it showed he was the nominee. He and Hubert Humphrey ran against Barry Goldwater and carried forty-four states with a wal-

---

[3] He was also called "King Lyndon" and "Uncle Cornpone." Kennedy aides called him "The Great Guided Missile." (He called *them* "The Georgetown Jellybeans.")

[4] He always did.

loping sixty-one percent of the popular vote. (Goldwater's slogan was "In Your Heart You Know He's Right," but the Democrats retorted, "In Your Guts You Know He's Nuts.")

To start with he had a Democratic Congress, and when he told them to haul off and pass a law, they said yes-sir, which was what he liked to hear. Lady Bird said she'd married him because "sometimes Lyndon simply takes your breath away." Others complained about this too. He had a lot of energy. If he wanted to tell you something at four in the morning, he just called you up and told you.

People went around telling Johnson stories. It didn't seem to matter if they were true or not because they were all pretty much the same story.

Sample #1: At the airfield an army sergeant sees Johnson headed for the wrong helicopter, so he goes up to him and says, "Excuse me, Mr. President, but that's your helicopter over there." Johnson beams and throws an arm over the sergeant's shoulders and says, "Son, they're *all* my helicopters."

Sample #2: A Texas state trooper chases a car doing around a hundred and ten. When it finally pulls over, the trooper strides up to it and looks in the driver's window and recognizes his victim. "Oh, my God," he says. Johnson says, "That's right, sonny, and don't you forget it."

If you want any more you can make up your own.

People would have gone right on liking him because he was sort of like Andy Jackson, noisy and bossy but real down-home, and Americans don't mind people thinking they're king as long as they don't put on airs. Johnson wouldn't have known airs if they'd blown his hat off, and he invited folks over to the ranch and served a chili that made your shoes smoke.[5] Sensitive people said he shouldn't pick up his beagles, Him and Her, by their ears, but he said they liked it. Prudes said he shouldn't pull up his shirt and show off the surgical scars on his tummy for the press, but the press said they liked it. He was fun to write about and that is always the main thing.

There was this war, though. Well, not exactly a war, not at first, but we kept sending over people we called "advisors" to advise the South Vietnamese, and we sent more and more of them, and they were advising pretty strenuously, and somehow they turned into troops.

It wasn't at all like World War II, because it didn't have Hitler, and besides, most people had known where Europe was and nobody knew where Vietnam was, even after they'd been there for years. They started to resent having to go die in a country they couldn't find on the map.[6]

Suddenly students on both coasts took to letting their hair grow clear down their backs, abusing substances, writing subversive folk songs about peace, and burning their draft cards if they were boys and their bras if they were girls until the air was quite blue with smoke. In the Seventies, this era was known as the Sixties. It wasn't a bit what Johnson meant by the Great Society and he was pretty miffed.

He lost Congress too. It filled up with Republicans, and they took his Great Society money away from his social programs and

---

[5] Lady Bird had a terrific recipe for spoonbread too. You should try it.
[6] Some thought it was still really Korea, because of having places with funny names and good guys in the south and bad guys in the north, but it wasn't. It was south of Korea. For all I know, it still is.

sent it off to war. From time to time there were riots. The whole country divided up into two teams, the Hawks, who thought we should keep fighting till the last Commie bit the dust, and the Doves, who floated around with forgiving smiles and poked daisies into the business end of other people's rifles. The Hawks thought that a half-million troops in Vietnam wasn't half enough and the Doves thought it was a half-million too many.[7] The only thing they agreed on was that it was all Johnson's fault and they didn't like him anymore.

Johnson got so irritable there was no living with him. In his dreams he thought even his best friends were out to get him. Then he started thinking they were out to get him when he was awake too. Sometimes he heard planes coming in to land at National and thought they were going to hang a left and drop bombs on him.

In March of '68 he said all right, if that's the way we felt about it, then he wouldn't run for re-election, so there. He said maybe if he just went away we'd all stop quarreling and be friends again. In November he stopped the bombing in Vietnam and peace talks started.[8] In January he gave Nixon the door key[9] and went home.

Nothing ever did come of the Great Society, but Lady Bird had planted daffodils all along Rock Creek Parkway, and they're still there, and in the spring they look very nice indeed. Friendlier than the cherry blossoms, somehow.

---

[7] This would have led to arguments at dinner parties, only Hawks and Doves never went to the same parties.

[8] Then they stopped. False alarm.

[9] Halfway through FDR, new Presidents had been showing up for work in January instead of March, so the weather for the parade could be even worse, if possible.

RICHARD MILHOUS NIXON

★ ★ ★

1969–1974

THERE'S A LOT to be said about Nixon. Nixon himself said a lot about Nixon, since whenever he didn't have time to write books and memos and speeches about himself, he was recording every word that fell from his lips, for posterity, a practice he had second thoughts about later. He was his own favorite subject, and if you want to know a whole lot more about him, well then, there's a whole lot more waiting for you. If you laid it all end to end, you'd be surprised.

Some people liked Nixon and some people didn't, but say what you will, he was definitely our manliest President. You could see it in his navy-blue jowls. His language was so manly it was around forty percent unprintable and made Truman sound like a nun, and all his acquaintances were manly too. Even his worst enemies could never prove that, aside from siring two daughters, he'd ever had anything at all to do with women. The closest thing to a sex scandal in his administration was when he and a couple of his buddies were out on a yacht, and they'd brought along a life-sized, inflatable female doll. They'd hide this doll in each other's beds, frightening themselves out of their wits and then laughing themselves sick.[1]

Nixon was manly since childhood. A schoolmate remembered, "Oh, he used to dislike us girls so! . . . As a debater, his main theme in grammar school and the first years of high school was why he

---

[1] The Kennedys let real girls get into their beds, and smear lipstick on their shirt collars and hang stockings over the shower-curtain rod. You're either manly or you're just not.

hated girls." Nothing in later life altered his opinion and he vetoed the Mondale-Javits day care bill just to keep them in their place.

He liked to play poker and talk about football and run for office, especially against effeminate pinkos like Helen Gahagan Douglas.[2] Whenever he thought about pinkos and perverts his testosterone shot off the charts and his beard grew half an inch.

Nixon was born[3] in a lemon grove and grew up in southern California, but if you're trying to imagine him sprinting across the beach in a Speedo with a surfboard on his head, pursued by shrieking blondes, I don't recommend it. Not without some preliminary warm-up, like imaging Woodrow Wilson in a gorilla suit.

He was a Quaker, or said he was, which embarrassed other Quakers. He went to Whittier College and then to Duke University Law School. Classmates referred to him, perhaps lovingly, as "Gloomy Gus." As a young lawyer he had no luck at all and tried to sell frozen orange juice in little plastic bags instead, but back then people weren't used to drinking out of plastic bags. Then he joined the Navy. When he came home he was manlier than ever and trounced the congressional incumbent by calling him a "lip-service American . . . fronting for un-American elements." He was the first to point out to voters that secret pinkos are wily, and naturally the wily thing to do is to sound and vote like conservative anti-Communists, which is how you can tell they're secret pinkos. This revolutionized American politics for years to come.

---

[2] All he had to do was call her "The Pink Lady." It worked like a charm.

[3] His mother gave him a shove by naming him after Richard the Lion-Hearted, who was famous for his battles with his father, his brothers, Saracens, and anyone else he could poke a sword into.

He settled right down in Congress to be the shining light of the House UnAmerican Activities Committee. He was the only person who believed Whittaker Chambers when he said Alger Hiss was a secret pinko.[4] Hiss went to jail and Nixon moved up to the Senate and on to be Ike's Vice President.

Ike often sent Nixon off traveling around the world, and then went out to play golf.[5] Nixon would come home from these good-will tours with spit and vegetables all over his suit, and Ike would let him wash and change and then send him somewhere else. In the 1956 election, Ike suggested that he look around for another job, but Nixon didn't want another job and went on being Vice President and going places. He went clear to Russia to give Krushchev a piece of his mind. Krushchev said Nixon didn't "know anything about Communism—except fear," which was silly since Nixon was our national authority on Communism, and when he came home he was a national hero too.

Ike couldn't be President again, so Nixon ran instead. You remember the debates with Kennedy? You remember he lost? Well, he always hated losing, so he went home to California and ran for governor, and lost *again*. He could hardly believe it. He was *furious*. He charged up to reporters all rumpled and sputtering and said, "You won't have Nixon to kick around anymore because, gentlemen, this is my last press conference!" He was in such a wax that bystanders thought he was having a nervous breakdown, but he said no, he was perfectly cool inside, he was always perfectly cool.

---

[4] He figured pretty much everyone else was, so why not Hiss?

[5] He thought Nixon was a giant pain, and wouldn't show him where the Oval Office was and avoided him as much as possible, which was pretty much. That may have been what he was doing out on the golf course.

A television network ran a special called "The Political Obituary of Richard Nixon." People teased them about it for years.

In 1968 he made a surprise comeback and beat Johnson's Vice President, Hubert Horatio Humphrey, because who could vote for a man with a name like that? His first official act in the White House was to throw away everything Johnson had ever touched, even the rugs and the telephones, and scrape the paint off the office walls because Johnson had been sitting inside them.

He spruced things up to be properly impressive and dressed the White House guards in fancy new costumes that reminded some of the chorus of a comic opera. Right from the start he referred to himself as "The President," because he thought it had more of a ring to it than "Nixon" or "me," which it does. When an old friend called him "Dick," he said, "I am the President of the United States! When you speak to me you call me 'Mr. President.'" In fact, he didn't much like people speaking to him at all. Sometimes, when he was off relaxing with his buddies, nobody spoke for days.

He wasn't a very cuddly President. He liked to go for long manly walks on the beach all by himself, wearing black business shoes and black socks pulled clear to his knees. He never, ever unbuttoned his suit jacket, so that when he threw his arms up in his favorite public greeting, it climbed up his neck and swallowed his head, and his tailor buried his face in his hands and wept.

He did have a wife, called Pat,[6] and sometimes he remembered this and sometimes he didn't. Sometimes he forgot to introduce her to people, even when she was standing right there with her hand stuck out, or absentmindedly went home from the party alone and left her behind to call for a taxi. When he thought she should know

---

[6] Her real name was Thelma Catherine, if you must know.

something, he sent a memo to one of his aides to go tell her. In emergencies he'd even send her a memo directly, like about the end table by the bed, and how it had to be bigger because "RN has to use one dictaphone for current matters and another for memoranda," and besides, the bedroom worktable "does not allow enough room for him to get his knees under it." She was used to this so she knew right away who RN was.

Sometimes, in the White House, they'd have dinner together, if he remembered and wasn't off in the Bahamas or Camp David with his buddies, or if photographers were expected. I have no idea what, if anything, they said to each other.

Pat seemed like a nice woman with a slightly stunned expression, and avoided interviews. She'd had a tough time in early life, but never quite like this.

You mustn't think he didn't have his sentimental side, though. He was really fond of a nice fire in the fireplace, and sometimes he built it up so cozily that alarms went off and firemen rushed in. In July and August he turned the air-conditioning down to superfreeze and *then* he built a nice fire in the fireplace.

Vietnam was still going on and on. Sometimes The President said he had a secret plan for stopping it, and sometimes he said peace was at hand, and sometimes he just bombed it a lot harder. Nothing seemed to work. Students let their hair grow even longer and camped out on the Mall muttering discontentedly.

To take our minds off it, we went to the moon. This was in July of '69, and Neil Armstrong and "Buzz" Aldrin got out of the spaceship and walked around on the actual moon, making footprints. The President rang them up on a special telephone and said, "Because of what you have done the heavens have become part of man's world."

Well, they hadn't, really, but it was fun at the time. It really was. We'd been feeling kind of closed in down here, now that we'd found out what was in places like central Africa and Marie Byrd Land, and here was a whole new place to go. Then it turned out that it was specialized work, going to the moon, and nobody was going to send us up there to jump around in the funny gravity making footprints and peer down at the world to try to find our houses, and if we were going anywhere it would probably be the same old hotel in Ocean City with the same old sand in the beds. By and by we all stopped thinking about it and went back to feeling closed in.

In 1972 The President and his peculiar Vice President, Spiro Agnew, beat George McGovern.[7] Their slogan was "Four More Years," because at the time people still thought Watergate was just an apartment building on the Potomac.

Early in '73 Henry Kissinger, The President's international branch office, managed to stop us from fighting in Vietnam, so we took to bombing Cambodia instead, because we still had all these bombs and who could tell Cambodians from Vietnamese anyway?

Time for Watergate. It seems that during the '72 election, The President's people had been so staunch and loyal and devoted to The President that they'd formed a committee called CREEP. This stood for "Committee to Re-Elect the President," but some felt, later, that it made an unfortunate acronym. Because it was in such a good cause, they did some things a person could misinterpret, like burgling the Democratic headquarters in Watergate, and some exceptionally nosy reporters made a big deal out of it. The President said he didn't have anything to do with it, because he was too

---

[7] Some people can never remember which was McGovern and which was Mondale. It doesn't matter.

busy thinking about affairs of state to even think about getting re-elected, let alone burgling, and no, nobody could go poking through his memos and tape recordings for evidence because he was The President. He said he'd *tell* the Senate and the special prosecutor what was on the tapes, if they really wanted to know, but the whole thing was ridiculous. As an afterthought he fired the special prosecutor, but wouldn't you know another one popped up?

As if The President didn't have enough on his mind, it turned out that Spiro Agnew, the peculiar Vice President, had been sticking to some little envelopes full of money that he was hard pressed to explain, and quit quite suddenly, leaving his desk a mess. The President had to knock off work early and go over to the Hill and pick out a new Vice President. It's always something.

The House Judiciary Committee had no sense of humor and was making a federal case out of the Watergate caper and even ordinary folks were taking an interest.[8] In July of '74 the committee recommended impeaching The President three times, once for doing things he shouldn't have done, once for trying to stop us from finding out about them, and once for not answering the door when people came with subpoenas. The President said all right, all right, we could *have* the f____g tapes, or some of them, or parts of some of them, if that's how we felt. Well, it turned out that recording your every word isn't always the bright idea it seems like, even if you're The President and every word is precious. Many people were more upset by his vocabulary than they were by Watergate,

---

[8] The President called this "wallowing in Watergate" and urged us to cut it out before he put us on his Enemies List and sent us tax auditors and parking tickets and dead mice in the mailbox. We went right on wallowing. We couldn't help it. It was on radio and television every day, and it was even more fun than the moon landing and lasted even longer than "Upstairs, Downstairs."

and various key Republicans hinted that he should start packing before things got a lot worse.

He announced his departure on August eighth, the hundred-and-sixty-second anniversary of Napoleon getting punted off to languish on St. Helena. The Dow-Jones went up twenty-seven points. Historian Henry Steele Commager said, "Other things being equal, we haven't had a *bad* President before now. Mr. Nixon is the first dangerous and wicked President."

As soon as it wasn't on television anymore we all stopped wallowing in Watergate and sort of forgot about it, and in a few years Nixon started turning into an elder statesman. He wrote manly books about himself and foreign policy, himself and world peace, and himself and Southeast Asia. Serious people clustered around him and asked him deep questions, like what he thought about China, because he'd spent a week there in '72 and that was more than most people had spent.

Everyone agreed that Watergate had been a fine chance for the children to learn about the Constitution, and besides, Nixon had made it respectable to be a right-wing Republican again for the first time since Hoover, and if it hadn't been for Nixon we might not have had any Ronald Reagan, and how would you like *that?*

At his funeral in '94, Senator Bob Dole called him "the largest figure of our time, whose influence will be timeless," and said, "the second half of the twentieth century will be known as the Age of Nixon." Then he wept.

Many years later, as the century ended, the folks over at Archives released a few more miles of tapes. On them The President freely and frankly shares his views on "little Negro bastards on the welfare roles," whose immoral parents "live like a bunch of dogs;" on Mexicans ("They steal, they're dishonest"); and the

Catholic Church, which "went to hell three or four centuries ago" because it was "homosexual," unlike the Popes themselves who were "layin' the nuns." He deplores San Francisco, "the most faggy goddamned thing you could ever imagine . . . I can't shake hands with anybody from San Francisco." And he rather admires Russia because it doesn't put up with perverts: "Goddamn, they root 'em out. I don't know what they do with them."

Some think this wasn't a nice way to talk. Others, bored with the correctitude of our political discourse, find it curiously refreshing.

GERALD RUDOLPH FORD JR.

★ ★ ★

1974–1977

ON THE VERY first morning that Ford was President, he came to his front door in his blue-and-white striped pajamas and reached out to retrieve the morning paper, and looked around, and mercy, the yard was full of reporters and cameramen and he was all embarrassed.

When the American public heard this, we were overcome by a great wash of relief. In the typical subject this sensation began somewhere at the back of the neck and spread slowly in a warm tide down to the soles of the feet: *Here was a President we didn't have to think about.* We were tired of thinking about the President. We'd been thinking about Richard Nixon, man and boy, for twenty-six years, since HUAC days, and day and night for the past two years, and now we wanted to think about ourselves for a change, and when Gerry Ford came to the door in his pajamas many broke down and wept for joy.[1]

Gerry seemed to be something of a dingbat, and this was a relief too. It was suggested that more than his nose have been damaged on the football field. Lyndon Johnson said he'd played too often without a helmet and called him "the only man I ever knew who can't fart and chew gum at the same time,"[2] but we didn't care. We all smiled and told each other Gerry jokes, because nobody'd been able to think of any Nixon jokes.

---

[1] Nobody could imagine Nixon coming to the door in pajamas, or even going to bed in them. We took it for granted that he slept in his suit, and maybe his shoes too.

[2] The nicer newspapers revised this statement for publication.

Then he pardoned Nixon. He said he didn't know what Nixon had done, exactly, that was against the Presidential rules, but whatever it was it was okay with Gerry and Nixon couldn't be punished or even asked about it anymore.

This was unpopular. The usual cynics thought there'd been prior hanky-panky. Here Nixon had gone over to the Hill, after that little problem with Spiro Agnew, and picked out what folks called "a spectacularly average congressman" to be Vice President. Now ten months later the fellow's President and pardoning Nixon and the question was, why did Nixon pick him? Hints were dropped that he'd lined up rows and rows of Republican congressmen and said, "Okay, which of you b_____s would pardon The President if the s__t hit the fan?" And Ford jumped up waving his arm and knocking over his chair and said, "Me, sir!" and got the job.[3]

Hey, maybe Nixon picked Ford because he *looked* like an easy mark for a pardon.[4] Anyway this was before Nixon turned into an elder statesmen, and a few hotheads thought he should go to trial, just to tell us what really happened at Watergate. Others said it wouldn't look right if push came to shove and there was The Ex-President of the United States in the pokey getting his breakfast slipped in through a slot, because things like that give the place a bad name.[5] Anyway, he was pardoned and he stayed pardoned.

Other than that, the main controversy of the Ford Regency was

---

[3] Gerry *liked* Nixon. He said Nixon was exactly like Abraham Lincoln, and he always ate Nixon's favorite lunch, cottage cheese with plenty of catsup, whenever it was on the menu.

[4] Sometimes, for photographers, Gerry set his jaw and tried to look manly, mostly managing to look like a little boy pretending to be an alligator.

[5] Later on, many people felt President Clinton would look perfectly swell in the pokey, but that was different.

just how dumb Gerry really was. Some supporters claimed he was only pretending to be dumb, since nobody could be *that* dumb. Journalist Larry L. King said, "He is so average one almost suspects it to be deliberate."[6] An old friend said that instead of trying to outsmart his opponents, he outdumbed them, and this was a very effective ploy though it's hard to see quite how it worked. Some asked how come the loyal voters of Grand Rapids, Michigan, sent him to Congress thirteen times in a row if he was so dumb?[7] His wife, Betty, said, "I think a President has to be able to think like the people think."

It may be that Gerry was just permanently confused. When he was born his mother named him Leslie Lynch King Jr., after his father, and then several years later thought it over, divorced King, married Gerald Rudolph Ford and, as a gesture of respect, renamed the child after *him*. It was a mercy she decided to stick with Ford, but even so this kind of thing can rattle a child. It can cause him to trip over furniture in later life, and bean old ladies with golf balls, and turn up for his wedding in one black shoe and one brown one.

The major problem of the time was inflation. It was one of those spells when supermarkets hire fleet-footed extra help to race up and down the aisles all day raising prices, and housewives sprint to stay ahead of them and snatch the cans of soup before they go up another fifty cents. Ford tackled the problem head-on. He had millions of big round buttons printed up that said "W.I.N.," which stood for "Whip Inflation Now," and promised that if we wore them every time we went out in public, soon prices would stop going up and then slowly but surely start going down. Unfortunately

---

[6] As a child he had a dog named Spot, honest.
[7] Nobody answered.

not enough people remembered to wear them—you know how it is when you're dressing in a hurry in the morning—so it didn't work, but it might have.

Now it turned out that over the Vietnam years quite a number of young men of draft age had unaccountably disappeared into foreign countries and stayed there, leaving gaps in the population. The public began to notice, and ask each other, "Where's Eddie? I haven't seen Eddie since '71." So Ford said they could all come home and be pardoned, like Nixon, and not go to jail as draft dodgers if they'd apologize by doing community service work. Community service consists of jobs nobody in his right mind would dream of doing except to stay out of jail,[8] and most of the missing told Ford to stick it in his ear and stayed where they were. In April of '75 the war finally stopped,[9] but they still wouldn't come home. By this time they'd learned to speak Swedish, or Canadian, or whatever, and got used to being missing.

The *Mayaguez* was the only exciting thing that happened, and even that didn't last long. It was a U.S. merchantman that had gotten itself captured at sea by some Cambodians, who were still pretty cheesed about being bombed, and Gerry made his alligator face and sent for it back. In the scuffle ninety-one Americans got killed or wounded, but the thirty-nine on the *Mayaguez* were rescued, and we'd definitely showed the Cambodians what was what. It was Gerry's manliest act, but by the following Tuesday we'd forgotten all about it and gone back to telling Gerry jokes.

Squeaky Fromme and Sara Jane Moore both tried to shoot him

---

[8] You didn't catch Nixon doing community service.
[9] No, of course we didn't lose. Americans don't lose wars. We *withdrew,* which is quite different.

and failed dismally. They didn't even wing him. They were hysterical types and not from your better class of assassin, but no really reputable assassin could be bothered.

The W.I.N. buttons hadn't worked and the price of soup was still going up, so we didn't elect Gerry for a term as a real President. However, his fans did get together and set up the Gerald R. Ford Museum, a treasure trove of memorabilia and well worth the trip to Grand Rapids.[10] I recommend the golf balls, autographed by Gerry himself. Last I heard, they were $6.95 apiece but they've probably gone up, inflation being what it is.

---

[10] It's in Michigan; you can't miss it.

JIMMY CARTER

★ ★ ★

1977–1981

IT'S HARD TO explain to foreigners and small children just why Jimmy Carter was such a joke. You had to be there. He wasn't a funny joke, like Gerry Ford, more an embarrassing joke. Right from the beginning, when he insisted on carrying his own suitcase into the White House, we were embarrassed.

A quick survey among friends and neighborhood bartenders offers a broad spectrum of reasons:

a. Peanut farming. This is not a manly occupation, like raising cattle. Never mind that you graduated with distinction from the Naval Academy; when your father dies and leaves a peanut farm for you to manage, you should just say no. Peanuts are silly.

b. His religion. It's a modern political essential to call yourself a devout Christian and speak at length of religious values, but actual Christianity is something else again. As *Harper's* magazine put it, he "campaigned for the presidency in the robes of a Christian saint, barefoot and without guile," and "argued that the business of governing the American republic mattered less than the mending of the American soul." He kept muttering about our spiritual malaise. This was insulting as well as embarrassing.

c. His family. His brother Billy sat around whittlin' and spittin' and brewin' up Billy Beer, which was such an instant failure that the remaining cans sold to collectors for incredible sums. Last I heard, a six-pack went for twelve hundred bucks.

His sister was religious or psychic or something and rode a bicycle, and his mother—his *mother*—joined the Peace Corps when she was about a million years old and went to someplace like Africa. His daughter Amy had a Siamese cat instead of a dog. His wife, Rosalynn, had opinions.

d. Being governor of Georgia. Georgia is not a real place, like Massachusetts or Illinois. Georgia is funny, except for downtown Atlanta, and gives you an accent.

e. He talked funny. See above.

f. He was serious about Nature. Not in a manly way, like Teddy Roosevelt, to go do manly things in, but just to have it lying around.

g. The rabbit. Even he thought the rabbit was funny, and actually went around *telling* people how his rowboat had been pursued by a vicious seagoing rabbit, when any sensible pol would have murdered the witnesses and sunk their bodies in the river. Voters found the rabbit a worse joke even than the peanuts. Go out and vote, and what do you get? A President who gets publicly pushed around by rabbits.

h. His sweater. It was a dismal baggy old cardigan, and you know perfectly well he had better stuff in his closet. The public has a right to expect a President in attractive garments. Not Matty Van Buren and the orange necktie, necessarily, but *not that cardigan.*[1]

---

[1] It's true Thomas Jefferson also slopped around in shabby old clothes, but on him it looked distinguished.

i. His earnestness. All pols from sheriff on up are expected to care deeply about a few items, called "issues," chosen for them by the prospective voters, such as crime, or car insurance, and keep caring right through the week after the election, but nobody wants a pol who *really* cares. It's unbusinesslike. Carter really cared, and about things like pollution, housing for the poor, and peace in the Middle East, wherever *that* is.[2]

j. His name. Nobody ever thought of him as James, which is a traditional and dignified Presidential handle. He let us think of him as Jimmy. He *encouraged* us to think of him as Jimmy.

k. His honesty. Maybe people like to call Lincoln "Honest Abe," but you never caught Lincoln saying the wrong thing just because it was true. Honesty in politicians is a sign of mental deficiency, as in telling a *Playboy* interviewer that you've lusted in your heart after women you aren't married to.[3] American Presidents are supposed to be simple, straightforward, hometown folks, but a President who really *is* simple, straightforward, hometown folks is a national humiliation and a dork.

We were particularly offended by the time he was out jogging, and overdid it and collapsed. He was wearing black socks. Only dorks jog in black socks.

Worst of all were the hostages.

For reasons too Middle Eastern to go into, a bunch of Iranian students cut class and barged into our embassy in Teheran and

---

[2] Car insurance had gotten just *appalling*, but did Carter care?

[3] A President should either not lust, like Nixon, or do something about it, like Kennedy. Lusting in your heart annoys all of the voters all of the time.

took fifty-two Americans hostage, and Carter *let* them. Oh, he tried to get them back, and kept fiddling around working on this deal and that deal,[4] but he was mostly dealing with the wrong people.[5] All the deals fell through, so he decided we should just go crashing in there and rescue them.

Well, *that* was a joke and a half. There were helicopters that wouldn't even *start,* for heaven's sake, but did Carter get out there with a can of grease and a Phillips screwdriver and start them? No. There was one that did start, and what happened? It bumped into a transport plane and eight of our boys got killed. People spoke wistfully about Nixon, and how *Nixon* would have made those helicopters straighten up and fly right, and here Carter can't even get them off the *ground.*

Not only were the hostages still hostages, but now the whole *world* was laughing at us.

The hostages stayed on and on, playing pinochle and getting bored and depressed. We all sent them Christmas cards, but even that didn't cheer them up. They stayed there for four hundred and forty-four days, and besides, we still had all that inflation and our fuel bills were something shocking. So much for President Carter.

Even after he lost the election, he kept on working to get the hostages back, but they didn't come home until the very last day of his term, which was much too late, and anyway wouldn't have made up for the price of heating oil and for being a dork.

Foreigners and small children, who never understand jokes, may think Jimmy Carter looked like a thoughtful, decent sort of

---

[4] He tried to tell us it was a complex situation. We promptly replaced him with a President who never saw anything complex about anything.

[5] Iran is like that. It's hard to tell the right people from the wrong people. They all look like Iranians.

President who cared about poor people and Nature and peace, and lost thirty pounds in the White House from worrying and working late, and afterwards, instead of playing golf like any sensible retired President, climbed around on ladders with a mouthful of roofing nails building houses for poor people.

All I can say to them is, you had to be there. Ask anyone.

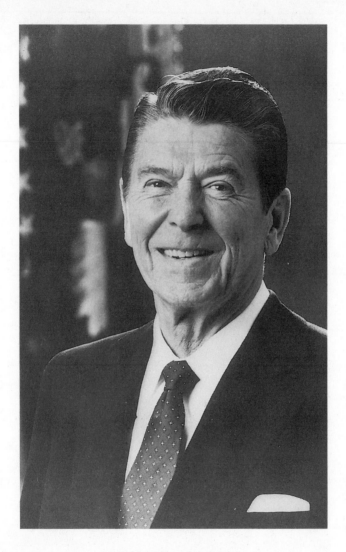

RONALD REAGAN

★ ★ ★

1981–1989

A PRELIMINARY CHECK among friends, neighbors, and colleagues warns that writing about Ronald Reagan will be a perilous task. There simply aren't words to describe him. He was—and at this point still is—the most beloved President in our history. Oh, some might make a case for George Washington, object of almost hysterical adoration, but George wasn't half as embraceable.

Reagan's legacy towers, literally: Washington is in the process of renaming most office buildings, bridges, highways, landmarks, and airports after him—there's talk of re-christening the Washington Monument[1]—but even the tallest building can never outshine the magic of his spell when he was with us.

Reagan was our first President trained as a movie actor and the effect was almost hypnotically pleasing. His voice alone was like a full-body massage. Biographer Edmund Morris describes it as a light, fluid baritone but with "a fuzzy husk to it, rather like peach fuzz" and "almost sensually appealing . . . so that people got physical pleasure out of listening to Reagan talk." Those who were young in the '30s when he was a sports announcer remember being uplifted by the merest snatches of his words on radio, and realizing that life was okay after all.

His excellent speechwriters made the most of it and he was known as The Great Communicator, at least when he had a script. Ad-libbing, he could seem a bit spacey, but *endearingly* spacey.

What he communicated was a serene and joyful optimism that,

---

[1] Some have also suggested "The Reagan National Debt."

after fussy Carter, fell upon our souls like sunshine and into our ears like wine. It was, he told us, morning in America, and we were a shining city on a hill. The long-held hostages landed from Iran at the very moment of his inauguration, as if he had produced them like fifty-two rabbits from a hat, and we forgot about Carter's dogged negotiations and blessed Reagan for their return.[2] It was an auspicious beginning, and it went on like that.

He didn't just rise to the occasion, he soared. He levitated into the Oval Office on wings of confidence, shining like a lighthouse and spreading inspiration like a benediction. Forget Carter's "spiritual malaise," our souls, he said, were just fine the way they were,[3] and so was everything else. Great was America. All was well.

He was a happy man, a happiness professional, sent from the world where they manufacture the stuff. It was a whole new experience in Presidents.

Part of his optimism was natural temperament, but some of it must have been vocational. An actor on stage must always be braced for unscripted disasters, but a movie actor sails risk-free through the working day. The director will show him where and how to stand; the story's end is already in place, with each step planned in advance by committees of screenwriters; the producer guarantees that all will come out for the best in ninety minutes or so. Should the actor sneeze or fluff his lines, he has unlimited second chances to get it right. If there's anything dangerous to be done, it's the stand-in or stunt-man who breaks an arm. And even

---

[2] A few of the usual cynics claimed they'd been packed and ready to go for quite a while, but got delayed so they could make this timely entrance.
[3] Excepting only the souls of student radicals, secret Socialists, welfare cheats, and people who had abortions.

if the whole enterprise is a turkey from the get-go, who could blame the actor for that?

And who could blame an actor who, after fifty-some movies, deeply believes in the kindness of Fate and the inevitable happy ending for the good guys? It's enough to make anyone cheerful, right through the fairly serious recession of '82, the swelling of the national deficit, and the hotting-up of the Cold War.

Reagan had a vision, later called "The Reagan Revolution." Indeed, he was a man of almost pure vision, like those shimmering light-swords in "Star Wars." It was a vision of "national pride," of the "new patriotism," and of "freedom of enterprise" as our most sacred right. As he put it in a nutshell, "What I want for this country above all is that it may always be a place where a man can get rich."

Not that Americans hadn't always wanted to get rich. It was just that some previous Presidents had made us feel guilty about it, forever urging us to worry about other things instead. Reagan told us it was not only the right thing to want, it was sublimely, quintessentially American, and stood for all that shone most brightly over this great land of ours.

He'd started out as a New Deal Democrat, but when the Red scare hit Hollywood, it opened his eyes to the menace of Communist infiltration and he changed his tune, voluntarily supplying the FBI with names to watch out for. He moved as far right as it gets, and frankly, some of the folks over there can seem, well, *mean,* but Ron was clearly a puss-cat. He took thought for the poor, as long as they stayed off welfare. When people asked what would happen to them as the rich rose, freed from "confiscatory taxes" and petty business regulations, through strata of increasing wealth, he explained his trickle-down theory: when allowed to get sufficiently rich, the rich can provide the poor with jobs walking their dogs and washing their cars, so all will prosper together.

In one of his best-known movies, "Bedtime for Bonzo," he co-stars with a chimpanzee who learns to eat with a spoon and ride a tricycle.[4] His grand triumphant curtain line, as he drives off in his convertible with the girl (and the chimp), is "By golly, I'm the richest man in six counties!" It resonated. Here was a President we could relate to. Hordes of Democrats started buttonholing strangers and explaining that they were actually *Reagan* Democrats, and became a formidable voting bloc.

Back to basics.

He was born and raised in Illinois, son of a humble shoe salesman, and graduated from Eureka College there, then went to work announcing for a couple of Iowa radio stations. In California in 1937 to broadcast spring-training stories, he wangled a screen test and got hired by Warner Brothers to play a radio announcer in "Love Is On the Air." His career was off and running.

It was interrupted for several years by World War II, in which he served with distinction in California making training films for the armed forces, though sometimes he remembered it differently.

Afterwards, he took up politics, and served as president of the Screen Actors' Guild, where he worked to expunge subversive elements from the movie world. His wife, the actress Jane Wyman, got so bored she divorced him.[5]

Then General Electric hired him to appear on "General Electric Theater" and travel around the country giving speeches. It was

---

[4] Some actors make movies called "films" and give themselves airs, but Reagan's were by-gosh *movies* that anyone could understand.
[5] He was great with an audience, but up close he faded out.

mostly the same speech, which he tinkered with constantly, and it got further and further right, denouncing creeping Socialist projects like Medicare and Social Security, and labor unions, and government meddling, all explained with stories and anecdotes lifted from *Reader's Digest*.[6]

Influential California Republicans realized he'd make a great President, so as a warm-up they ran him for governor. Readying him for the campaign, his backers were alarmed to find that, after thirty years there he knew "zero about California . . . I mean zero," and even less about governments. He was good at taking directions, though, and a quick study, and memorized his note cards, which toned down his views considerably. His backers had plenty of money too, which never hurts, and he trounced the startled Democratic incumbent, who'd thought he was a joke.

As governor, he could kick back and relax. His staff took care of everything, including hiring and firing themselves, and cued him when he forgot the issues. (Sometimes he misunderstood them, like the time he accidentally signed a bill liberalizing abortion.) Then he ran for re-election as an anti-government reformer, complaining about the way the state was being run and the mess things were in, and won. His opponent was flabbergasted. Only Reagan could convince voters that he didn't have anything to do with his own government.

He surprised the liberals with some good environmental bills, and got a welfare-reform bill passed.

Welfare was always a sore spot with Reagan. Unlike some Presidents, he'd worked for his money, making all those movies and Arrow Shirt ads and real-estate investments, and he hated a deadbeat. Somebody once told him that mothers on the dole regu-

---

[6] What this had to do with electricity I cannot say, but he was a big hit.

larly went to pick up their checks in chauffeur-driven Cadillacs, and he couldn't get them out of his mind. He spoke of them often. "Welfare Queens," he called them.

It was time for the Presidency. In '76 he gave Ford a run for his money, speaking out strongly against détente with Russia and arms control, but Ford took unfair advantage of being President already and beat him out, and then got beaten by Carter. Then at the '80 convention, Reagan buried George Bush up to his armpits and went on to lick Carter, and lo! morning broke over the land. The man we'd dismissed as an aging actor turned into the rising sun.

Early on, he got shot by a fellow named Hinckley. Now, Hinckley was in love with the movie actress Jodie Foster, and felt that if he shot a President, this "historic deed" would win him her "respect and love."[7] He'd had a try for Carter but accidentally left his guns in the hotel room, so now he went for Reagan and got him in the chest. (A couple of guards were felled too and his press secretary, James Brady, got it in the temple and was permanently paralyzed.[8]) Well, Reagan was a perfect trooper. He smiled and waved as they carried him away.[9] In the hospital he quoted Jack Dempsey's line, "Honey, I forgot to duck," and W. C. Fields's tombstone quip that he'd rather be in Philadelphia, and any remaining sourpuss holdouts were charmed out of their socks. Hinckley was found insane and locked up.[10]

---

[7] There must be lots of ideological reasons to shoot Presidents, but our assassins all seem to have strangely personal agendas. (See McKINLEY.)

[8] Later his wife stumped around trying to limit our constitutional right to carry guns, but you wouldn't catch Reagan whining like that.

[9] You could almost smell the popcorn.

[10] A theory, so far uninvestigated, is circulating on the Internet that the Democrats got hold of Hinckley and induced his psychosis and told him to shoot Reagan. Just like in the movie "The Manchurian Candidate."

It's possible that Reagan stayed so cool because he thought he'd been shot in a movie. Sometimes it wasn't clear whether he was actually in the White House or in a movie about the White House, or perhaps about football players or fighter pilots. Nasty people claimed he couldn't tell reality from the movies, but on him this was charming and gave his administration a dream-like glamour too often lacking in politics. Besides, it rang our bells, because we'd seen the same movies he had; when he called Russia the "Evil Empire," we too saw Darth Vader.

He said, "As a kid, I lived in a world of pretend. I had a great imagination . . . I used to make up plays and act in them myself." Early habits are hard to break.

He was deeply interested in UFOs and the possibility of attack by space aliens. It's said that when he saw "E.T," the movie about a visitor from space, he took it for a documentary and congratulated Spielberg on exposing the issue. In several speeches, he spoke warmly about how the space invaders would unite the countries of Earth in self-defense, and mentioned it to Soviet Secretary Gorbachev as the best hope for world peace. It may be that his tireless efforts to hoist the Strategic Defense Initiative into place[11] were aimed as much at Mars as Russia.

And take Grenada—which he did. Many of us thought that was a movie. We could close our eyes and see it. Grenada is a dot of a place in the blue Caribbean, maybe twice the size of Washington, D.C., described by fans as "a rolling, mountainous island covered with fragrant spice trees and rare tropical plants, bordered by stunning beaches and picturesque towns," simply pleading to be a

---

[11] He'd played a secret agent in a movie, "Murder in the Air," that had something like it, only in the movie, it worked, and didn't cost as much.

movie. Well, you have to have a villain, and the bad guys (Marxists) had taken over the government, clearly an invitation for Cuba to turn it into a military base and nuclear threat. Besides that, a thousand suntanned young American medical students were studying there, no doubt attracted by the superior education and not the stunning beaches, and must need rescuing from the Marxists. The script has everything. We stormed in with seven thousand troops and mopped up the place in a few days, losing only nineteen men[12] and replacing the bad Marxists with good capitalists.

Our European buddies thought it was silly and we should have asked the United Nations, but we thought it was swell. It was a decisive military victory, our first since before Vietnam, and showed the world that Marxists better not mess with Reagan. As he put it, we stood tall again.

His second wife, Nancy, was in some ways the perfect First Lady and an adoring helpmate who coordinated her husband's schedule with advice from her astrologer back home. Her worshipful upturned gaze at him, as unto a shrine, filled all other American husbands with discontent. She was a tiny, elegant little thing with a big, perfectly sculpted yellow coiffure, so that the envious went around saying, "Did you hear about poor Nancy? She fell down and broke her hair." Her guests from back home were better-looking than any previous White House guests and her splendid gowns were greatly admired until some snoop reported she got them free from famous designers, as advertising.

The White House was afraid this made her seem shallow, so they drafted her into the War on Drugs. Suddenly she was everywhere, urging young Americans to "Just Say No" to drugs, and

---

[12] I can't find out whether the med students allowed themselves to be rescued.

countless thousands of teenagers, previously unaware of this option, threw away their reefers and opium pipes.

In his seventies, Reagan always seemed pink-cheeked and boyish, with a full head of rich wavy hair that sometimes looked auburn and sometimes just brown, but people did say he took the occasional unscheduled nap.[13] This is why nobody could blame him for Iran/Contra. He said he hadn't had the slightest clue that his national security advisor Admiral Poindexter and his aide Oliver North were illegally selling arms to Iran, of all places, and then sending the money to help some guerrilla insurgents in Nicaragua.

Many Presidents we wouldn't have believed for a minute, but we believed Reagan. The scandal was thoroughly investigated, and the report concluded that even when he was awake, he wasn't *very* awake, and hadn't noticed.

This was approvingly called his "relaxed management style," but you mustn't suppose he was idle. Far from it. He unshackled businesses from many petty rules and gave their advertising people free rein, so that "Caveat Emptor!" again rang out in the land. He beefed up the military something marvelous and clamped down on the spread of birth control and the arrogance of labor unions. When the Professional Air Traffic Controllers said their jobs were making them crazy and went on strike, Reagan outlawed their union and fired the whole crybaby bunch and replaced them with unprofessionals.[14] He talked to Gorbachev, who was the first sane thing in Russia in ages, and the Cold War cooled down again.

All was well. In his second term he had cancer surgery and the

---

[13] So did Taft, but on Reagan it looked sweeter.

[14] Some passengers, coming in to land at O'Hare, wondered who exactly they were and what their previous jobs had been, but nobody got killed, or not that I know of. Luckily Reagan's own plane used separate arrangements.

public was treated to exhaustive coverage of his lower bowel; afterwards he seemed a bit spacier than before, but we didn't mind. Some Presidents get blamed for everything from earthquakes to flu, but Reagan was our dear Teflon President and only good flowers were laid on his doorstep. The common wisdom holds that he single-footedly kicked down the Berlin Wall and went on to personally destroy the Soviet Union, leaving it a rubble of squabbling statelets with ludicrous names, and without Reagan we'd be either a dismal Russian satellite eating turnips or a smoking nuclear wasteland at this very minute.[15] He did this without firing a shot, simply by spending so much money on the military that the Evil Empire went broke trying to keep up with us. It was a master stroke.[16]

And he did it all without breaking a sweat. Some fuss-budget Presidents stagger gaunt and pale from the White House, but after eight years, Reagan look relaxed, tanned, fit, and more serene than ever. His departure would have capsized the country into devastating national grief, but he promised to leave us his Vice President, George Bush, as a stand-in, and we'd hardly notice the difference.

In our hearts we saw him leaving on horseback at an easy lope, with "Red River Valley" or maybe "She Wore a Yellow Ribbon" pouring from the soundtrack.

He turns in the saddle, and smiles, and waves his hat.

So universally did we love our Ronald that when he was diagnosed later with Alzheimer's disease, only three people *in the entire country* echoed the Dorothy Parker crack about Coolidge's death, "How can they tell?"

---

[15] Perhaps even a province of Cuba. Put *that* in your pipe and smoke it.
[16] He tripled the budget deficit and quadrupled the trade deficit, but it was worth every cent.

GEORGE HERBERT WALKER BUSH

★ ★ ★

1989–1993

IF PERHAPS THERE was less to Reagan than met the eye, perhaps there was more to Bush than met it, but these days the eye is what counts.

Bush, for instance, had fought in the actual war, in the flesh, flying fifty-eight combat missions as a bomber pilot and winning the Distinguished Flying Cross for bravery in action. When his plane took a hit and burst into flames, he wobbled it over to his target, an island near Japan, and nailed it before heading off to sea and bailing out.

But he didn't *look* like a war hero, or even like a pilot. He looked like a man in a suit.[1] He looked like a wimp in a wimp-suit. He had the very best handlers and advisors, but nothing could be done about it.

He'd been captain of the baseball team at Yale, but he didn't look like a baseball player either.[2] As President, he pitched horseshoes. This is sportier than Coolidge bouncing on his electric horse, but not much.

He looked, somehow, short. People meeting him in person were stunned to find he was nearly twice as tall as they'd thought.

He looked rather like a dry stick, though actually he was a compulsive party-thrower who couldn't be stopped from hauling home unexpected guests. He kept telling everyone he was a good ol' yee-hah Texas oil-man, but he didn't look like a Texan either, though

---

[1] Reagan, now, *he* looked like a war hero. Did you see him in "Hellcats of the Navy"?

[2] Reagan, *there* was an athlete. Did you see him in "Knute Rockne—All American"?

he did have a hotel room in Houston and a bunch of oil and a big hat. He'd grown up in posh Greenwich, Connecticut, son of a senator, and spent much of his time in the posh seaside enclave of Kennebunkport, and that's what he looked like.

And, though nobody else is rude enough to mention it, he had a tooth problem. Over the past decades, teeth—large, white, sparkling, assertive teeth—had become a major political asset. Gone were the days when a Wilson or a Coolidge could keep his mouth shut and forebear to expose them. Cameras were everywhere, and teeth were expected. Certainly Bush had the usual number of them, or if he didn't he could afford the very best replacements, but apparently they were set too far back in his jaw and, photographed informally, his mouth opened on empty darkness. Even when artfully lighted in a studio, his teeth seemed not nearly large enough or white enough for true leadership.

His hair wasn't leadership quality either. However commanding his international actions, his hair looked meek.

His family and all his oldest friends called him "Poppy."

In short, he was no Reagan. Some of the lingering fairy-dust of Reagan rubbed off on him, lending a faint phosphorescence, and public loyalty followed its light, but it wasn't the same. All most people remember about him is that he threw up on the Japanese prime minister at an official dinner.[3]

Even his staunch political allies sometimes eyed him with suspicion. He had a degree in economics, and way back when folks first explained Reagan's vision of balancing the budget by cutting rich folks' taxes and pouring money into the military he'd called it "voodoo economics," which was rude, and the liberal media had

---

[3] Apparently it wasn't the sushi. It was something he'd taken to fight off jet lag.

snapped it up. And though he certainly tried to sound just like Reagan,[4] there were rumors that he'd once been a closet moderate, perhaps even open to the Equal Rights Amendment. It was whispered that back in Congress, before his Reagan conversion, he was in favor of birth control and referred to by colleagues as "Rubbers."

And sometimes his wife, Barbara, who had a mouth on her, strayed off-message and let a moderate opinion slip out.

In general, though, Bar was the greatest possible asset. She supplied the human side. She was in every way the opposite of her predecessor, and made people think Nancy had been, perhaps, a bit *spindly*. Bar was heartily built, as befits a woman who's had six children, and however often her friends dragged her off to buy clothes, she never looked even slightly elegant, and she didn't care. Apparently she combed her gray hair with an eggbeater. She went sledding with her grandchildren. She was potty about her springer spaniel, Millie, and when George was Vice President, she was sometimes caught in her bathrobe, out walking Millie in the early morning.

Democrats told each other she couldn't possibly be a Republican.

Bush ran against Massachusetts Governor Michael Dukakis, who was un-American by his very name, which Bush people claimed they couldn't pronounce, and soft on crime. Bush kept saying, "Read my lips. No new taxes."[5] Best of all, he had Reagan's fabulously poetic speechwriter Peggy Noonan. He (or she) promised a kinder, gentler nation gleaming with a thousand points of light.

Later some people stomped around grousing that they'd voted for Peggy Noonan and got Bush instead, sort of like Cyrano de

---

[4] It wasn't as good without that velvet voice, though.
[5] He was sorry later.

Bergerac crouching in the bushes and feeding that other fellow all his good lines. After Peggy's speeches, they'd expected a lot more inspirational stuff, but poor Bush admitted he had problems with what he called "the vision thing." This was a letdown after Reagan, who was vision through and through.

The office of President carries grave responsibilities, as Bush realized all too soon. Right off the bat, he said he hated broccoli. At that time, broccoli was the single most important human health factor since the smallpox vaccine, and the mothers of America rose up in their wrath: if the *President* won't eat his broccoli, how can they force it down their children? He became the anti-nutrition President.

Bar countered by having Millie bred, and the free world waited breathlessly for the pups. There were six of them. They were cute. Millie was the most popular First Dog since Fala,[6] and *Millie's Book—As Dictated to Barbara Bush* made number one on the bestseller list and solid money for Bar's literacy campaign.[7]

Out in the great world, things were happening. The Soviet Union collapsed and the Cold War stopped, and we all cheered ourselves hoarse for Reagan's victory. Well, yes, Bush was the President-apparent, but Reagan seemed to have just handed him the mike for a moment while he stepped offstage to powder his nose.

George Bush is not on record as ever saying a harsh word about Reagan, but he must have had private thoughts. Barbara may have turned the bedroom blue with private thoughts. Later, in 1995, after Bush had slipped out of the White House, Peggy Noonan wrote in *Newsweek* about "the party's undiminished hero" and the empty

---

[6] Fala, however, always stood at attention for the national anthem. Millie seemed to be quite unmusical.

[7] She really did care about people reading. She thought it would solve a lot of problems. This was before computers changed the rules of the game.

feeling of "his big absence," but she didn't mean Bush. "Reagan," she wrote, "looms like a sun, lighting the stage on which the year's contenders stand. But his light is so bright they squint in the glare and seem paler, washed out."

Even now, in another century, Republicans of every stripe and stance can get anything done by saying Reagan would have wanted it.

Still, everyone gets to be famous for fifteen minutes, and Bush finally got his lucky break. Saddam Hussein, evil despot of Iraq, invaded tiny little Kuwait on the Persian Gulf. Bush may have had a brotherly feeling for Kuwaitis as fellow oil entrepreneurs, and the place was just *leaking* with oil, so we rushed to their aid. It was an enormously popular crusade and brightened the nation right up.[8] We tied yellow ribbons on lampposts and mailboxes and car aerials and went around giving the victory sign.

Almost nobody said the Kuwaitis were famous scum-buckets and who cared if Iraq ate them for lunch?

These days you can damage a country badly by throwing things at it from a safe distance, and we massaged Iraq with over a million tons of hardware and some seven hundred Tomahawk missiles. They lit up the sky something marvelous and the television coverage was gorgeous to behold. (In the White House, officials lit a candle every night in hope of something landing on Saddam Hussein's bunker, wherever it might be, but nothing did.)

Then we went in on the ground. This was called "Desert Storm" and lasted a mere hundred hours, after which we left. It turned out that we hadn't done nearly as much damage as we'd

---

[8] In radical places like San Francisco, crackpots risked life and limb to paint NO BLOOD FOR OIL on bridges and water towers, and lay down in the roads in protest, but nobody paid them any mind.

hoped, and if we'd stayed longer we might even have found the main man, who came out safe and sound and went right on making trouble, but modern Presidents always think of poor Lyndon Johnson trying to sleep with all those people out there chanting, *"Hey, Hey, LBJ! How many kids did you kill today?"*

Otherwise it was a fantastic success and Bush's approval rating roared up to ninety-one percent, or about as good as it gets. A Bush Web site calls the Gulf War "one of the proudest moments in American history." Bush himself said it had vanquished the memory of Vietnam for good and all. Certainly it vanquished what was called Bush's "wimp factor": Bush had made a fist.

Whole days went by when nobody mentioned Reagan.

Then the moment passed.

There'd been important arms-limitation talks with Russia, and the Clean Air Act, and the Americans with Disabilities Act, and free-trade negotiations, but they weren't half as much fun as a war and our minds wandered. A recession came along, the help-wanteds dwindled to a couple of pages in the back of the sports section, and we blamed Bush. He was no Reagan. In 1992 he lost to Clinton, a Democrat without a single sparkle of Reagan-dust on him and coming from Arkansas too. The Bushes went back to Houston.

He celebrated his seventy-fifth birthday by parachuting out of a plane, something most people do only if absolutely necessary. When asked about it, his son, the one we call W., said, "I agree with my mother's assessment when they named the Central Intelligence Agency building after him. She said, 'I can't believe they'd be naming any facility with the word intelligence in it after George Bush.'"

Some people just can't get any respect.

WILLIAM JEFFERSON CLINTON

★ ★ ★

1993–2001

BILL CLINTON WAS a very smart man who'd been a Rhodes scholar and knew way too much about most things, including such un-Presidential matters as modern literature. This would have disqualified him for President, or even— or especially—governor of Arkansas, if he hadn't kept doing really dumb things with bimbos that everyone could relate to.

Bimbos, like FDR's wheelchair, cut him down to popular size.

As with Jefferson, we'd best get the sex over with first, even if you're already oversupplied on the subject, because otherwise you'll just be sitting there fidgeting at your desks and waiting. It's something we'll just have to go through, like adolescence.[1]

You may not care as much as you should. At the time, many key legislators and opinionizers were outraged that we weren't more outraged. They were dismayed that the people who hated Clinton didn't hate him any more than they always had, which would have been difficult anyway, and the people who didn't hate him weren't interested. Pundits said it just showed how godless we were getting, and assured us that this was morally much, much worse than Watergate, since Nixon never had sex with anyone, but the trouble was, there wasn't enough *story*. Watergate offered us a cliff-hanging narrative, with strange new characters popping up and bizarre events unfolding, but Monicagate could be explained in a sentence: The President fooled around with a young woman he wasn't married to and then denied it.

---

[1] Quite a lot like adolescence, actually.

Once you'd absorbed that and registered either horror or boredom, there wasn't much more. Well, I mean there was lots more, thousands of pages, fifty million dollars in expenses, possibly billions in book contracts, and eons of television programming, but there wasn't much more plot.

Presently it turned out that some of the angriest of the opinionizers had been having affairs of their own, but they retorted that *theirs* were dignified Republican affairs and not squalid Democratic ones.[2] Besides, they said, it wasn't the affair, it was the lie. If a President lied to a grand jury about his sex life, wouldn't he lie if he planned to, like, nuke Nebraska? And unless you've got CIA connections, lying is illegal. "Jail to the Chief," advised one famous columnist.

A few elderly voices spoke up saying that where *they* came from, any man who *didn't* lie about his sex life was considered an unspeakable cad, and besides, if you ask people questions that are none of your business you deserve to get lied to. Nobody listened.

Clinton was a Baptist, and a Baptist spokesperson said he wasn't really lying, because according to their rules, "sex" meant what used to be called "going all the way," and the Prez and his tootsie were just fooling around. This was clearly a quibble. The Republicans thrust aside their usual distaste for pornography and insisted that the public find out exactly what "fooling around" entailed, in a blow-by-blow account, so to speak.

It was very instructive. One woman, in a customer review of

---

[2] One of President Harding's girlfriends wrote a memoir describing sex in a coat closet in the Oval Office, but that was long ago.

the Starr Report on Amazon.com, wrote, "Amazingly, I learned new ways to have sex!"[3]

The investigation and impeachment used up all of 1998 and parts of '99 and the President's sex life was *the* hot topic. No one could see the world's top leader trying to broker peace between heads of state without imagining his trousers around his ankles, which was highly indecorous though of course his own fault. Our European friends found the whole uproar either insane or hilarious[4] and the French commentary frankly envied us our lusty leader; in France a brisk sex life, like a hearty appetite, is a mark of mental and physical vigor. Europeans have no moral sense.

As did the unfortunate James Buchanan and Andrew Johnson, Clinton put his foot in the wrong time slot. Many a President had come and gone with his amours unprobed, back before the invention of body wires, phone taps, DNA testing, talk shows, and the Internet. For instance, you may ask, what of President Kennedy, whose total scores were perhaps far higher than Clinton's, though undocumented by special prosecutors? But that was quite different: Kennedy was allegedly schtupping class acts like Marilyn Monroe and Marlene Dietrich, but Clinton appeared to be trolling the trailer parks. Class counts. And remember Kennedy was from Massachusetts and Clinton from Arkansas.[5] Besides, few people hated Kennedy the way they hated Clinton.

---

[3] The *New Yorker*'s review said the report was "so overwrought that the reader gradually realizes that the point of the story is not that the hero is wicked but that the narrator is mad."

[4] Or perhaps dangerous, since he ought to be keeping an eye on the world instead of spending the working day answering detailed questions about his once-private parts.

[5] So were the friends he brought with him, and the Georgetown establishment howled as if he'd filled K Street with free-range razorback hogs.

There's always a pretty steady supply of hate on hand, but for most of the twentieth century we'd been shipping it abroad. After the collapse of the Soviet Union, it kind of backed up on us with no place to go. Hating ethnic minorities had fallen out of fashion and hating Communists began to seem silly, so presently the stuff gathered its forces together and headed for the Clintons.

The only people who didn't hate Clinton were people who'd met him personally. Happily for his ratings, he was friendly and energetic and millions and millions of people met him personally, or thought they had. He was a big affable fellow who hugged total strangers and felt their pain, like some ancient Norse bear-god, probably named Potus, good-natured but with a weakness for milkmaids.

Previous Presidents like Franklin Roosevelt got hated for ideological reasons, but it was hard to pin those on Clinton, though many Republicans hated him for filching their best ideas, like booting people off welfare, and many Democrats hated him for filching Republicans' best ideas, like booting people off welfare. Labor unions hated him for free-trade agreements giving their jobs to a bunch of foreigners. Health types hated him for his cheeseburgers and cigars. Reporters hated him because he knew all the answers and then some. Golfers hated him because he liked to go out and play a few holes but didn't care much about winning. Lumberjacks hated him for not letting them cut down their trees; enviros hated him for letting them cut down other trees. Anti-drug people hated him for trying marijuana; pro-drug people hated him for not inhaling. In 1994 Republicans took over the House and Senate and hated him so much they said he wasn't really President at all and shut down the government to prove it. Hawks hated him for draft-dodging. Dog-lovers hated him for having a cat named Socks instead of a dog named Buddy.[6] Millions of deerhunters hated him for trying to take away their Uzis.

In 1996 he ran against Senator Bob Dole, saying he would build a bridge to the twenty-first century, and won because Bob Dole had an irritating habit of referring to himself as Bob Dole, as if the two of him were barely acquainted.[7] (Nixon, his hero, had the same problem, even when talking to his wife.) Bob Dole hated Clinton. Back in '92, Bob Dole said that people who didn't vote for Clinton needn't consider him President; Bob Dole would act as their President instead.[8]

All the people who mattered in Washington hated Clinton because he'd never even heard of them, and besides, maybe it's leaderly to be governor of a real state like California or Texas, but what's with this Arkansas joke,[9] where the poor chump was only making $38,000 a year and never got to meet people who mattered? One important *Washington Post* columnist lamented, "He came in here and he trashed the place, and it's not his place." The press called him "Bubba." Author John Updike giggled that his hair looked like 'possum fur, or maybe plastic carpeting.

Mostly, though, they just figured, what's not to hate? In the beginning, they didn't have much to work with but they made do, and there were some jolly fund-raising scandals, like asking for money from the phone on his desk instead of putting on his coat and walking down the street to a pay phone like a normal person. Worse, apparently if you were a friend of Bill's and brought some

---

[6] Presently he did get a dog named Buddy, but Socks was there first.

[7] Later he went on to fame and fortune advertising his penile shortcomings on television. It was the Decade of the Phallus.

[8] There is no Constitutional provision for this.

[9] Carter was from Georgia, but at least Georgia has Atlanta. Arkansas has Little Rock.

campaign funds and your pajamas, you got to sleep over in the Lincoln Bedroom. Not the Grover Cleveland Couch, mind you, but the *Lincoln* Bedroom, where naturally out of respect nobody'd changed the sheets since Abe last lay between them. "Obscene," one Washington insider called it. Who wouldn't hate a guy like that? I mean, if *you* had a room Lincoln slept in, and you let somebody else sleep in it, what kind of scum would *you* be?

Besides, there was trouble about a savings-and-loan scam, way back when in Arkansas, and his wife, a public-service lawyer, did okay in cattle futures back at the law firm.[10] People hated her even more than him. She hadn't even hung up her coat before the bumper stickers bloomed saying, "Who elected her?" and "Impeach President Clinton—and her husband too." People were driven mad with rage at the way she wore her hair, and however she changed it, they hated it more. She was earnest and hard-working—"Homework Hillary," they called her—and wanted to do good for people, which is always infuriating, especially to those who don't need doing good for, and she fired Barbara Bush's cook and talked about health insurance and child care, which were none of her business. (She'd come in with some nutty health scheme to wrench us from the arms of our kindly doctor, the one who nursed us through chickenpox, and replace him with government agents. She got slapped down hard for it. So did he.)

People hated the Clintons so much it gave them a rash and interfered with their sleep. They called in to talk shows about it. They logged on to the Net, where free speech rules and by morning anybody's midnight paranoia is everybody's common knowledge.

---

[10] It wasn't very *nice* of her to make money, but at $38,000 a year, they needed all the help they could get.

The Internet came of age just as the Clintons arrived, and it all but collapsed under Clintoniana. In a twinkling we'd learned the names and résumés of all forty of the people who'd died more or less at the hands of Bill and Hillary—"Arkancide," it was called—and that wasn't even counting White House deputy counsel Vincent Foster, billed as a suicide but actually offed for being Hillary's lover.[11] (Later, when Rudolph Giuliani got prostate cancer and had to drop his New York Senate race against Hillary, everyone nodded sagely. Nobody knew quite *how* she gave him cancer, but it was clearly her doing.)

After the Monica scandal broke, the Hillary-watchers split into two camps, those who hated her for being such a sentimental wimpy spineless doormat that she stayed with that dirtbag, and those who hated her for being such a steely, ambitious, political schemer that she stayed with that dirtbag.

Most hateful of all, clear through the earlier bimbo and fundraising scandals and then the endless investigation and trial, Clinton *went right on being President.* Oh, he did say he was sorry about the Monica thing, but he wasn't half sorry enough; the public had a right to expect at least tears on prime time.[12] Many had assumed he'd just throw some things into a suitcase and slink out the back door into remorseful oblivion. He didn't. He didn't even look angry, as any sensible person would, or shout "Let them impeach and be damned!" like Andrew Johnson. He hardly seemed to notice. With breathtaking arrogance, he went on smiling and hugging,

---

[11] Some Netsters said no, she was way too busy with her endless stream of lesbian lovers to bother with Foster, but others held that she was insatiable.
[12] Some, though, agreed with Mr. Starr that tears are a thin substitute for blood.

conferring with the world's leaders and dropping the occasional bomb on the world's troublemakers.

He even seemed to be having a good time. Like Teddy Roosevelt, he'd always found the Presidency the greatest possible fun and said he couldn't understand why previous fellows griped about the job. He was still having fun. This is pretty darned insulting, after everyone's hard work, and proof that he was slime beyond shame.

Clinton thought he was the world's playground monitor, and prowled the globe trying to get folks to play nicely in the Balkans, Israel, Pakistan, China, Africa, Russia, Colombia, and even Ireland. This was quite futile, as people are programmed to squabble and if it isn't one thing it'll be another, but maybe he just wanted to get out of the country occasionally. They liked him in other places.[13] In June of 2000 he became the first American President to receive the revered Charlemagne Peace Prize in Europe and get proclaimed an honorary European.

Back home, he cut the deficit down to pocket-change, doubled Head Start, got universal childhood inoculation, and covered several million more children with health insurance, though he never managed to haul the country into the civilized world on health and child care. He bullied businesses into hiring some pretty weird folks off welfare. He got the Family and Medical Leave Act, and money for drug counseling and college tuition, fortified gay rights, taxed the rich, and went right on dishonoring the office by sitting in it.

He was still there because those who wanted him out had a couple of problems. One was that people were pretty happy. When he was first elected, chanting, "It's the economy, stupid," a person

---

[13] They even liked *her*. They adored her in Belfast and Beijing and Bangladesh when she nattered about maternity clinics and women's rights. Foreigners. Go figure.

could hardly get a job shining shoes. Shortly afterward, things took off and flew. It was called the "New Economy," and pimply youths with bad hair blossomed into billionaires overnight by promising to produce future virtual profits. Everyone else—or everyone else who counted—got rich on the stock market and kept buying ever-larger cars and building ever-statelier mansions on former corn-fields. The anti-Clintonians kept pointing out that this had nothing to do with him but was all thanks to someone named Alan Greenspan, chairman of the Federal Reserve, but just the same it's hard to get people to rock the boat while they're wondering where to park the yacht.

The other problem, they suddenly realized, was that if they gave Potus the shove for his high crimes and misdemeanors, they'd get his Vice President, Al Gore, who didn't seem like a bimbo man, and there he'd be already in the White House when Election 2000 rolled around.

The House voted for impeachment but the Senate turned it down.

When asked about his future, Clinton said he planned to list on his résumé, "Designed, built, and painted bridge to the twenty-first century. Supervised Vice President's invention of the Internet. Generated, attracted, heightened, and maintained controversy."

As the end approached, even the fiercest columnists wondered what they'd find to write about in the future. One said, "Let's face it, we're going to miss the big guy." Clinton nostalgia swept the media. They'd been used to a high-octane diet. Blandness loomed dark on the horizon. Then everything started exploding at once like a string of cherry bombs, and the media rejoiced until the rafters rang.

As a warm-up, Hillary had bought a house in a high-class out-post of New York, for her Senate run, and everyone called her a carpetbagger and complained that the house was too expensive. Then she got elected and bought another house, in Washington, so she wouldn't have to stay in bed-and-breakfasts while Congress was in session, and this was a bit too pushy if not downright larcenous. It's so much nicer to already *have* houses than to be homeless and have to go buying them.

Then there was the election, which reminded the pundits of the Hayes/Tilden brouhaha, and George W. Bush moved into the White House without anyone being quite sure who'd actually won the thing, though the Supreme Court voted for Bush and that settled it. The Clinton folks moved out, followed by rumors that the outgoing staff had removed the "W" key from some of the office computers. This story ballooned gloriously, and anonymous Bushies claimed Clintonians had smashed the computers and piled them in corners, cut all the phone lines, filled the desk drawers with unspeakable substances and stuck them shut with Crazy Glue, and gutted Air Force One. The new President said he was paying it no mind, but of course he couldn't stop his followers from laying on the details. A few days later it turned out none of it was true except the missing Ws, but it was great while it lasted.

Then we learned that the Clintons had walked off with every stick of furniture in the White House and some of the lightbulbs, which made for hilarious political cartoons.

This wasn't entirely true either, but he *had* submitted a list and he did stick to $190,000 worth of gifts, much of it furniture sent by loyal fans, while his predecessor hauled only $160,000.[14] He sent some of it back and paid for a lot more of it, but the looter label

---

[14] The Bushes already had plenty of furniture, while the Clintons had always lived in publicly furnished housing.

stuck. Actually, looting is quite traditional. Millard Fillmore drove off with the Presidential coach and six bay horses, which he promptly sold for a pretty penny. Nancy Reagan waltzed out of the White House with over a million dollars worth of gift dresses, shoes, and handbags, and moved into a nice little ranch worth two and a half million, bought for her husband by his loving supporters.

Still, you can see this was beside the point, the point being that the Clintons were scum and the others weren't. Arlen Specter of the Senate Judiciary Committee announced he was impeaching Clinton all over again; he couldn't be thrown out of office since he'd already left, but at least we could cut back his pension. Talk of a prison sentence resurfaced.[15]

Then the furniture story shrank to a few chairs and tables and faded. The op-ed columnists again despaired. Then the pardon scandal broke. This was so juicy that nobody even tried to resist, and liberal commentators and opinionizers and senators and congresspersons roared the loudest of all. They'd been suffering in silence for eight years, coming to a slow boil because the other side got all the fun stories, and now they all caved in chorus and dashed into the fray, each vying with the others to be more shocked, appalled, and disappointed. Even the most dignified used words like "trailer-park trash" and "slime."

It seems Clinton, on his way out the door with his coat over his arm, not only protected a whole bunch more wilderness and upped the ante on some of his pet projects, like clean drinking water, but he pardoned a lot of people. This is a President's prerogative, but he's supposed to pardon only *good* people, though really good

---

[15] Nobody mentioned the new President. He couldn't get a word in edgewise, or a minute on the evening news, or his picture in the papers.

people rarely need it. Chief among the undeserving was the nicely named Marc Rich, a stock swindler who'd left the country to avoid paying taxes. Shockingly, his ex-wife had donated money to Clinton's library and that must have been why he did it, though perhaps he misunderstood her; the Riches' divorce had been quite ugly, Rich had a new wife, and his ex may have hoped Bill would have him poisoned instead of pardoned.

The uproar was deafening. True, there'd been outrage over the pardons granted by Washington, Adams, Jefferson, and Madison. Lincoln may have been the worst. Senator Elihu Root wrote that he was "all the time pardoning people who ought to be shot." Taft, Wilson, Harding, Coolidge, and Carter all handed out scandalous forgiveness, and six Presidents pardoned folks who'd tried to assassinate other Presidents. Ford pardoned Nixon. Reagan pardoned a bank robber who went home and killed his wife and cut her remains up into small pieces. Bush Sr. pardoned the Iran/Contra gang, before we could find out what they were up to and what he himself had been doing at the time, and a Cuban terrorist and a Pakistani heroin smuggler.

All trumped by a runaway tax-dodger.

Never you mind. The important thing isn't what's done but who's doing it. Once word goes round that you're sleaze, you look sleazy even while you're flossing your teeth. You probably stole the White House floss.

Clinton went out not with a whimper but a series of bangs, a rousing end to the bang-filled years. This was a great blessing, because it took our minds off who'd won the election, and everyone was tired of wondering.

GEORGE W. BUSH

★ ★ ★

2001–

THE ELECTION WAS between Clinton's Vice President, Al Gore, and George W. Bush, son of President George H. W. Bush, Sr.

George W. was more fun than Gore. Gore had held all these boring important offices and talked like an encyclopedia and sometimes gazed at his opponent as if he couldn't *imagine* how they were applying for the same job. Bush, on the other hand, was lovably tongue-tied and said hilarious things like, "How hard it is to put food on your family?" and "Is our children learning?" (He made former laughingstock Dan Quayle sound like Daniel Webster.) Endearingly, he never pretended to be one of those heavyweights who know where foreign countries are and read a bunch of books.[1]

His history was more fun than Gore's too. Gore admitted to smoking a spot of pot in his youth, but other than that you could tell he was the Eagle Scout type, while Bush had done the playboy thing with all his heart. *Newsweek* said that in college "he seems to have majored in beer drinking in the Deke House." Later there was a drunk-driving arrest, and rumors about a cocaine conviction that got expunged by community service, and a clever way not to go to Vietnam, and some wild stories about women. W. forgave himself fully and freely, though, because he was young and irresponsible then, and he assured us he hadn't touched coke for at least seven years.

---

[1] His parents had always expected his brother Jeb to carry on the Presidential tradition. Jeb was the smart one. Perhaps influential folks felt he was too smart.

At forty he'd had a religious experience, coupled with the love of a good woman, and reformed. God rewarded his newborn virtue with rivers of money, somehow involving friends of his father, and gas and oil and part of a baseball team. The stuff just poured in. Vindicated, he went around urging everyone else to profit from the mistakes of his wild past and stay away from sex and booze and drugs.[2]

Sobriety didn't make him stiff-necked, though, not a bit of it. On the campaign trail he gave everyone silly nicknames and clowned around on the plane making faces and sticking his tongue out and prancing in the aisles like, one reporter noted, a four-year-old. It was a riot, much funnier than Al Gore, who was doing his homework the whole time.

To complicate the campaign Ralph Nader, the man who made us wear seat belts, ran on the Green Party, or Seat Belt, ticket and siphoned off a lot of dreamy-eyed Democrats. The two main men, though, were running pretty neck-and-neck, to widespread public apathy.

Then came the election and the media gave a whoop of relief. It was as rowdy an event as any since the Hayes/Tilden brouhaha. Everyone on the country's edges voted for Gore and everyone in the middle voted for Bush. Gore won the popular vote in a walk, and the electoral count boiled down to, of all places, Florida, where they had ballots in funny shapes and missing ballots and people who got turned away from the polls for being possible felons, or black, or otherwise unacceptable, and it was downright embarrassing. Ballots were counted over and over, using different

---

[2] As governor of Texas, he made it very very tough on those who tried making their own mistakes.

rules, and if you counted them one way, Bush won, and another way, Gore won. Everyone learned a new word, "chad," formerly a country in Africa but now a tiny scrap of paper dangling from a ballot punched with insufficient force.

Since under the Constitution we have to have some sort of President, and since it's impractical to have more than one at a time, Bush the Younger was awarded the post, courtesy of friends on the Supreme Court, and moved into the White House. The usual whining ensued. Many newspapers and other periodicals avoided calling him "President Bush" and referred instead to "the White House," "the Administration," or, more casually, "The Bushies." More than a year after the election, *The Economist* ran a printed correction, saying various correspondents had chided them for referring to him as "President" when it was still too close to call: *"The Economist* regrets any inconvenience."

Bush was no workaholic and cut himself a bit of slack on the job. He was crazy about fitness and worked out for hours, and he spent quite a lot of time back in Texas where, he said, the real people lived, on a place he called his ranch.[3] Nobody minded, though, since it was understood that there were plenty of grownups around to run things, old Cold-Warriors and friends of his father, Vice President Dick Cheney and Colin Powell, Secretary of State and Gulf War hero. If Clinton had loomed alarmingly larger than life, Bush seemed somewhat smaller than life and was sometimes pictured as an elfin-eared doll in Dick Cheney's breast pocket.

Then came September 11, 2001. For the benefit of those just ar-

---

[3] He was no Ronald Reagan and kept no visible livestock; he didn't like horses and rode around the place in a golf cart, but "ranch" sounds much manlier than "estate."

rived from a galaxy far, far away, a handful of Moslem malcontents highjacked some planes and flew them into both towers of the World Trade Center in New York, one after the other, and the side of the Pentagon in Virginia. The towers fell down. Dust and smoke and flames filled the air. Thousands died. The country screeched to a horrified halt. New York's mayor was seen striding boldly through the flaming rubble. President Bush was nowhere to be found.

Later it turned out he'd followed orders from the Secret Service to make himself scarce and was being sequestered in remote Western states and air bases. This was quite right and prudent of him. One can only imagine what a previous Texan President would have said, no doubt something like, "Boys, I'm going back to the White House, get on the teevy, and speak to the Amurrcan people, and if you're not taking me there, then get your sorry ass out of that cockpit and I'll fly this dang thing myself." That would have been reckless and irresponsible.

Nobody called W. a sissy, though, because as soon as he got back home he declared war on Afghanistan. America rose to its feet and cheered. The questionable President was instantly reborn as a national hero. A great tidal wave of patriotism and religion engulfed and uplifted us. Wherever three or more Americans assembled, they linked arms and sang "God Bless America." "God Bless America" was sung in supermarkets and parking lots and hardware stores all across the country. American flags of every size were sold out by sunset, so people had to carry red, white, and blue ribbons instead, while all over China seamstresses toiled around the clock making more flags, and all around them factories stamped out literally millions of flag lapel pins. In even the most sophisticated circles, no lapel was without its pin, and any car or truck without at least one flag, a couple of flag decals, and a "God Bless America" bumper sticker looked downright subversive. All along America's roads, movable-letter signs that used to say "No Money Down" or "Tuesday Meatloaf Special" now read "God Bless America."

All the pundits agreed that September eleventh was the pivotal, defining moment in American history, more far-reaching than the Revolution, more profound than Pearl Harbor. Nothing would ever be the same again. Some looked back with nostalgia at September tenth, but most agreed that the new sincere, spiritual us were better than the old shallow, materialist us. We had learned that nothing is more important than our loved ones. We would never again indulge in satire or irony, or speak flippantly of our elected officials, or sow divisiveness on late-night television, or pull our sister's hair. And above all, we stood united behind our leader. Even hardened Gore supporters agreed that their man wouldn't have been half so bold and decisive, but would probably still be looking things up in the Koran or reading Central Asian history.

George W. Bush, Commander-in-Chief, was never again shown as a puppet with pointy ears and a freshman beanie, dangling from strings in fat-cat hands. Suddenly he reminded a lot of people of Teddy Roosevelt.[4] He was a lion of a leader, a towering pillar of strength, and so admired that frivolous European papers suggested he'd arranged the attacks himself, to boost his ratings. His people warned us that any criticism of him, or his military budget, or his ears, would be a traitor's blow to America itself, but who would criticize?

We bombed Afghanistan. This is a steep pile of rocks in Central Asia, wedged in among Pakistan and Iran and places with names like Tajikistan, though it doesn't really matter who the

---

[4] Others said no, he was more like Winston Churchill.

neighbors are since you can't get there from there. The British Empire had much admired the Afghans for their fierce and warlike natures; male and female, they were born with a knife in one hand and a chip on both shoulders and were wonderfully handsome, with ferocious green eyes.[5]

It's tough to hold a war there. The roads are called "roads" only by courtesy and the locals resort to unfair tactics like hiding in caves. There are no maps. After the Russians, there were few identifiable cities. Nobody we knew spoke any of the local languages. However, President Bush had it on good authority that the nuts who knocked down the World Trade Center were under the auspices of a rich Saudi named Osama bin Laden, who lived in a cave there and had plenty more nuts waiting in the wings. Bush vowed to get him, "dead or alive." This was easier said than done, since there were hundreds and hundreds of caves and all the inhabitants, good and bad, looked pretty similar, in beards and turbans, and the people in charge of Afghanistan, called the Taliban, didn't want to give us bin Laden, either dead or alive.

We bombed the place to a fare-thee-well, reducing many large rocks to smaller rocks and even, in some places, gravel. Victory was declared. Then we went in on foot, peering into cave after cave after cave, calling for bin Laden, but there was no answer. Apparently he didn't wait around for us. Presently he faded from the front page and Bush stopped talking about him. He had bigger things in mind.

He had the greatest agenda of all time. The grandest vision in

---

[5] The Russians said we ought to think twice about the place. They'd tried invading it, back in the '80s, and had to creep back out again.

the history of the American Presidency, possibly in the history of the world: he vowed to stamp out evil and evildoers everywhere, something God himself had never achieved.

A few cautious voices warned that the evil he'd targeted for starters—Iraq, Iran, and North Korea, the "axis of evil"—weren't the whole story, and there were evildoers lurking in as many as sixty countries around the world that would need stamping out, but he never flinched. The Global War on Terror, he called it, or GWOT for short. He admitted it would take a long time—at least through his second term—but he called it a crusade.[6] It was. It is. Finding and identifying evil everywhere, and scouring it from the face of the earth—isn't this bigger than Social Security? More important than unemployment or global warming?

Boldly he established the Homeland Security Department to keep us posted on how scary things were at any given moment, with color-coded alerts from not-so-scary (yellow) to seal-your-windows (orange) to run-for-your-lives (red). The liberal media hinted that these alerts were neatly timed to distract people from financial scandals and dubious legislation, but talk like that just aids the enemy.

Security was spiffed up all over. People took off their shoes in airports and submitted their e-mails and library books for inspection, and helicopters flew low over Manhattan looking for terrorists in turbans. Pink-cheeked National Guardsmen marched around carrying rifles and looking nervous.

The President, always calm himself, urged us to stay calm too

---

[6] Some of our Eastern friends have long memories and didn't like the word, but he assured them this wasn't about non-Christians specifically, just evil non-Christians. People who, he said, so hated freedom that they'd gladly blow themselves to smithereens rather than put up with freedom even for a minute.

and keep shopping, to boost the economy, but to be very alert around hot targets like shopping malls, banks, apartment buildings, sporting events, the Brooklyn Bridge, the Statue of Liberty, and the Fourth of July. Dangers to watch for included anthrax, radiation, bacteria, and men with beards carrying suitcases full of smallpox.

Even in wartime, Bush remembered his compassion. In his effort to create new jobs, he slashed the punitive taxes rich people had been groaning under and stamped out the Death Tax.[7] Without the Death Tax people who, through thrift and hard work, have parlayed the family farm or the mom-and-pop grocery store into billions of bucks can leave them intact to their little children so they don't starve in the streets.

The tax cuts were hard on the bank balance, and in no time flat the greatest budget surplus in history turned into the greatest budget deficit in history, but compassion has its price. Besides, deficits are good: without money, we can't waste it on social programs.

However, this didn't mean the President hated poor people. He was sure that if he ever met any, he'd like them just fine. He said, "First, let me make it very clear, poor people aren't necessarily killers. Just because you happen to be not rich doesn't mean you're willing to kill."

Jesus himself couldn't have put it better.

With all he had to worry about, Bush never neglected his exercises. For him, fitness was what his father had called "the vision thing." Much as he hated talking to reporters, he did give an interview to *Runner's World,* saying, "It's interesting that my times have

---

[7] Democrats called it the Estate Tax, but that gives the wrong impression.

become faster right after the war began. I guess that's part of the stress relief I get from it. For me, the psychological benefit is enormous . . ." He ran six days a week, but told the reporter, "It's sad that I can't run longer. It's one of the saddest things about the Presidency."

He holed up in his gym every morning and nothing was allowed to distract him. Someone suggested he watched the news while treading the treadmill, but his aides said no, he concentrated on the fitness.[8] When he had to visit foreign countries, he took his treadmill along on Air Force One and treaded his way across the oceans.

Some malcontents muttered that since we were paying this man to spend the best hours of his day in a gym, we had a right to expect someone, well, brawnier. More Arnold Schwarzenegger. In photo ops, especially when wedged between Dick Cheney and Colin Powell, he looked a bit rabbity. Even fans admitted that when he sat in a chair, the chair kind of dominated the scene. But he really was fit. He could bench-press one eighty-five and his cardiovascular system was in the top one percent of men his age. "President Buff," some called him.

He slept well too. Shakespeare or somebody said, "Uneasy lies the head that wears a crown," but President W. turned in at nine-thirty every night wearing the top crown on the planet and slept like a kitten.

In perilous times, a President who's fit, fleet-footed, and perfectly calm is a comfort to all.

---

[8] He had people to watch the news and read reports and newspapers and tell him in a few plain words what they thought he'd want to know. This saved hours of valuable time.

Out beyond the gym, Afghanistan was somehow even messier conquered than unconquered, but everyone lost interest and the reporters had come home. Word leaked out that it was dangerous to go for a walk there, because the warlords had reverted to their old ways, gunning each other down all over. Freed from the repressive Taliban, everyone went back to planting opium poppies; the whole countryside was a blanket of blooms and entrepreneurs processed them into heroin and sold it. The economy perked right up.

Since we never did find bin Laden, object of the enterprise, we were told he'd died of natural causes, probably kidney disease. Unfortunately he kept releasing tapes urging his followers to keep killing Americans, and on the second anniversary of September eleventh, a new videotape showed him strolling among some peaceful pastures looking fit as a fiddle, but nobody cared anymore. We had other fish to fry.

Saddam Hussein was still in Iraq (see BUSH I). He hadn't done anything to us yet, but he wasn't a nice man at all, and someone told Bush he was stockpiling poison gases and nuclear weapons and suitcases full of smallpox to drop on us, and then lying about them. Besides, he'd once threatened to assassinate Bush Sr.; he was "the man who tried to kill my dad."

The President decided to go back and finish the job his father started, and this time hang around and make Iraqis choose somebody friendlier. After Iraq, we still had Iran and North Korea, both of them bragging about their nuclear weapons, and other countries yet to be announced, but was Bush dismayed? Not a bit. In youth he and Cheney had shown the liveliest distaste for warfare, but now they were in touch with their inner soldiers, and Iraq was the easiest place to start.

Bush wanted to invade it all alone, for the greater glory, but

Colin Powell and some other pussyfooters told him it would look better if we talked to the United Nations first. Bush said that if they didn't approve the project, we'd do it anyway, and make them look pretty foolish—"irrelevant," he said. The U.N. said they'd send some inspectors in to see what the Iraqis were hiding in the way of Weapons of Mass Destruction, or W.M.D., and if they found some, we could go ahead.

Back here at home there were some scandals about friends and former employers of the Administration lying about profits and doing funny things with the stock market, but Republican scandals made pretty dull reading and only accountants understood them. They weren't about real evil, like Clinton and Monica. Just good old American entrepreneurs getting a bit rambunctious.

Well, it was time for the mid-term elections, when the President's party traditionally takes a pasting, but Bush dropped everything and went to work. He spent the fall traveling all over the country, wherever a Republican was running for anything, raising untold sums of money and dropping his final "Gs" all over. His top advisor marveled at how he got more and more like Andrew Jackson: a straight-shooting down-home frontiersman beloved by the common man.

By some silly accident—perhaps a mix-up in the hospital nursery—he was born into a rich Eastern Establishment family with useful friends, but anyone could tell by listening to him that he was a simple Texas cowboy who knew right from wrong.[9] He hadn't just ducked education, like Lincoln; he'd stood up to it like a man, face-to-face, and wrestled it to the ground, striding untouched from

---

[9] They still couldn't get him to pose for a picture with a horse, though, or even a pony.

the fanciest schools money could buy, still using "drug" as the past tense of "drag."

The election was a smash. The Democrats couldn't think of a word to say. We were in a war against evil, Bush was our Commander-in-Chief, and anything they said would have sounded pretty darned unpatriotic. It was pretty unpatriotic to be a Democrat at all, actually.

Not since 1882 had a sitting President made such a clean sweep. The Republicans now stood firmly astride the White House, the Supreme Court, the Senate, and the House, and the road ahead lay clear. The President was monarch of all he surveyed. As he'd said himself, we'd misunderestimated him.

Well, the U.N. weapons inspectors had poked around and poked around in Iraq and hadn't found anything, proving what incompetent bumblers they were. Bush said, "Facing clear evidence of peril, we cannot wait for the final proof, the smoking gun that could come in the form of a mushroom cloud." We were going to invade the place and find those weapons for ourselves, and the rest of the world could join us.

Alas, our former allies like France and Germany and Russia— the "axis of weasels"—turned out a bunch of sniveling cravens. Only England was ready to help.[10] We were naturally disgusted, especially by the sissy French, who ate snails and thought about sissy things like clothes and perfume. We made French jokes and ate Freedom Fries with our burgers and all the better restaurants uncorked their priceless stocks of French wines and poured them down the toilet.

---

[10] Well, not the English, exactly, but their prime minister, Tony Blair, which was all that really mattered.

Quite a few millions of other cowards protested in peace marches, some in funny places like Athens and Madrid but some right here in America. When aides told Bush about it, he stood firm as a rock, saying he wasn't the kind of leader who got swayed by "focus groups," and either you know right from wrong or you just don't.

Prudently, the U.N. weapons inspectors scuttled out before we roared in.

It was glorious. We bombed and bombed and bombed the place. We called it Operation Shock and Awe, since everyone would be shocked and awed to learn we had so many planes and bombs. Then the army poured in. We expected poison gas and smallpox and mushroom clouds and fierce resistance from the elite Republican Guard. However, almost nothing happened, at least not at first, and the Republican Guard simply vanished.[11] We also expected the population to pelt us with flowers, but that didn't happen either.

We marched into Baghdad. Our troops couldn't be everywhere at once, of course, and we needed tanks and soldiers to protect the Oil Ministry, and people who fuss about such frippery complained that looters broke into the museum of antiquities down the street and made off with a lot of antiquities. This was too bad but it couldn't be helped.[12]

Like bin Laden, Saddam Hussein, the object of the enterprise, was nowhere to be seen, even though we offered a large reward. We did find a statue of him and knocked it down, which looked grand on television, but the Iraqis thought it wasn't the same as the

---

[11] They filtered back again later, wearing civvies and carrying AK-47s.
[12] The Administration apologized handsomely, even though some of the antiquities must have been fraudulent, since they were claimed to predate Genesis.

man himself. In America, though, everyone felt that Hussein and Osama bin Laden were the same guy, possibly named Osaddam, and the fact that we couldn't find him—or them—pretty much proved he was dead. Revenge was sweet.

Victory was sweet. The President got an aircraft carrier to park off San Diego and had himself flown to it on a fighter plane. He jumped out of the plane in a borrowed flight suit, looking every inch the pilot back from a victorious mission, and declared the war over. The assembled troops cheered themselves hoarse and miles of film were shot for use in his re-election campaign.[13]

Some things were still a bit messy, it's true. Not exciting things, like the invasion, just domestic things, like we couldn't get the electricity or the water to come back on, and people kept blowing up the oil lines, and nobody spoke English so we couldn't explain things like checkpoints to them and had to shoot them. Often they shot back. As in Afghanistan, with the tyrants gone, people celebrated freedom by settling old religious and ethnic and tribal grudges with grenades and arson. In the general confusion, assorted terrorists from all over the world moved into Iraq and threw bombs at our troops, and the U.N., and the Red Cross, and the bystanders. People got killed, though never more than a few at a time.

Our leaders remained confident, as leaders should be.

President Bush said we had indeed found the Weapons of Mass Destruction, or at least a couple of suspiciously empty trailers, or, if we hadn't, we certainly would if we had another $600 million to spend looking. With 1,400 of our own trusted experts digging through the sands, we were bound to find something. And when the attacks stepped up, the truck bombs just proved how well

---

[13] Campaigning is more fun if you can arrange for the right props.

things were going, driving our enemies to despair. The more we succeeded, "the more desperate these killers become, because they can't stand the thought of a free society."

Besides, that wasn't the point. The real, *real* reason we invaded was to liberate the Iraqis, who were pining for a democracy like ours.[14]

From his Undisclosed Location, Vice President Cheney told us that Saddam Hussein, not bin Laden, was really the man behind the September eleventh attacks, and Iraq, not Afghanistan, was really home to the evil al Qaeda.

Besides, it was all worthwhile because of the money American corporations were going to make mending stuff and managing all that oil.

Attorney General Ashcroft said we'd have no more terrorists in America because he was keeping an eye on everyone, even you and me, all the time.

Defense Secretary Rumsfeld said Iraq was exactly where we wanted terrorists to flock to from all over, so we could keep an eye on *them,* and everything was going according to his original plan.

It was getting expensive, though. Bush told Congress we needed $87 billion more to hang out in Iraq, just for starters, and this seemed like a lot of money, especially since we still had a lot of other countries to take out.

Because it's only Christian to turn the other cheek and show forbearance unto them that have despitefully used you, Bush went back to the United Nations. He said that now that we'd won the war, they

---

[14] Turned out they just wanted the electricity back on. It was hotter than the hinges of hell and they couldn't work the air-conditioning or even the ceiling fans. We'd brought them sixty thousand soccer balls to lighten the mood, but it was too hot to play soccer and they kept whining for electricity.

could all chip in and send troops and money. We'd be in charge, of course—whose war was it, anyway?—but we'd let them help.

And yet they did harden their hearts against him. One U.N. official said, "They're on their own. It's just between them and the American taxpayer." Besides, somebody'd blown up the U.N. headquarters in Iraq.

Lesser Presidents would have shown signs of strain. Polk was a wreck after the Mexican War and LBJ went right round the bend over Vietnam and Carter wasted away to a shadow during the hostage crisis. Bush was made of sterner stuff. Fit as a fiddle, refreshed by regular prayer and long brush-cutting vacations in Texas, he even found time to travel, always a learning experience.

He'd once called Africa an "important country," but when they told him it was actually a whole bunch of countries, he went to visit some of them[15] and had his picture taken with Africans and told them the only cure for AIDS was abstinence. After fitness, abstinence was his favorite thing. Remembering Clinton, everyone was hugely relieved by the distaste for sex that came with his moral clarity.

On sex, as on terrorism, he followed the highest advice. Quite aside from the scheduled White House Bible Study classes, his relationship with God was close and personal. The two of Them conferred constantly on matters like stem-cell research, condoms, and preemptive wars, so that we all knew that whatever was all right with Bush was all right with God.

For thousands of years we'd trusted kings, however peculiarly they behaved, because we understood they ruled by Divine Right. They were appointed by God, who knows what He's doing. In a

---

[15] He brought his own food and cars and chairs to sit on. You can't be too careful.

democracy, anxiously adrift on shifting piles of ballots, it's always a joy and a consolation to know the President too is under His special wing and privy to His every word. In the days to come, through good times and other times, this was a comfort to us all. Even if he hadn't quite won the election, he was clearly God's personal choice.

It's a great country. Anything can happen. Stay tuned.

BARBARA HOLLAND was "born in the shadow of the White House and never recovered." A long-time observer of the Washington scene, she's been called "shameless" by Russell Baker, "outrageous" by the *Wall Street Journal,* and "a national treasure" by the *Philadelphia Inquirer.* Concerning *Hail to the Chiefs,* she insists, "I am not making this up." She has done all American citizens a service with this indispensable reference work, reminding us of history lessons long forgot, illuminated by haunting sidelights our textbooks never told us.